CW01418324

Anatomy of the Ship

The Naval Cutter

ALERT

1777

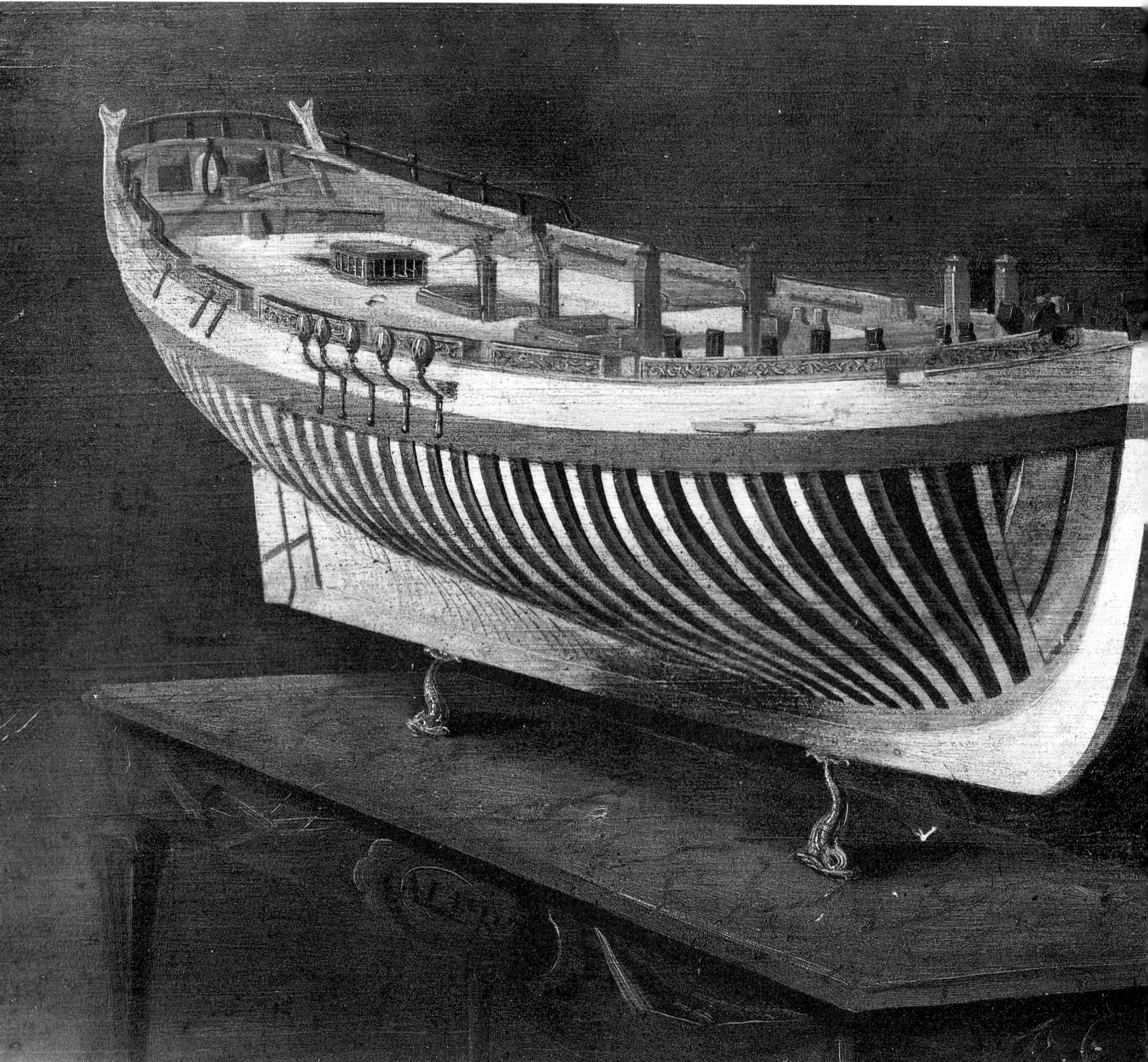

Anatomy of the Ship

The Naval Cutter
ALERT
1777

Peter Goodwin

Frontispiece. An oil painting of the *Alert* cutter model dated 1775, painted by Joseph Marshall. Various features comply exactly to the modified draught of the *Rattlesnake* used for the 1777 *Alert*. These include the squared gunports, the five shroud deadeyes and three backstay chain plates. This painting formed part of the George III Collection of ship model paintings.
(Courtesy of the Science Museum)

First published in Great Britain 1991 by
Conway Maritime Press Ltd,
101 Fleet Street,
London, EC4Y 1DE

British Library Cataloguing in Publication Data
Goodwin, Peter
The Naval Cutter Alert. — (Anatomy of The Ship).
1. Warships
I. Title
623.8225

ISBN 0–85177–592–6

Designed by Roger Lightfoot
Typeset by Inforum Typesetting, Portsmouth
Printed and bound in Great Britain by
The Bath Press, Bath

Contents

Foreword

The *Alert* was one of many armed cutters that were either 'bought in' or purpose-built to supplement the British fleet between 1763 and 1835. These small, swift vessels were generally deployed for minor roles such as conveying dispatches, routine inshore patrol work and reconnaissance duties; they were also used to assist the Revenue service engaged on preventive duties against smuggling. Often, the careers of these cutters were short lived: most were payed off after brief employment while others less fortunate, like the *Alert*, fell to the enemy. Although the origins of the cutter lie in mercantile and leisurely pursuits, these vessels were for a short period turned into compact and successful fighting units.

Information concerning most cutters constructed after about 1790 is well documented in surviving dockyard records and other contemporary sources. Prior to this date, however, the majority of these vessels were built in private yards and so documentary evidence is unfortunately scarce and rather fragmented. In describing a cutter of the 1770s it has been necessary to look at a wide range of sources.

The *Alert* was constructed to the lines of the *Rattlesnake*, an identical vessel which was built by Farley at Folkestone and launched in June 1777. This master draught, believed to have been prepared in 1776, appears to have been modified before actual build commenced and the relevant amendments governing gunports and deadeyes are marked up and annotated accordingly.

Rigging details for the *Alert* have been based on the contemporary model of the *Hawke* cutter dated 1777 and currently on display at the National Maritime Museum, Greenwich. Though there is some controversy over the name attached to this model it is perhaps the only reliable source of earlier cutter rig. Of considerable interest is the fact that this particular model has also been rigged with sails, a rare circumstance which has proved a great asset towards the compilation of this work.

Naturally, I would not have been able to produce this work without the kind assistance of various colleagues and institutions. First, I must express my gratitude towards the staff of the National Maritime Museum – Dr Eric Kently, David Lyon and Ian McKenzie, and Simon Stephens for providing much detailed information and arranging suitable models for close examination; also David Topliss and Graham Slatter of the Draught Room for the provision of suitable plans, and David Spence for arranging the necessary photography. Special thanks are also due to Keith Percival for his excellent photographs of the model of the *Hawke* cutter.

Further gratitude must also be extended to the staff of the Public Records Office, Kew, and to Wendy Sheridan of the Science Museum, Kensington, who kindly permitted access to the George III collection of ship model paintings which were undergoing restoration. I must also express my thanks to Rob Gardiner, Julian Mannering and the staff of Conway Maritime Press for guidance and production of this work.

Last and most important I must thank my wife Jan for her dedicated assistance, both in research matters and in typing my manuscript with its unfamiliar terminology, and for her overall understanding, patience and support for which I am once again indebted.

Peter Goodwin, 1991

AUTHOR'S NOTE

The two paintings of the *Alert* were done as part of the George III collection during the 1770s and yet both appear to be dated 1755. If the date of 1755 were to be believed then it could be assumed that the original draught of the *Rattlesnake* precedes the actual date of the ship by some 20 years.

Introduction

DEVELOPMENT

In all probability, the armed cutter and its counterpart, the single-masted sloop, originated from the two-masted yachts commonly used by the Dutch during the early part of the seventeenth century. These yachts, specifically designed for use in shallow coastal waters, were simply rigged with a gaff sail on each mast. Finding the addition of headsails proved more advantageous for both sailing closer to the wind and for manoeuvring, this rig began to be modified around 1650. The foremast with its gaff sail was eliminated and replaced with a foresail set up on a stay rigged between the remaining mast head and the stemhead. The foresail was then supplemented by a jib set on a jibboom which could, if required, be removed. The remaining gaff main sail was enlarged and its foot extended on a boom and it was termed the 'bezaan' sail. Consequently, this type of vessel became known as a 'bezaan yacht'. One vessel of this sort, presented to the British Navy by the Dutch in 1661, was actually listed as a 'Bezan Yacht'.

From the bezaan yacht, the Dutch developed the staten yacht, a swift manoeuvrable craft employed for conveying dispatches and important personnel, and for scouting duties. Initially these vessels set a large mainsail which was sprit-rigged. The sprit was soon superseded by a standing gaff and the loose footed mainsail was furled by being brailed up. Later still a boom was introduced in the same manner as previously employed on the bezaan yacht. A foresail and jib were rigged in the conventional manner.

When England's monarchy was restored in 1660, yachting became a popular recreation of the royal entourage. This new activity, primarily encouraged by Charles II, had evolved from his active interest in sailing while he had been exiled in Holland. Following this, smaller vessels of similar design, often referred to as advice boats, were soon utilised for dispatch duties in the King's Navy.

Merchant shipbuilders quickly realised the potential of adapting the yacht design to meet the requirements of coastal trading and by about 1710 the forerunner of the standard English cutter had been developed. These shallow draughted vessels were built with a length to breadth ratio of 3:1, and with hollow floors to the midship section. Following the established north European practice, all cutters at this period were clinker built, a lapstrake system of planking commonly used on all small vessels which greatly enhanced longitudinal strength. One particular feature of most cutters was the rockered keel. The sail plan at this period still remained simple and consisted of a large mainsail set on a gaff and boom, and a triangular foresail and jib. The bowsprit was set on one side of the stemhead and could be retracted. The mainmast now carried a single loose-footed square sail set on a yard rigged to a halliard running through a block at the mast head. No topmast had yet been introduced, though a short slender pole fitted abaft the lower mast head existed. This was later replaced, about 1730, with a short topgallant mast on which a small square sail was set in light breezes.

Initially, Folkestone served as the major building centre for cutters though by 1757 shipyards at Dover and Shoreham were also supplying vessels. Not only did the cutter prove very suitable for coastal trading, but they were very soon utilised for more clandestine purposes: smuggling. This illicit trade which spanned most of the southern coast of England had attained epic proportions by this period. Many Kentish and Sussex towns of smuggling notoriety such as Dymchurch, Hythe, Romney and Rye, to name but a few, would have been served with contraband brought in by cutters built at Folkestone and Dover. In retaliation against the smugglers identical craft were soon adopted by the Revenue men.

Precisely when cutters were first used by the Navy is uncertain. Contemporary evidence (The Vernon Papers, NMM) verifies that a number of 'Folkestone Cutters' were hired by Admiral Vernon in 1745. Under orders from Vernon aboard the *Royal George* stationed in the Downs, these vessels were employed specifically for inshore surveillance of the French invasion fleet assembling at Ostend and Dunkirk. France, supporting the cause of Charles Stuart intended to land a considerable force to assist the rebel army. The Admiralty order to Vernon was as follows:

September 4, 1745

[One Dutch ship to be detached to convoy Dutch troops to England.]

You are also to keep a clean, tallowed cutter constantly off of Dunkirk to watch the motions of the enemy in that port, & to relieve her every day; and you are to send us up daily accounts of the intelligence the said cutters bring to you. Given etc. etc.

VERE BEAUCLERK
By command of their Lordships, G. ANSON
THOS. CORBETT. GEORGE GRENVILLE

Only by maintaining a constant blockade and reconnaissance of the French and Belgium ports would England thwart the intentions of the Young Pretender. Vernon replied to the Secretary of the Admiralty:

Deal
September 27, 1745.

Sir; – I am pleased to find their Lordships approve of the orders I have detached the 'Nottingham' and 'Folkestone' to act under, and I sent with them two of the Folkestone cutters, one under the command of Capt. Gregory who is to look into Ostend before he returns, and the other, Lt. Lucas who will keep company with them till he is windward of Dunkirk, and then look in there to bring me the speediest intelligence he can from thence, and had I a sloop . . .

E.V.

The two cutters referred to were the *Mayflower* and the *Two Brothers* which had been hired since late August of that year. By December a further three cutters were hired to augment Vernon's Channel squadron.

With the exception of the major dimensions of those entered for service in 1763, documentary evidence pertaining to English cutters is rare, and the earliest contemporary draught in existence is dated 1757. A second draught (now held in the Rigsarkivet, Copenhagen) shows a 'Shoreham Cutter' dated 1765, built at Portsmouth for use in the Revenue service. Though simple, this draught indicates all the regular features common to the cutter, including the broad beam and the offset bowsprit. Of particular interest on this draught is the bowsprit heel which is supported by two independent vertical bitts set abaft the windlass, which implies that the common practice of using the windlass pawl bitts as the bowsprit step had not yet become fully accepted.

Officially introduced into the Navy in 1763, twenty-two cutters were bought in for service during that year, and all were purchased from the south coast yards. In addition, three dockyard-built vessels were added to the Navy List. As might be expected, most of the 1763 vessels varied in size, tonnage and armament; no specific standardisation of hull form, layout and rig can be fully ascertained. This new policy of supplementing the fleet with small craft to carry out coastal duties may well have been influenced by the shortage of financial resources caused by the cost of the recent conflict, the Seven Years War.

Contemporary models, which are unfortunately few, indicate many contradictory practices. Some show open as opposed to built up bulwarks; different methods of stepping the topgallant mast; considerable variations in the number of yards and sails carried; and alternative sides for stepping the bowsprit. During this period no single type emerged though some moves towards standardisation did begin to take place after 1780. With the close of the War of American Independence and the end of conflict with France, Spain and Holland more time and resources became available for the development of the type.

Between 1777 and 1782 thirty-four cutters were entered for service. Twenty-six were purchased and the remainder were built at Dover and Folkestone. Since 1763 there had been a marked increase in the overall dimensions of cutters by around 40 per cent, though this point should not be considered as a consistent trend as some later vessels were considerably smaller. In general, as these ships became larger and sturdier their armament was modified to up-rate fire power. Initially, this was implemented by replacing the light 3-pounders with 4- or 6-pounder guns; then further developments in ordnance were to improve cutter armament by a greater degree. This was due to the introduction of the carronade, a short barreled, lightweight gun that discharged a much heavier shot. This type of gun was officially introduced into the Navy in 1779. At first, 6- or 12-pounder carronades were utilised to supplement the main armament and were used as stern or bow chase guns. One exception at this period was the *Nimble*, purchased in 1781, which carried an entire armament consisting of ten 18-pounder carronades. After 1800 most cutters carried a main battery of carronades (generally 12-pounders) with two 3- or 4-pounders for chase guns.

By 1785 the rig had become more standardised and somewhat simpler. The square sail, which had been set flying on its respective yard, was now bent to what once acted as a spread-yard for the foot of the topsail and this reduced the running rigging. A further modification in rig was the introduction of a longer topgallant mast which was now fitted in the conventional manner afore the lower mast head instead of abaft as before. Following the conventional method this mast was rigged with shrouds, backstays and a forestay and, in addition, spreaders were introduced. These took the form of extended crosstrees set athwart the lower mast tressletrees, and two shorter crosstrees were added to produce a platform at the same point. Some vessels now carried a jibboom which could be temporarily rigged to permit a flying jib to be set in light winds.

During the next three decades thirty-three vessels were entered for service; nineteen were purchased, nine built in private yards and the remaining ones constructed in the Royal dockyards. The most significant change to these craft during the period concerned their construction. Early cutters were built, following the north European practice, of clinker planking, but this technique did have its limitations especially when applied to long hull forms which were prone to leaking. This problem was overcome by introducing carvel-built cutters which, with their frames, were far stronger. From around 1800 there was a transitional period of about ten years when cutters were built in either fashion. It may be that the growth in carvel construction was a result of increased building by the Royal dockyards which favoured the system.

By 1820 the naval cutter had attained its zenith in hull form, armament and rig. Though the mainsail area was marginally reduced, overall sail area had been increased by the introduction of the gaff topsail in the 1780s. Likewise, studding sails were in some cases now employed for use in light breezes. With the exception of a small number of purchased vessels, the building of naval cutters was now governed by the Royal dockyards; all private contractural work was abandoned. Between 1815 and 1832 some fifteen dockyard-built cutters were entered for service and a high proportion of these were constructed at Pembroke. After this period, what few cutters were built were mainly employed for revenue, survey or coastguard duties; with the end of the European Wars there was no need for the armed cutters. Employed for more peaceful roles the development of these vessels was directed towards greater refinement. No longer requiring a full complement of guns, breadth was reduced to give finer hull lines and greater speed. The cumbersome square sails disappeared which made the vessels more manageable for a small crew.

During the nineteenth century the cutter was adapted for all sorts of uses. The Bristol pilot cutter, for example, was a wonderfully seaworthy boat which was sailed in the rough waters of the Bristol Channel. On the east coast the basic cutter rig was adapted by the smacks which fished for herring in the North Sea.

HISTORY

The *Alert*, one of fifteen cutters built for the Navy during the years 1777 and 1778, was built at Dover, one of the principal ports where vessels of this nature were constructed. The contract was allocated to Mr Henry Ladd whose expertise in constructing such craft had been recognised by the Navy Board. During the construction all work was overseen by the Surveyor of the Navy, Sir John Williams. The keel was laid in January 1777 and five months later, on the 24 June, the *Alert* was launched. The overall cost for completing the hull reached an estimate of £1391 18s 5d. Directly after the launch the *Alert* was handed over to the naval authorities.

Dover, June 24, 1777.
Ref. 26.

Honourable Sirs,
I Pray leave humbly to acquaint your Honours that the Alert Cutter built by Mr. Henry Ladd for His Majesty was this day launched and delivered safe to the Officer appointed to receive her –

Draught of Water as follows:-	ft.	ins.
Afore	4	2
Abaft	8	11

I am Honourable Sirs
Your Honrs Most humble
and Obedient Servant
Wm Raydon.

The Honourable Navy Board.

(Ref. PRO: ADM 95/64 Letter No. 79)

The vessel was taken to Deptford for fitting out and reached the dockyard on the 30 June. Two days later the ship was put into the graving dock to be sheathed with copper below the waterline. This was a relatively new method of protection against fouling and ship worm which had been introduced in the 1760s. The *Alert* was re-launched on the 22 of July. While at Deptford she also received her masts and yards, rigging, stores and armament. Her main armament consisted of ten 4-pounders. The cost of her rigging and stores was £912 10s 11d, while the remainder of the work on her hull, including the masts and spars, amounted to £496 9s 3d. The final cost of building and equipping the *Alert* for service came to £2,800 18s 7d.

On Monday 11 August 1777 the vessel was moored 'at the Jetty Head' awaiting orders. Two days later, while at anchor at Galleons Reach, her commander, Lieutenant John Bazely, received orders to proceed to the Channel. After anchoring off Sandwich on the 20th the *Alert* reached Dover on the 4 September. The following eight days were spent cruising between the Downs and Beachy Head carrying out surveillance on all merchantmen proceeding through the Channel and preventive duties against smuggling.

Further orders sent the *Alert* to the western approaches of the Channel. Since the start of the American War of Independence in 1775, colonial privateers had continuously harrassed the British mercantile fleet and had captured a number of ships. These actions were undertaken primarily to equip the revolutionaries with supplies, arms and munitions for their struggle against the British Army in the colonies. France, though at peace with Britain at this period, openly supported the American cause by permitting the privateers refuge within her ports for replenishment and repairs.

The *Alert* anchored off the Scilly Isles on Sunday 14 September. According to the Captain's log the ship was still off Beachy Head only two days earlier and so it can be reckoned that the *Alert*s average speed was about 6–6½ knots. The ship then steered a course S.S.E. arriving off Ushant on the 18 September. Early the following morning a small vessel was sighted and the *Alert* altered course to intercept:

Captain's log: Friday, 19 September, 1777; 'Light winds mixed with Calm; at 5AM saw a sail to the —— [word illegible], let the reefs out of the Mainsail and set the outer Jib, got the Tops'le Yard up set the Topsail and Royal, cleared the Cutter for Action.' The ship altered course; the Master's log records; 'Tacked and Steerd towards the place found her to be a Brig under English Colours. . . .' The Captain's log continues; '. . . ¾ after 6 Tacked and stood too then fired a swivel to bring her too . . .'; Bazely was then challenged by the other vessel. 'She hailed us we answered from Whitehall, we then hailed him when she answered Guernsey she then hauled down English Colours and hoisted American, gave us a broadside which we returned and an engagement ensewed which lasted from ½ past 7 to 10 o'clock when she bore up made use of his sweeps and endeavoured to get off . . .' During this action the *Alert* received considerable damage to her rigging. The American Commander, knowing he had little shot remaining to continue the fight took advantage of the *Alert*'s situation and veered off from the engagement. Bazely immediately prompted his crew to make running repairs to the rigging and quickly resumed the chase. Henry Peake, the Master, stated in his log; 'wore round after him . . . reev'd new rigging and set the smaller sail; At Noon in chase with the Enemy; the People empld [employed] making wads, filling Powder and preparing for Second Attack.'

Bazely's log proceeds: 'Fresh and middle breezes to Light Breezes and Fair, latter Fresh Gales with some Rain; at ½ past We bore up with the Enemy, cut and let run the small sails overboard and renewed the action . . .' The second engagement only continued for an hour until the Americans ran out of ammunition. The log continues; 'When at ½ past 2 she struck, [lowered her colours] Found her to be the Lexington Brig assured by the American Congress, Henry Johnstone Master, mounting 14 fours and 2 pounders, 12 swivels and 84 men'. Further details regarding the *Lexington* were recorded in Peake's log; 'from Morlai [Morlaix, on the coast of Brittany], bound for Boston with dispatches'. Bazely's log gave account of the casualties. 'The Enemy had 7 killed and 11 wounded, in the former was the Master and Lt. of Marines, in the latter the 1st Lt. and Gunner; The loss on our own side was 3 men wounded and 2 killed, with both Masts and Rigging very much damaged. Sent a midn (Midshipman) and 17 men on board to take charge of the Prize; received 68 prisoners from her'.

Measures were then taken on board the *Alert* to minimise the dangerous condition of her rig, the responsibility of which lay with the Master, Henry Peake who recalled; 'got the Topyard Down, Struck the Topmast, set the 3rd Jib . . . reefd Mainsail; at 10 made sail the Prize in Company; at ½ past 7AM the Prize lost her mast, brought too at Noon the Prize in Company'.

The remarkable defeat of the *Lexington* by the smaller cutter was due mainly to two causes: surprise, and the American's shortage of shot. During the previous five days the *Lexington*, in company with the *Dolphin* and *Reprisal*, had managed to capture fourteen ships and had used up most of her ammunition. The *Alert* then proceeded to Plymouth with her prize and underwent repairs to her masts and rigging, having moored alongside the sheer hulk in the Hamoaze on Thursday 26 September. The ship remained in port for some time and on 1 November superficial work was still being undertaken: 'scraped the side and payed with Varnish of Pine'. This substance, generally referred to as rosin, is a residual obtained from the distillation of turpentine and was commonly used at this period to protect ships' side planking from the elements. Ten days later having embarked provisions the vessel anchored in Cawsand Bay off Penlee Point, southwest of Plymouth Sound, awaiting favourable winds to proceed to sea.

On 13 November 1777 the Captain's log states: 'At 2 got a Pilot on Board, at ½ past ran over the Bar and came too off the Town of Falmouth with the small Bower; Veered off to ¼ of a Cable; Carried out the Kedge Anchor and Hawser to the N.W. to steady her; Sent the casks to be filled; the carpenters employed repairing the Horns of the Gaff'. This entry suggests that the *Alert* had met with heavy weather after her departure from Cawsand Bay and had made a run for the safety of Falmouth Roads.

Two days later the *Alert* passed Ushant and on Wednesday 19 November joined company with the *Egmont* (74) and the frigate *Hussar* off Oporto. After transferring dispatches intended for the *Egmont*, the *Alert* and *Hussar* sailed north to rendezvous with the 60-gun ship *Medway* off Cape Finistère. Three days later, on Sunday 7 December, these three vessels were further joined by the *Asia* (64), and this squadron then proceeded with surveillance duties off the Iberian coast between Finistère and Lisbon. Parting company on the 17th, the *Alert* sailed south towards Tangier anchoring 'off St. Julians Fort, Cape Spartelle' the following evening. For the remaining weeks of December the vessel participated in routine patrol and dispatch work, operating off southern Portugal before returning home, eventually reaching the safety of the Hamoaze at Plymouth on Saturday 18 January 1778.

Throughout February the *Alert* underwent an overhaul at Plymouth.

During this refit some alterations were made to her hull. In addition, her main armanent was replaced with twelve 6-pounders. Guns of this size were more commonly used and so the availability of replenishment shot was greater. Furthermore, apart from these additional two guns, her overall weight of broadside power was raised by over 30 percent. To supplement these heavier guns her original complement of sixty was increased to eighty men. The vessel was then recommissioned under a new commander, Lieutenant William George Fairfax. Unfortunately, the log books covering the remainder of the *Alert*'s career no longer exist. In May, Fairfax was promoted to Commander and the *Alert* was re-rated as a sloop to comply with Admiralty requirements.

With the entry of France into the War, the need for Britain to achieve a naval victory at this moment was important and so a fleet comprising three First Rates, twenty-seven other sail-of-the-line and nine lesser Rates (including *Alert*) was swiftly mobilised. In the early summer of 1778 this fleet, under the command of Admiral Keppel sailed from Spithead in search of the French in the Channel.

On 17 June, while undertaking reconnaissance duties for the fleet, the *Alert*, in company with the Frigate *Arethusa*, intercepted the French frigate *Belle Poule* and the armed lugger *Coureur*. The *Coureur* armed with two 3-pounders, eight 2-pounders and six swivels, carried a crew of fifty men. While the *Arethusa* invited an engagement with the *Belle Poule*, the *Alert* overhauled the lugger and ordered her to surrender. The *Coureur*'s commander, Enseigre de Rosily adamantly refused and was immediately fired upon. During the ensuing engagement, undertaken at musket range, the *Alert* received several shot between 'wind and water' and suffered severe damage to her rigging. After an hour and a half, de Rosily, having had five men killed and twelve wounded struck his colours. The *Alert*, though seriously mauled, had suffered only four wounded. The action between the *Arethusa* and the *Belle Poule*, however, was inconclusive and the engagement was discontinued after a warm fight. Shortly afterwards Keppel's fleet returned to Spithead along with the *Alert*'s prize.

On 8 July 1778 the French fleet under the Compte d'Orvilliers finally broke out of Brest. Keppel, flying his flag aboard the 100-gun *Victory* received this news the following day. Immediately, the Channel Fleet weighed anchor and put to sea in pursuit. Keppel was supported by two Vice Admirals: Sir Robert Harland aboard the *Queen* (90) and Sir Hugh Palliser in the 90-gun *Formidable* (commanded by Captain John Bazeley, previous commander of the *Alert*). By the 15th Keppel's fleet lay off Ushant. His escorts, including the *Alert*, were each deployed independently, seeking out the location of enemy fleet, and on 17 July 1778, the *Alert*, taken by surprise whilst executing these duties, was captured by the French Frigate *Junon*.

Six days later the elusive French fleet was sighted and Keppel, giving chase, pursued the enemy into the Atlantic. Suddenly on 27 July d'Orvilliers shrewdly wore his entire fleet around and precipitated an action on opposing tacks. In line-ahead the two fleets converged. The action opened at about 11.45am, the *Victory* pouring her murderous broadsides into the *Bretagne* and *Ville de Paris*.

For nearly two hours the heated battle continued, during which many of the British ships suffered considerable damage aloft. Keppel soon realised that his ships were in no condition to tack and at 1.30pm signalled the fleet to wear, which imposed less strain on the damaged rigging. Unfortunately, Palliser's rear squadron, which had received the severest onslaught from the enemy, at first failed to respond to the order and precious time was lost while Keppel waited to re-group his fleet. As daylight faded the French made good their escape and all chances of re-engagement were lost.

CONSTRUCTION

When first introduced into the fleet, exact specifications for cutters were not included within the established dimension lists authorised by the Navy Board. This was because the majority of cutters were initially built in private yards and 'bought in' for service. Detailed dimension lists for this type of vessel only appeared later once the standard armed cutter had become fully established after 1780. A complete table of scantlings for a cutter of 273 tons are included within the Shipbuilders Repository of 1789.

The various timbers used in the *Alert* were procured from the Wealden forests of Kent. The keel, of elm, was made in three lengths which were joined with vertical scarphs bolted together. Elm was chosen for its durability under water and for its irregular grain pattern which permitted it to receive innumerable bolts without splitting. Rising vertically from the after end of the keel was the sternpost and its supporting inner post, both made from oak. Each of these timbers was fashioned with a tenon at its heel which fitted into a corresponding mortice cut into the upper face of the keel. Further support for these two posts was achieved by means of the deadwood, a series of horizontal timbers forming a bracket upon the keel. Similarly, at the fore end of the keel a stempost and its supporting apron was erected. Because of their curvatuve, these timbers were made from pieces of compass oak scarphed and bolted together. The heel of the stempost was joined to the keel by means of an intricate scarph termed as the boxing, while the heel of the apron extended aft to converge with the deadwood. Next the hog (or rising wood), also of oak, was laid longitudinally along the top of the keel. Its upper surface was scored to receive the floor timbers and cross chocks of the ship's frames. The scarphs of each length of rising wood gave shift to those of the keel. As the hog extended fore and aft its height increased to meet the deadwood accordingly thereby giving the desired rise to the floors.

All naval draughts at this period indicate station lines at every second frame position (ie B,D,F,H, etc, or 2,4,6,8). In the case of the *Alert* the station lines were spaced at intervals of 4ft, which when divided by two produced a 'room and space' of 2ft. This measurement implies that each frame had a siding of 12in though this was not the case with the *Alert*. The draught of her sister vessel, *Rattlesnake*, clearly indicates that each floor timber and first futtock had a siding of 8in giving a total of 16in for one complete frame. This dimension leaves a 'space' of 8in which is considerably larger than the accepted practice of the period. With fewer frames the weight of these vessels was reduced and their speed enhanced.

The framing system used at this period had double frames fitted at every station line (every 4ft as indicated on the draught), with two filling frames evenly disposed between. The double, or main, frames as they were generally referred to, were made up in two 'slices', one half consisting of a floor timber, second futtock and lengthening piece, the other half a first futtock and top timber. With her small size no third or fourth futtocks were needed. Once these components had been assembled to form each half of the full frame the two halfs were fayed and bolted together at the joint line. The single filling frames were made in an identical manner to each half of a main frame. All frames were made from compass oak.

The square frames extended between station 12 aft and H forward;

beyond these points cant frames were fitted. Unlike the square frames these did not extend across the centre line of the keel but were fayed and bolted to the deadwood. The angle at which each were set corresponded to the curvature of the ship's hull as it diminished towards the centreline at each end of the vessel. To accommodate this requirement the 'room and space' was decreased by fitting an additional filling frame between the station lines. The maximum angle to which cant frames were set was 45 degrees. The aftermost cant (18), known as the fashion piece, supported the extremities of the wing transom. Beyond the foremost cant (N) a series of hawse timbers and bollard timbers formed the structure of the bow.

Once all the frames had been set up in position the whole structure was locked rigid by a series of longitudinal members. The first, and most important, of these was the keelson, which ran fore and aft along the centreline directly above the keel. The fore end of the keelson terminated a little above the heel of the apron, while at the after end the keelson was married into a large knee called the sternson, which gave additional support to the sternpost. Running parallel to the keelson were two longitudinal strakes of planking, the limber strake and its adjacent footwaling. Together these acted as a clamp to hold the floor timbers. Next to be fitted was the thickstuff, which comprised a number of strakes of heavy planking laid over the inner faces of the frames at a level corresponding to the joint lines of the first futtocks and top timbers. In a similar fashion the deck clamps which supported the ends of the upper deck beams were wrought over the joint lines of the second futtocks and lengthening pieces. The remaining surfaces within the hold between the limberstrake and the thickstuff were covered with thinner planking, known as the ceiling. For this type of vessel the ceiling was continued upward to the upper deck beam shelf forming a lining to the lower deck and after platform accommodation spaces.

The deck beams, made from pitch pine, greatly enhanced the strength of the vessel in its transverse plane. The ends of the upper deck beams which located into scores cut in the upper surface of the deck clamp were also supported vertically with hanging knees and horizontally with lodging knees. The timber from which these knees were made was carefully selected, or even grown to shape, to ensure that grain curvature gave the maximum strength required. The beams of the after accommodation platform, lower deck (fore platform) and magazine were not supported by hanging or lodging knees; their ends were simply fayed and bolted to the internal planking.

Worked within the upper deck beams were a series of lighter timbers called carlings and ledges. The carlings were laid longitudinally in two tiers, the innermost tier forming the boundaries of the hatchways and skylights. The ledges were worked transversely between the tiers of carlings usually three between each deck beam.

The deck planking was generally laid with either a three or four butt shift, a technique which ensured that adjacent plank ends did not terminate at the same beam. This system increased the overall strength and reduced timber wastage. All planking was laid 'heart down' to prevent the boards warping upwards at their ends. Most of the upper deck, with the exception of the binding strakes and margin planks was laid with 2½in deal boards. Plank ends which terminated with the curvature of the hull at the fore and after ends were 'sniped' and joggled into oak margin planks which were laid parallel to the waterways. For extra longitudinal strength, binding strakes made from 3in oak plank were extended the full length of the upper deck. These were laid in two strakes to either side of the centreline fittings. Being thicker boards, the binding strakes were scored down onto the beams for a depth of ½in so as to be flush with the adjacent deal plank.

Plank fastenings included iron spike nails and trennails. The former secured the plank butts to the beams while the latter retained the planks at the various beams and carlings between. The heads of the spikes were driven below the surface of the plank and capped with a small wooden disc. Unlike the spikes, trennails were always driven from below. Their upper ends were split, expanded with a wooden wedge and caulked. The lower deck, after platform and magazine were laid with 2in deal boards but margin planks and binding stakes were omitted.

All transverse and longitudinal bulkheads were berthed up with either 2in or 1½in planking. Being permanent fixtures, bulkheads were supported by 3in to 4in vertical stanchions which were tenoned into beams and decks accordingly.

Prior to the turn of the eighteenth century all cutters were clinker-built. With this system, the lower edges of one strake of planking overlapped the upper edge of the strake below, the two mating surfaces being clenched with copper nails and roves. All planks were in turn fastened to the frames with bolts and treenails. The principle disadvantage of the system lay in the difficulty of replacing damaged boards because it entailed removing the adjacent planks. All of the bottom planking was 2½in thick and approximately 12in broad amidships. The ends of these planks, which were set into the rabbets at the stem- and sternposts, were called hood ends.

The main wale was wrought in a single strake across the frame joints at the second futtock heads. Each plank, made from oak 5in thick and 15in broad was joined together by 'hook and butt' scarphs. These wales added strength to resist the hogging and sagging stresses generally incurred in wooden ship construction. The bulwarks above the wales were planked up with 2½in boards.

Internally, waterways were wrought along the bulwarks over the ends of the upper deck beams; these formed a watertight seal between the deck planking and the ship's side. Directly above the waterway a deep band of planking called the spriketting was worked up to the level of the sheer rail which coincided with the gunport sills. Spirketting was generally wrought top and butt fashion.

The stern of the ship was built with a square tuck, a flat transom formed by the fashion pieces, terminating at the wing transom. This, like the bottom planking, was closed in with 2½in thick boards. The framing of the stern above this point consisted of six counter timbers which were set up with their heels bolted to the wing transom. These counter timbers were braced laterally with deck transoms and transom beams accordingly, the latter forming the sills for the chase ports. The remaining surfaces of the counter were planked up with 2in boards. At the fore part of the hull the entire structure was stiffened with deck hooks and breast hooks wrought transversely across the inboard side of the hawse pieces.

DECORATION

Few, if any, cutters were embellished with elaborate decorations and carvings at the head and stern. Most of the vessels were either hired or bought in for service from owners who cared little for superfluous and expensive ornamentation. Cutters, therefore, were in general plain. The external hull was 'bright', payed with rosin, and the wales painted black. All inboard works, the bulwarks and various deck fittings were, following general practice at this period, painted red. To comply with standard men-of-war at the turn of the nineteenth century the later cutters adopted the colour scheme of buff painted sides and inboard works while the wales remained black.

The two paintings in the Science Museum, Kensington, however, portray the model of the cutter *Alert* with a certain amount of decoration. The upperworks are decorated with a whorled frieze painted in gold and highlighted with red on a bluish-green earth. Similarly, the transom and counter are adorned with various motifs embellished with the same colouring. Whether this vessel was actually painted in this manner is conjectoral, and it seems more likely that such enhancement was merely artistic licence either on the part of the original modelmaker or the painter himself; the addition of such work on small vessels would seem to have been unlikely.

The two paintings of the *Alert*, which originally formed part of a collection assembled by George III, clearly depict her decoration. They were executed by Joseph Marshall in 1774–75. There is a close resemblance between the painting of the model of the *Alert* and the draught of the *Rattlesnake* upon which the cutter was based. Of particular note are the squared-off gunports and the additional deadeye and chain, irrespective of other minor details.

LAYOUT & INTERNAL ARRANGEMENT

The *Alert*, like all armed naval cutters, only had one complete full length deck. The remaining space below the upper deck consisted of two platforms divided by a single main bulkhead. In comparison with other naval vessels the general layout and internal compartment arrangements for cutters were relatively simple albeit rather cramped.

The upper, or main, deck layout consisted of a series of centreline hatchways, companionways and skylights. At the foremost end of this deck, on the forecastle, were positioned the windlass, bowsprit step and catheads. Perhaps the most prominent feature of cutters was the running bowsprit which would be retracted in heavy weather or when the ship was moored in confined waters. It was fitted off-centre to the port side of the vessel and held in position by a large iron gammon ring bolted to one side of the stempost. The heel of the bowsprit was square in section and fashioned with a series of horizontally bored square holes through which passed an iron fid which retained the bowsprit in position against the bitts. Each bitt head was similarly furnished with horizontal square holes to receive the iron fid. The adjustment of bowsprit length was easily attained by the realignment and relocation of the iron fid to an alternative hole in the bowsprit heel itself.

Other fittings on this deck included the jeer bitts which were situated abaft the mainmast. In addition to their regular furnishings and crosspiece, these bitts were also fitted with a winch to raise or lower the large and heavy gaff and incorporated in this winch was a pawl and rachet mechanism. Crank handles could be detached from the winch spindle when not required. Afore the mainmast was the galley flue leading from the firehearth below. Shot garlands on this particular ship were placed along the bulwarks adjacent to the gunports. The practice of having shot garlands fitted amidships around hatchways had not yet become standard in all vessels at this period. At the aftermost end a short low deck was raised over the counter. This served both as a housing for the rudder stock and as a support platform for two stern chase guns. Records of the *Alert* do not indicate that she carried guns at this position, but some later vessels did carry two 12-pounder carronades here.

The after platform which comprised the main cabin accommodation was subdivided into three sections by transverse bulkheads. The foremost section consisted of a central lobby and two separate cabins, one for the Master, the other allocated for the surgeon. If necessary (subject to the size of the crew) the surgeon also shared his cabin with the Master's mate. Access to the lobby was attained by either a companionway reaching from the upper deck or by a door leading from the fore platform (or lower deck). This lobby also served as a form of wardroom for the Warrant Officers. At the fore end of the lobby was a small scuttle which lead to the magazine light room below.

The entire centre section incorporated the Captain's accommodation. His quarters included a central day cabin and a bed place, the latter furnished with a fitted bunk and commode. The day cabin, which served as both his office and dining quarters, was illuminated from the skylight on the upper deck. A second cabin sited on the opposite side of the ship was generally used as his personal storeroom though it could be refurbished to accommodate the Master. Aft of the Captain's quarters was the breadroom which contained casks of flour or biscuits. Entry to this compartment was generally made via a door in the Captain's day cabin. For provisioning purposes, however, stores were loaded from a hatch on the upper deck.

Below the after platform lay the magazine, access to which was made through a scuttle leading from the Captain's day cabin. Although the magazine was rather cramped, it followed the conventional plan and was divided into two separate areas. At the fore end was the powder room, which contained the main supply of gunpowder in small kegs. The after end was termed the filling room and this was where the powder was measured out into the cartridge cases. When filled these cartridges were stored on racks either side to be ready for use. At no time was a naked light permitted inside the magazine and so, centred at the fore end of the powder room, there was a lightroom which housed the light for illuminating the entire magazine. For safety purposes the lantern within this room was retained behind a glass screen which was further protected by a fitted copper grill. For additional safety when the vessel was in action, anti-flash precautions were implemented. This was achieved by fitting wetted hides or canvas over the magazine scuttle and lobby door. Each cover was furnished with a flap through which the cartridges could be passed.

The fore platform (or lower deck) which accommodated the majority of the crew extended from the main transverse bulkhead forward. The foremost end of this deck, divided off by a single transverse bulkhead, was longitudinally sub-divided into three storerooms: the boatswain's store, the carpenter's store and the steward's room in between. Access to the fore peak was made via a small scuttle within the boatswain's store.

The remaining area throughout this deck was primarily used as the crew's living quarters and there was space to hang a maximum of thirty hammocks either side. When required, mess tables were slung from the overhead deck beams. To permit access to the wings of the hold complete portions of the deck area between the beams could be lifted. On the centreline between the main hatch leading to the hold and the mainmast was the sailroom fitted with doors on either side, while afore the mainmast was the ship's galley with its iron firehearth. To reduce any possible fire hazard the deck area in this vicinity was covered with a layer of stone tiles. Adjacent to the main after bulkhead were two storerooms, one for dry provisions and the other, on the starboard side, for the gunner's store.

Below the fore platform was the hold, which contained most of the ship's provisions. These stores included various casks containing salted pork and beef, pease, oatmeal, water and beer. To prevent them shifting around with the roll and pitch of the ship these barrels were meticulously arranged in tiers amid a packing of dry shingle.

Fitted aft on the centreline was an integral structure which combined both the pump well and the shot locker. Amidships, within the vicinity of the main hatch, was the cable tier where the anchor hawsers were stowed and allowed to drain off into the bilges. The fore part of the hold afore the forward access hatch was partitioned off by two transverse bulkheads, between which lay the coal hole and the spirit room which held the seamen's rum issue or, on occasion, brandy. Access to each of these compartments was made by way of scuttles from the deck above.

STEERING GEAR

The *Alert* was simply steered by means of a rudder and tiller; a wheel was considered unnecessary for a vessel of this size. The rudder was made from two baulks of timber: a main piece and back piece. The main piece, which was made from oak, extended the entire length of the rudder. The fore face of this timber was bearded to 45 degrees on each edge to permit rotation and fashioned with four recesses to receive the pintles. Unlike conventional rudders the fore end of the heel was cut back to conform to the angled face of the end of the keel. This portion itself was also bearded. The back piece, made from fir, was fayed, dowelled and bolted to the after edge of the main piece. Being of shorter length its uppermost edge was fashioned with a hance which reduced the width of the rudder to that of the main piece. To the heel of the rudder a sole piece made from elm was fitted which served to prevent damage to the vulnerable end grain of the rudder timbers.

The rudder was suspended from the sternpost by four pairs of wrought iron pintles and gudgeons. The gudgeons were wrought with integral iron faces which were bolted directly on to the hull. Similarly, braces formed with the pintles gave additional stiffening to the rudder itself. The uppermost recess for the pintles and gudgeon was fashioned to receive a wooden rudder lock, fitted to prevent the rudder riding up and unhinging.

The head of the mainpiece, the rudder stock, extended upward through the helm port in the counter and terminated about 2ft above the level of the upper deck. The head of the rudder stock was fashioned with a mortice to receive the after end of the tiller. The timber at this point was strengthened with a series of iron hoops and straps to prevent the head splitting.

The tiller was made from ash which is flexible and shock absorbent. The after end of the tiller was suitably formed into a tenon which fitted into the mortice of the rudder stock. The other end was formed into a rounded handle grip for the helmsman. Under normal conditions only one helmsman would have steered the vessel but assistance would have been necessary during heavy weather.

TABLE 1: **TYPES OF ANCHOR, SIZES AND WEIGHTS**

DIMENSION	SHEET				BOWER				STREAM		KEDGE	
	18cwt		17cwt		15cwt		14cwt		6cwt		3cwt	
	ft	*in*	*ft*	*in*	*ft*	*in*	*ft*	*in*	*ft*	*in*	*ft*	*in*
Length of the shank	12	2	11	10	11	2	10	10	8	3½	6	10
Size at the throat	–	7	–	6⅞	–	6⅝	–	6½	–	4⅝	–	3⅝
Size at the small	–	5⅝	–	5 7/16	–	5 3/16	–	5 1/16	–	3 15/16	–	2 15/16
Length of the square	2	1	2	0¾	2	0	1	11¾	1	5¾	1	2½
Size of the square	–	5½	–	5⅜	–	5⅛	–	5	–	3⅞	–	2⅞
Outer diameter of ring	1	11	1	10¾	1	10¼	1	10	1	4½	1	1½
Inner diameter of ring	1	8½	1	8¼	1	7⅞	1	7⅝	1	2⅞	1	0¼
Hole diameter for the ring	–	3¾	–	3¾	–	3½	–	3½	–	2¾	–	2½
Length of the arms	4	2	4	0⅜	3	10	3	8⅝	2	10	2	4
Size at the throat	–	7 5/16	–	7 3/16	–	6 15/16	–	6 13/16	–	5	–	4
Size at the small	–	5 15/16	–	5¾	–	5½	–	5⅜	–	4⅛	–	3
Length & breadth of palms	1	11½	1	11¼	1	10¾	1	10½	1	5	1	2
Thickness of palms close to blade	–	1½	–	1½	–	1½	–	1½	–	1¼	–	0⅞
Thickness of palms at the edge	–	1	–	1	–	1	–	1	–	0¾	–	0⅝
Estimated cost at £1.10s/cwt	£27 20s 0d		£25 10s 0d		£22 10s 0d		£21 0s 0d		£9 0s 0d		£4 10s 0d	

GROUND TACKLE

In accordance with the authorised regulations, vessels of between 180 and 190 tons like the *Alert* carried a total of five anchors comprising one sheet (or 'best bower') anchor of 18cwt, two bower of 15cwt, one stream of 6cwt, and one kedge of 3cwt. Irrespective of these specifications, the weights given for the sheet and bower anchors do appear to be a little excessive, thus it can be assumed that alternative smaller and lighter anchors of 17cwt and 14cwt may have been used at the discretion of the ship's Master.

Two anchors, the sheet and one of the bowers, were secured at all times to their respective cables ready for instant use, and each was stowed, suspended from its cathead, and lashed to the ship's side. The sheet anchor was always stowed on the starboard side of the ship. Whether the second bower was stowed abaft the sheet anchor is uncertain; if this were the case the smaller kedge anchor would have been stowed, lashed to its shank. Alternatively, both the second bower and the kedge may have been stowed below in the hold along with the stream anchor and with their stocks removed to permit better storage.

Most cutters were equipped with six cables all of which were 100 fathoms long. Five of these cables were 11½in circumference and two were permanently rigged to the sheet and bower anchors; the remaining three were kept as spares. The sixth cable of 7½in circumference was used mainly for the kedge anchor, and its lighter weight (approximately 11 tons per 100 fathoms) made it easier to handle when warping the ship. Each main anchor cable passed through its respective hawse hole at the bow of the ship and was then passed around the windlass spindle. It then ran aft to the main hatchway where it descended to the cable tier in the hold.

The windlass comprised two stout vertical timbers called carrick bitts which supported the horizontal spindle. The spindle itself was retained in position by removable cheeks forelocked to the after side of the bitts. The carrick bitts were further supported on their fore side by long standards, and the whole assembly acted as a set of riding bitts when the ship was at anchor. The windlass was turned using wooden handspikes which were inserted into square sockets disposed radially around the spindle. Warping heads for hauling lesser sized hawsers were fashioned at the extremities of

TABLE 2: **GUN DIMENSIONS**

TYPE	Length of piece		Bore diameter	Weight of piece			Shot diameter	proof		Powder required for charges: Service		Saluting		Scaling		Gun crew
	ft	*in*	*ins*	*cwt*	*qtr*	*lb*	*ins*	*lb*	*oz*	*lb*	*oz*	*lb*	*oz*	*lb*	*oz*	*Number*
6pdr gun	7	0	3.668	17	1	14	3.494	6	0	2	0	2	0	0	8	5
6pdr gun	6	0	3.668	16	0	14	3.494	6	0	2	0	2	0	0	8	5
4pdr gun	6	0	3.205	12	2	13	3.053	4	0	1	8	1	8	0	6	4
3pdr gun	4	6	2.912	7	5	0	2.774	3	0	1	0	1	0	0	4	4
½pdr swivel	3	0	1.602	1	2	0	1.526	0	8	0	3	0	3	0	1	1
18pdr carronade	3	3	5.160	10	0	0	5.049	4	0	2	0	2	0	1	0	5
18pdr carronade	2	4	5.160	8	1	0	5.049	4	0	2	0	2	0	1	0	5
12pdr carronade	2	2	4.520	5	3	0	4.403	3	0	1	8	1	8	0	12	5
6pdr carronade	2	8	3.668	4	3	0	3.494	2	0	1	0	1	0	0	8	4

Cost of ordnance power and shot			
6ft long 6-pounder – Weight 16cwt 14lbs	£16	0s	0d
1 barrel of powder (weight 100lbs)	£ 5	0s	0d
1 ton of 6lb shot (approx 374 balls)	£10	0s	od
(1 individual shot; each approx)	–	–	6½d
Grape shot, 100 (weight 5cwt 1qtr 12lb)	£ 2	13s	6¾d
Tin or cannister shot, 100 (weight 5cwt 1 qtr 12lb)	£ 2	13s	6¾d

(Note: Each single grape or cannister shot comprised of twelve half pound balls giving a total weight of 6lb. The estimated cost of each was 6½d)

the spindle and a ratchet arrangement was provided to lock the spindle. This mechanism consisted of two iron pawls, each of which were fitted to two respective pawl bitts, (these bitts also served as a step for the bowsprit). When required, these pawls engaged with corresponding iron pawl rings fitted integrally with the spindle. Disengagement of the pawls permitted the windlass to veer and allow the cable to run freely. When weighing anchor the windlass was operated by about ten men, and others stood by to tail the cable. In most cases the ship's side was protected from the anchor flukes by an anchor lining, a series of elm boards that sheathed the hull planking. The windlass also served to hoist the yards, embark stores, and the ship's boat.

PUMPS

The vessel was furnished with two identical elm pumps. Each pump casing was made from elm, bored out parallel to its entire length and shaped to the desired external diameter. The complete casing was reinforced with a series of iron hoops which were shrunk onto the timber when the wood was dry. Two pistons or 'boxes' were fitted within the tube of the pump, one of which was fixed and the other free to reciprocate. The lower box, which was fixed, was set a short distance from the lower part of the casing and was held in position by its own weight and the swelling of the timber when wet. The complete box was fitted with a non-return valve, often referred to as a poppet valve, and an iron staple. The latter was fitted to allow the box to be retrieved by a hook for inspection and maintenance.

The upper box was the same as the lower box except that it was free to move within the casing. An iron shaft known as the spear was attached to the staple of this box. The upper end of the spear was loose fitted to the operating handle, or 'brake', and the brake was allowed to pivot on a pin set between two 'ears'. The ears were made integral with the uppermost part of the casing.

Operation of the pump was simple, though not particularly efficient, and the output was approximately 25 gallons per minute. When the brake was operated to lower the upper valve box, the water between the two boxes was compressed until the non-return valve on the upper box lifted which allowed the water to pass up through it. The same compressive action kept the valve on the lower box shut. On the upward movement the water retained above the free box was lifted and discharged out of the top of the casing. At the same moment a partial vacuum occurred between the two valve boxes, the poppit valve on the lower box opened permitting water to be drawn up from below the lower box. As the water was pumped it flowed across the deck into the scuppers and overboard.

ARMAMENT

When first commissioned, the *Alert* was equipped with ten cast iron 4-pounder carriage guns, each of which weighed approximately 12½cwt. Each gun was 6ft long (excluding the cascable) with a bore of 3.20in including windage. The solid round shot itself had a diameter of 3.05in. The maximum range for a gun of this size was estimated at 1,700 yards and point blank range about 300 yards. The normal charge of powder required to fire the 4lb shot was between one third and one half of the weight of the shot (1½–2lb). There were different charges for other sorts of firing such as proof firing (4lb), saluting (1lb 5oz) and scaling (6oz). Other charges were set to attain variations in range. The standard gun crew for this type of weapon consisted of four men.

The gun was mounted on a conventional carriage made of elm which was resistant to fragmentation into small splinters if hit and able to withstand

TABLE 3: **GUN TACKLE SIZES FOR 4- AND 6-POUNDER GUNS**

	Rope circumference	Length of rope
	in	*ft*
Breeching	4¼	24
Gun tackle	2	30
Traversing tackle	2	26–30

the shock of the gun's recoil. The carriage consisted of two side cheeks, a front transom, and a bed which carried the quoin. The quoin was a wedge-shaped block of timber placed under the breech which was used to elevate or depress the gun. Axeltrees made from elm were fitted at the fore and after ends of the carriage, onto which trucks (wooden wheels) of oak were fitted. These were removable and the rear trucks might be taken off to give a greater elevation to the gun. The gun barrel was held to the carriage by iron hinges known as cap squares which fitted over the trunnions and were locked down by a pin inserted in the keep plate.

Each gun was furnished with gun tackle, traversing tackle and a breeching rope. The breeching rope was made of good-quality stout hemp which secured the gun to the bulwark and took the strain of the recoil. Fitted either side of the carriage was the gun tackle which was used to run the gun out ready to fire. At the rear of the carriage was the traversing tackle which could be used to simply haul the gun back for reloading, or to turn the gun to make the oblique fire possible, by transferring the tackle to an adjacent ringbolt in the deck.

After her refit at Plymouth in February 1778, all of the 4-pounders were replaced with twelve 6-pounders, and the additional two guns were mounted at the aftermost broadside ports on each side. This modification increased her broadside weight from 20lbs to 36lbs.

Each 6-pounder was 6ft 6in in length overall and weighed 18cwt and bored out to a diameter of 3.675in. The diameter of the shot in this case was 3½in. The maximum range for the 6-pounder was 1800 yards and point blank 300 yards. The charges for firing a 6-pounder shot were between 2lb and 3lb, for proof firing 6lb, saluting 2lb and scaling 8oz; a gun crew of five men was needed. The gun carriage was the same apart from its size, as described for the 4-pounder.

In addition to her main armament the *Alert* also carried between six and ten half pounder swivel guns, and there were ten pedestals on which these guns could be mounted. They were used primarily as anti-personnel weapons and could be loaded with cannister shot as an alternative to a single round shot. Each gun was 3ft long, weighed approximately 2cwt, and had a bore diameter of 1½in. The diameter of the solid shot was approximately 1¼in and in general was made from lead. The charge required to fire the half pound ball was 3oz, proof firing 8oz, saluting 3oz, and scaling 1oz. The gun was mounted by its trunnions into an iron yoke furnished with a pintle, which was inserted into a vertical hole bored into the timber pedestal. The pedestals were formed from the heads of the toptimbers, six aft and four forward.

As a preference, the British Navy generally used solid round shot. However, alternative types of projectiles were carried, principally for destroying spars, sails and rigging. These variations included bar shot, chain shot and expanding shot, all of which comprised two half spherical heads joined together by either an iron bar or chain. On leaving the gun these projectiles travelled with a rotary action and could scythe through cordage, spars and sails. Though potentially damaging the Navy seldom utilised this form of shot because of its inherent inaccuracy.

Cannister or grape shot was commonly used against personnel. The former consisted of a sealed tin cannister filled with musket balls which shattered on impact and released a deadly hail amongst the crowded decks of a ship.

Even more effective was grape shot which comprised a number of iron balls centred around an iron spindle set in a circular wooden base plate. The assembly was then covered with a canvas bag which was secured and laced externally with cords. The contrivance was then painted and sealed with tar giving it the appearance of a bunch of black grapes.

MASTS & YARDS

In general, the basic cutter rig resembled that of the single-masted sloop; the main difference between the two lay in the manner in which the bowsprit was fitted. On sloops the bowsprit was fixed permanently at a set angle whereas on all cutters a running bowsprit was used. All the spars were made from pine imported from either Riga or New England.

At this period all small vessels had the lower mast and top mast combined in a single spar and a separate topgallant mast rigged above. The main mast, made from a single tree, was furnished with a set of bibs to support the tressletrees at the mast head. At this period it is unlikely that crosstrees, spreaders and bolsters were fitted though their appearance on later cutters is almost universal. The heel of the mast was fashioned with a tenon which fitted into a mortice cut in the upper surface of the mast step. The step itself was made from a single baulk of oak set astride the keelson and securely bolted in position.

Contemporary masts and yards lists for cutters include two topgallant masts: one of standard length and another shorter one for use in heavy weather. The standard topgallant mast, (sometimes furnished with a long pole-head) was rigged with its heel set between the lower mast tressletrees and retained with an iron fid. Further support was given by means of a cap fitted at the extremity of the lower mast head. The shorter topgallant mast was fitted in an identical manner. General practice for this period indicates that the topgallant mast was fitted abaft the lower mast head, and that the alternative fashion (afore the mast head) was adopted later.

The bowsprit, located by a gammon ring on the port side of the stempost was fashioned with a square heel approximately 12ft in length. This portion

TABLE 4: **DIMENSIONS OF MASTS AND YARDS**

Pheasant cutter

Mast Length ft	in	Mast Dia in	Yard Length ft	in	Yard Dia in	
(89) 81		(22½) 22				Mainmast and topmast
33		9				Topgallant
25		9				Topgallant short
			44	5	8	Topsail yard
			54	9	9	Spread yard
			49	6	9	Square sail yard
39		9¾				Gaff
16		9½				Storm gaff
60		12¾				Boom (clamped)
37	2	6				Driver boom
56	6	18½				Bowsprit
41	6	9				Jib boom
37	2	8				Mizzen mast
			36	6	6	Mizzen yard

Author's Note: the *Pheasant* was purchased in March 1778. Her burthen by builders own measurement was 149 tons, length 66ft and breadth 25ft. Armament comprised twelve 4-pounders. She capsized in the Channel on the 20 June 1781.

Based on a letter from Deptford, dated 6 June 1778.

TABLE 5: **DIMENSIONS OF STANDING AND RUNNING RIGGING AND BLOCKS**

(Based on *Steel's Elements of Mastmaking, Sailmaking and Rigging*, 1774)

	Size	Length	BLOCKS Type	Size	No
	In	*Fathom*		*in*	
Bowsprit					
Shrouds	5½	14	–	–	–
tackle falls	2½	38	D*	10	4
Jib					
Halliard	5	35	Sc	14	2
tackle fall	3½	40	Trc	12	2
Jack	6½	24	Sn, Ibd, c	15	1
Sheets cable laid	5	18	S*	14	2
Downhauler	2	24	S	8	1
Inhauler	2½	15	Dc	8	1
Inhauler	2½	15	Sn, c*	8	1
Heel rope	3	21	Sn, Ibd	13	1
Flying Jib Halliard	2½	35	–	–	–
Sheets	2½	24	–	–	–
Jack	2½	30	–	–	–
Downhauler	2	24	–	–	–
Foremast					
Sail Halliards	2½	50	Dc	10	1
Sail Halliards	2½	50	S*	10	1
Downhauler	2	30	S*	8	1
Jack tackle	2½	10	S*	8	2
Bowline	3	14	S*	8	2
Sheets	3	7	S*	10	2
Mainmast					
Girtlines	2½	50	S	9	2
lashings	1	10	–	–	–
Pendents of tackles	6	26	Sc	15	2
Runners of tackles	5½	24	Lt, c*	20	2
Falls	3½	45	Sc*	11	2
Shrouds, cabled,	8	84	DE	12	8
Seizings, eye	1	68	–	–	–
throat	1	68	–	–	–
end	1	68	–	–	–
Lanyards,	4	40	–	–	–
Ratline	1½	120	–	–	–
Stay, cabled 4 strands,	13	16	DE	18	1
Seizings	1½	10	–	–	–
Lanyard	4	10	–	–	–
Worming	1½	60	–	–	–
Lashing	2	25	–	–	–
Preventer stay	6½	18	DE	9	1
(Cabled 4 strands)	–	–	Ib	9	1
Lanyards	3	4	–	–	–
Seizing	1	9	–	–	–
Boom topping lifts	4½	26	S. Ibd, c	12	1
Runner	4	12	Sc	12	1
			Sc	13	1
Fall	2½	32	Dc	12	1
			Sc*	9	1
Guy pendent	5	9	T	–	1
Tackle fall	3	30	D*	12	1
			S*	12	1
Gaff Span	4½	5	–	–	–
downhauler peak	2	28	S	8	1
throat	2	38	S	8	1
Inner tie	6	13	S, Ibd, c	14	2
halliard	3	56	Dc	14	2
Outer tie	6	19½	–	–	–
halliards	3½	90	S, Ibd, c	12	3
			Dc	12	2
Earings, inner	1½	18	–	–	–
outer	1½	18	–	–	–
Sheet	3	60	Trc	15	2
Tack tackle	2½	20	D*	8	1
			S*	8	1
Luff tackles	2½	40	D*	11	2
			S*	11	2
	5	7	–	–	–
Main reef pendents	5	7	–	–	–
	5	9	–	–	–
	5	10	–	–	–
Topmast					
Tackle fall	3	30	Lt*	20	1
			S*	11	1
Tie	3	26	–	–	–
Halliard	2	32	D	9	1
			S*	9	1
Horses	2½	8	–	–	–
Braces	2	60	S	8	2
Lifts	2	45	S	8	4
Parrel ropes	2	8	Par	12	1
Racking and seizing	¾	10	–	–	–
Clewlines	1½	44	S	6	4
Buntlines	1½	44	S	6	2
Bowlines	2	66	Tr	9	1
Bridles	2	7	T	–	6
Sheets	3½	42	S, Sho	10	2
Quarter blocks	–	–	D & Dsc, c	12	1
Trysail sheet	2	33	Tr*	11	2
Downhauler	2	24	–	–	–
Lacing	2	24	–	–	–
Studdingsail halliards	2	96	–	–	–
Sheets	2	38	–	–	–
Tacks	2	90	–	–	–
Downhaulers	2	30	–	–	–
Topgallantmast					
Standing backstays	2½	60	–	–	–
Tackles	2	28	S*	8	8
Stay	3	30	–	–	–
Halliards	2	40	S	9	2
Top Rope	4	28	D	9	1
Fall	2	45	S*	9	1
Tricing line	2	30	S	8	2
Crossjack Yard					
Clewlines	2	40	–	–	–
Braces	2½	60	S	8	2
Sheets	2½	14	–	–	–
Halliards	2 ½	50	Dc*	9	1
			Sc*	9	1
Lifts, running	3	35	S	8	2
Buntlines	2	40	–	–	–
Tacks	2½	14	–	–	–
Horses	3	12	–	–	–
Stirrups	2	8	–	–	–
Horse down the mast	5	25	DE	7	2
Strap	3½	4	–	–	–
Lanyard	2½	5	–	–	–
Necessary Ropes					
Cat falls	3	44	D, Ibd, c	12	2
Fish tackle pendent	4	3	H & T	1	1
Stoppers, sheet anchor	5	5	–	–	–
Best bower	5	5	–	–	–
Small bower	5	5	–	–	–
Stream anchor	2½	3	–	–	–
Kedge	2	3	–	–	–
Deck and bit cabled	6½	7½	T	–	4
Lanyards	2	10	–	–	–
Seizings	¾	20	–	–	–
Shank painters sheet-anchor cabled	4	6	–	–	–
Best bower	4	4	–	–	–
Small bower	4	4	–	–	–
Buoy rope sheet anchor					

cabled	4	18	–	–	–
Best bower cabled	4	18	–	–	–
Small bower cabled	4	18	–	–	–
Stream anchor cabled	3	20	–	–	–
Kedge cabled	2½	20	–	–	–
Entering	3	10	–	–	–
Wheel, white	2	12	S	7	2
Puddening of anchors	2½	50	–	–	–
	2	18	–	–	–
	¾	42	–	–	–
	2½	30	–	–	–
	1½	6	–	–	–
Slings, Buoy	4	12	–	–	–
Hogshead	3	3	–	–	–
Can hooks	4	6	–	–	–
Cable bends	1½	34	–	–	–
Nettings for the tops, quarters, waste, and barricades	¾	540	–	–	–
Halliard for ensigns	¾	20	–	–	–
Slings, pendent	¾	24	–	–	–
For different uses on	–	–	Sn, Ibd, c*	12	2
board the ship	–	–		10	2

	–	–	Bulkhd	9	2
Ridge ropes for the quarters	2½	108	–	–	–
Boat					
Main and fore halliards	1½	10	–	–	–
Main and fore sheets	1½	10			
Grapnel ropes cabled	3	35	–	–	–
Painter	3	5	–	–	–
Slings	4½	5	–	–	–
Seizings	¾	10	–	–	–
Rudder lanyards	¾	1	–	–	–
Sternfast	2	5	–	–	–

* Indicates that the block or heart is fitted with a hook and thimble.

c	– Coaked.	Par	– Parrel.
D	– Double block.	S	– Single block.
Dc	– Double block, coaked.	Sc	– Single block, coaked.
DE	– Deadeyes.	Sho	– Shoulder block.
Dsc	– Double block scored.	Sn	– Snatch block.
H	– Heart.	T	– Thimbles.
Ibd	– Iron bound.	Tr	– Treble block.
Lt	– Long tackle block	Trc	– Treble block, coaked.

of the spar was housed between the two windlass pawl bitts and secured with an iron fid passing horizontally through both the bitts and the heel. Additional fid holes allowed the bowsprit to be run out to various lengths.

Like the mast, all the yards, the booms and the gaff were made from pine. With the exception of the topgallant yard, and possibly the spread-yard, the middle portion of all yards were octagonal in cross section, while the remaining parts of the yards were round. Most of the yards were furnished with two cleats at their centre to retain the ties and, if rigged, the slings. These cleats were also employed for the retention of the parrel ropes. However, evidence suggests that parrels (if used) would only have been rigged to the topsail yard. Stop cleats for securing the various strops, brace pendants and blocks were also fitted to the fore and after faces of the yardarms at the ends. The square sail yard was, in all probability, made from two separate pieces of timber tabled and scraphed together and strengthened with battens nailed across the flats of the octagonal section. Whether the spread-yard was made in the same manner is not altogether certain but as it probably served as a spare yard for the square sail it is likely.

The mainsail was spread on a gaff and boom, both which had jaws which fitted the mast. For heavier weather conditions a small mainsail on a short storm gaff and driver boom was rigged.

Other than this standard rig contemporary records suggest that cutters also had a mizzen mast and yard, driver boom, outrigger and jib-boom. It would appear that in light winds a mizzen mast could be temporarily rigged at the aftermost extremity of the upper deck and a large lugsail set on the mizzen yard. The foot of this sail was extended by an outrigger projecting beyond the stern. Alternatively, this sail might be spread with a driver boom. According to Steel this sail could either be a square sail bent to a yard, or a spritsail bent to the mast and peaked with a sprit and a driver boom. When not in use, these additional spars were stowed on the upper deck alongside the hatchways.

The reference made to the jibboom is of particular interest. The inclusion of this item within the masts and yards lists implies that the rig of the cutter could, if necessary, be altered to that of a single-masted sloop and carry a flying jib.

RIGGING

The standing rigging consisted of forestays, backstays and shrouds. Up for long periods and exposed to all weathers these ropes were well treated with tar and served, parcelled or wormed as necessary. Unlike the rigging on later cutters it did not terminate at the mast head but at a position approximately midway between the mast head and the jaws of the gaff. The forestay of the combined lower and topmast was set up with an eye which passed around the hounds of the mast. A stop termed as a 'mouse' was raised on the stay to prevent the eye closing. The stay then passed forward to a five-holed deadeye which was secured by a lanyard rove through similarly sized holes bored in the stemhead. The lower end of the forestay was set up 'cutter stay fashion'. This practice entailed passing the end of the stay around the front of the deadeye, then crossing the end over the standing part of the stay and doubling it back around the deadeye and securing it with four seizings.

Directly above the forestay was the preventer stay, the lower end of which was seized in the conventional manner to a thimble which in turn was secured to the stemhead by a lanyard. Unlike larger vessels the practice of 'snaking' the preventer to the forestay was omitted as this would have impaired the raising and lowering of the foresail.

Generally, most cutters were rigged with four pairs of lower shrouds, each pair having an eye spliced or seized into a bight which was passed over the head of the mast. The lower ends of each shroud were secured to the channel with deadeyes and lanyards. The lower deadeye was fastened to the ship's side with a chain plate. The fore shroud either side was wormed, parcelled and served throughout its length to prevent chafe. Once all of the shrouds were rigged they were 'rattled down' with their ratlines which formed footholds for the crew. Contemporary evidence suggests that the *Alert* (and its counterpart *Rattlesnake*) was modified to include a fifth pair of deadeyes either side for the standing backstay. In order to facilitate this modification the third gunport had to be moved a short distance and the channels extended. Running backstays were fitted to iron plates bolted to the ship's side.

General practice of this period suggests that the topgallant mast was fitted abaft the head of the lower mast and in which case both shrouds and backstays were omitted, the mast itself being supported by virtue of its position. Rigged like this the topgallant mast could be swiftly struck and brought down when the wind got up. Shortly after this period the length of the topgallant mast was increased and it had to be fitted in a more permanent fashion afore the lower mast head and following the conventional practice used on ship-rigged vessels. When so fitted forestays, backstays and shrouds had to be introduced.

The running bowsprit was supported by a single shroud either side. Each shroud was spliced to a hook and thimble at their outer end which in turn was moused to an eye on an iron hoop driven on the end of the bowsprit. The inner ends of the shrouds were seized to a single block which was part of a tackle whose other block was hooked to an eyebolt fitted on the ship's side. The tackle fall was made fast to one of the adjacent timberheads.

The running rigging was left untarred to prevent the possibility of snagging in the block sheaves. The rigging for the yards simply comprised of ties (or halliards) and lifts which served to raise or lower the various yards as required. Lifts were only rigged to the topsail yard and spread-yard. Slings and parrels, used for holding the yards to the mast, appear not to have been employed during this period though they were generally used for the lower yards on later vessels once the cutter rig had become more standardised. At the extremities of the yards brace pendants and blocks for the braces were rigged. Contemporary sources indicate that braces were only fitted to the topsail yard and spread-yards and that the squaresail yard and topgallant yard were normally set 'flying'. Running rigging for the gaff and boom consisted of topping lifts and halliards which rove through blocks rigged to the mast head, their falls being spliced to a double block that connected by its own fall to a single block hooked to the channel or bulwark. Rigged a short distance from the outboard end of the boom was the main sheet block and tackle. This tackle comprised of two double blocks, the standing block itself being hooked and moused to an eyebolt fitted midships on the short platform fitted at the stern. The sheet fall was secured to the taffrail.

The running rigging for loosening and furling the sails comprised clewlines, buntlines and leechlines. These particular ropes generally applied to the squaresails. Reef points used for shortening sail were only rigged on the mainsail and foresail.

Most of the sails were furnished with tacks, sheets, bowlines and bridles which were used to set the sail. Bowlines and bridles were omitted from the square sail and topgallant sail as both were generally set flying.

The foresail was laced to the forestay and raised by a halliard leading through a block at the masthead. The foresail tack was rove through a block bolted to the inboard side of the stem, the fall being made fast on a nearby cleat. The foresail sheet tackle, which comprised a single and double block, was made fast to an iron horse fitted transversely across the upper deck afore the mainmast. The jib was set flying, the foot of the sail being run out on the bowsprit on a traveller, while its peak was raised by a halliard running through a single block at the masthead. The jib tack itself was clinched to an eyebolt on the traveller, then passed forward through a sheave fitted in the end of the bowsprit, and then returned via a block set on the side of the stem near the waterline, the tack fall then being made fast to a timberhead. Jib sheets without blocks were bent to the clew of the sail and lead either side to cleats adjacent to the mainmast shrouds. To haul in this sail from the end of the bowsprit an inhauler was led from the traveller to the stem. Both the foresail and jib were rigged with downhaulers, each making fast to timberheads or cleats at the fo'c'sle.

Whether the *Alert* carried a set of studding sails is uncertain though there are references in the ship's log books to additional sails being carried in light winds. If included within the sail plan the manner in which both the sails and booms were rigged would have varied little from the gear used on larger ship-rigged vessels. Each of the studding sail booms and yards were rigged with halliards, topping lifts and guy ropes. Each studding sail (or stunsail) had its own halliard, sheets and tacks, and the topmast stunsail would have had a downhauler. Studding sails were certainly carried on most naval cutters by the end of the eighteenth century.

The rigging for the mizzen mast, outrigger, yard and boom would have been of a temporary nature. The mast was set up off-centre on the leeward side and so two housings for stepping the mast were fitted. These simple housings, made in the form of a semicircular iron bracket, were bolted to the vertical face of the short platform at the after end of the upper deck, one fitted to port, the other to starboard. Once inserted within its step the mast was supported by two temporary shrouds each side. Likewise the outrigger was supported temporarily by two guy ropes while provision was made to retain the heel of this spar in its position. Running rigging for the mizzen sail would vary accordingly depending on whether the sail was set on a driver boom, sprit yard or transverse yard.

SAILS

For small vessels, naval cutters carried a large amount of sail. Three types of sail were set: square sails, foresails, and the large mainsail bent on to the gaff and boom. Not until after an Admiralty order of August 1783 was a gaff topsail set.All these sails were made up from a series of cloths known as bolts which were 2ft wide, and they were stiffened with bolt ropes stitched around the edges.

To strengthen the sails additional cloths known as linings were sewn on at various positions, particularly where excessive wear might have occurred. These were generally placed in way of buntlines and reef points, and also sewn to the leeches and foot of the sail to reduce possible chaffing from mast fittings or standing rigging. Along the leeches and foot of the sails small rope eyes called cringles were spliced into the boltropes. To these the buntlines, leechlines, reef tackle and bridles were rigged. Larger cringles were formed from the bolt ropes at each corner of the sail.

For securing the head of the sail to the yard a series of small eyes were formed across the head seam. Through these passed short lengths of rope called robbands, the two ends of which passed over the yard and were secured with a reef knot. The head of the mainsail was laced to the gaff with robbands in the conventional manner while the luff was secured to the mast with wooden mast hoops. These loose fitting hoops were seized to cringles at regular intervals, generally eight or nine in number.

When required, eyes for the reef points were set in parallel rows along the sail. Like the robband eyes these were positioned two to every sail cloth.

SHIP'S BOATS

For conveying stores, dispatches and officers and crew, the *Alert* carried a single boat. The size and type of boat carried on naval cutters at this period is uncertain. Invariably those boats used varied according to dockyard availability, the choice being governed by preferential allocation to larger men-of-war. In all probability, 6- or 8- oared cutters varying between 12ft and 18ft in length were employed. Alternatively, a long boat either 14ft or 16ft in length may have been used. A number of Admiralty orders made provision for cutters' boats. In December 1763 one such order decreed that

TABLE 6: ESTIMATED SAIL AREA OF THE *ALERT*

Sail	Area (sq ft)
Mainsail	2,313
Square sail	1,480
Topsail	690
Topgallant sail	981
Foresail	425
Jib	827
Mizzen	984
Flying jib	300
Storm Mainsail	912
Storm foresail	324
Storm jib	300
	Total:9,560

TABLE 7: SAIL SIZES

	Cloths at		Boltropes at			
Sail	head	foot	head	foot	Leech	Luff
Mainsail	16	26	1½	1¾	1¾	3
Square sail	20	20	1½	2¼	2¼	–
Topsail	18	24	1½	2¼	2¼	–
Topgallant sail	15	18	1	1¾	1¾	–
Foresail	–	12	–	2	2	3
Jib	–	23	–	4	1½	6
Mizzen	14½	18½	1½	2¼	2¼	2¼
Flying jib	–	14	–	3½	1¼	5
Storm mainsail	7	16	1½	1¾	1¾	3
Storm foresail	–	10½	–	2¾	1¾	3½
Storm jib	–	14	–	3½	1½	5

All the sail cloths are 2ft in width. Any fraction in the dimension of a sail is divided equally to each side. Rope sizes refer to circumference and are measured in inches.

during winter only one small 4-oared boat should be allocated and that it should be carried rather than towed to avoid being lost. An order of June 1779 mentions 16ft boats for cutters while another of July 1783 recommends the addition of a second boat; and in September 1783 an order decreed that cutters employed against smuggling should replace their 18ft boat with one of 20ft.

When not in use the boat was stowed on the upper deck between the main jeer and topsail bitts and the two elm tree pumps abaft. Although this position may have deterred access through the main hatchway, entry was not often necesary at sea. When required, the boat was either swung out or hoisted inboard from tackle suspended from the boom. Should the vessel encounter action the boat was towed astern to reduce risk of damage from enemy shot and to create more space on deck.

The ship's boat also served to convey boarding parties onto vessels ordered to be searched; and for laying out the kedge anchor for warping the ship; or for towing the ship when becalmed.

CREW

When first commissioned the *Alert* carried a complement of sixty men, who were divided as commissioned officers, warrant officers and seamen.

On naval cutters only the commanding officer, in this case, Lieutenant John Bazeley, held the King's Commission. His status as captain or commander of the ship was in name only. Holding the rank of lieutenant since 1760, Bazeley was promoted to commander on 1 October 1777. His successful action against the *Lexington* off Ushant no doubt led to the promotion. Promoted to captain on the 15 April 1778, Bazeley was appointed to the 90-gun *Formidable*, Admiral Palliser's flagship during Keppel's action off Ushant in July the same year. By coincidence, Bazeley was to see action off Ushant 16 years later when he commanded the 74-gun *Alfred*, which formed part of Howe's victorious fleet at the Glorious First of June.

The non-commissioned officers – those holding the Navy Board Warrant – comprised those whose professional skills maintained the organisation and running of the ship. Of this group the most senior was the Master, Henry Peake. The master was responsible to the Commander for the navigation, safety and general well being of the ship. Supporting the master was the boatswain whose duties lay with the vessel's masts, sails, rigging and ground tackle. The remaining warrant officers, often referred to as standing officers, consisted of the surgeon – named John Bennet – the gunner and the carpenter.

The ship's muster book for the period 17 July to 31 August 1777 makes no reference to a purser which suggests that men 'of this notoriety' were rarely borne on naval cutters. Those duties generally confined to this rank were either undertaken by the clerk or even the master himself.

The remainder of the crew, colloquially referred to as 'the People' during this era, consisted of petty officers, able and ordinary seamen. Most of these men were employed in sailing the ship and manning the armament, though the petty officers of this group were also allocated specified duties, acting as mates to assist either the master, boatswain, and gunner.

The quartermaster was generally a more senior petty officer who's maturity restrained him from the rigours of going aloft and his various duties included taking charge of the helm and the stowage of casks, ballast and anchor cables. On this size of ship he would also act as the coxswain in charge of the ship's boat.

The remainder of the ship's company embraced a variety of skills and ranks. There was one midshipman (transferred to the *Lexington* prize), the captain's clerk, one steward and the ship's cook who was an Irishman named John Murphey. Also listed on the ship's books were two servants, John and Henry Bazeley, who were the commander's two sons. During this period it was common practice for aspiring officers to volunteer into the Navy under the status of captain's servant, and their patron was often their father or a benevolent uncle. When old enough they would be rated as midshipmen and ascend in rank accordingly. John Bazeley junior was promoted to lieutenant on 19 April 1783 and commander on 5 June 1794. Promoted to captain on the 11 November 1794, he took command of the 98-gun *Prince of Wales* during Lord Bridport's victory off L'Orient on 23 June 1795. He later took part in the operations off Texel during August 1799 while commanding the *Overyssel* (64). By then his brother Henry had attained the rank of commander. While commanding the 18-gun sloop *Harpy* he assisted in the capture of the French frigate *Pallas* (38) off Cape Frehel on 5 February 1800. For his participation in this action he was promoted to post captain.

When the *Alert* was recommissioned in March 1778 under Lieutenant William George Fairfax, twenty extra men were added to the ship's books. Her total complement now stood at eighty men. This increase took account of the recent upgrading of the vessel's armament.

After the *Alert* was captured in 1778, most of the crew were detained as prisoners for the duration of the War, though it it likely that Fairfax, being of commissioned rank, was exchanged. Later, as captain of the 74-gun *Venerable*, he undertook an active part in Duncan's victorious action against the Dutch off Camperdown on 11 October 1797.

PROVISIONS

The following extract from a letter from Plymouth gives a good impression of the provisioning of a naval cutter.

Plymouth Yard 19th December, 1777.

In Obedience to your directions of the 4th of April 1775 we humbly send you the following accounts of the Draught of Water and Height of the Port Cells of His Majesty's Frigate, the Thetis and the Alert Sloop together with the Weight and Quantity of all Provisions they had on board when they sailed out of port . . .

[After referring to details of the Frigate *Thetis* the letter continues]

No. 3 Alert Sloop*

		ft.	ins.
Height of Ports from the Water	Abaft	4	9
	Midships	4	2
	Afore	5	5
Draught of Water	Afore	7	6
	Abaft	12	3

* The *Alert* was re-rated to sloop in October 1777. This rate was in name only, to comply with the Admiralty instructions, when her Commanding Officer, Lt Bazeley was promoted to the rank of Commander.

		tons.	cwt.	qtr.	lb.
Ballast –	Iron, 112 Pigs	16	0	0	0
Provisions with the Fare of Costs.	Beef 462 pieces in 6 Barrels		19	3	26
	Pork 777 D^o^ in 5 Barrels		15	2	17
	Beer 12 Barrels	2	7	0	4
	Water 56 Hogsheads, 26 casks of 18 galls each	19	4	1	4
	Bread 6048 lb. in 54 bags	2	14	0	0
	Butter 420 lb. in 7 Firkins		4	2	0
	Cheese 400 lb.		3	2	8
	Oatmeal 20 Bushels		7	0	16
	Pease 16 D^o^		8	1	4
	Flower, 1,300 lb in 4 Barrels		13	0	4
	Suet 82 lb in 1 Barrel		1	0	0
	carried forward	43	18	1	27

(Second page of letter)

		tons.	cwt.	qtr.	lb.
	Brought over	43	18	1	27
Provisions with the Fare of costs	Raisons 200 lb in 2 Barrels		2	2	0
	Rum 4 half Hogsheads		12	1	0
	Vinegar 1 Hogshead		5	3	26
	Wood and Chords	1	10	1	12
	Candles			2	24
	Coals and Caldron	2	8	0	24
	Total	58	18	2	9

We are,
Honble Sirs,
Yore most obedient humble Servants,

Henslow, J. Jenner, More.

Honble Navy Board

TABLE 8 **PROGRESS BOOK** – Cutter 10 Guns 'Alert', from the Abstract of progress for Cutters, folio 36.

Built by Admiralty Order.

At what Port	Arrived	Docked Grounded or Carreened	Where Sheathed	Graved	Launched	Sailed	Nature of the repair	Charge £.s.d. of Hull, Masts and Yards.	Rigging & Stores	Total	Observations
Dover (Hen^y^ Ladd)	Began	Jany 1777	–	Bottom painted June 1777	24th June 1777	June 1777	Built	Hull only 1391.18.0.			
Deptford	30th June 1777	2nd July 1777	Coppered July 1777	–	22nd July 1777	25th Aug 1777	Fitted	496.9.3.	912.10.11.	1409.0.2.	
Admiralty Order Octr 1777 to register her as a Sloop. See abstract of the progresses for ships & Sloops No.5. folio 435.											
Plymouth	24th Sepr 1777	–	Copper Repaired Octr 1777	–	–	10th Nov 1777	Refitted	130.3.8.	425.2.7.	555.6.3.	was the Alert Cutter. Admty Order 1st Octr 1777 to register her as a Sloop by the same Name, to have 12 Carriage Guns, 4 pounders, 10 swivels & 70 men. (Refer to Author's Note below)
D^o^.	16th Jany 1778	Grounded 13th Feby 1778	–	–	Hauled off 13th Feby 1778	Mar 1778	D^o^.	92.18.8.	404.4.4.	497.3.0.*	
Portsmouth	7th May 1778	–	–	–	–	22nd May 1778	D^o^.	13.7.9.	112.10.6.	125.10.3.	
Plymouth	23rd June 1778	Grounded 25th June	–	–	Hauled off 25th June 1778	15th July 1778	D^o^.	See expence included above at Ply*			

Taken by French 17th July 1778. Admty Order, 15th February, 1780 to dispense with the want of the Officers Books. &c.

Author's Note; This statement contradicts alternative sources which imply that *Alert* at this period carried 6-pounder carriage guns and had a complement of 80.

TABLE 9 **PRINCIPLE DIMENSIONS & SCANTLINGS FOR THE *ALERT***

	Ft		In
Length			
By the Keel for Tonnage	52		0
Of the Upper (or Main) Deck from the after side of the Rabbet at the Sternpost to the fore side of the rabbet of the Stempost.	69		4
From the fore part of the Stem at the height of the Hawse Holes to the after side of the Sternpost at the height of the Wind Transom.	71		8
Foremost Perpendicular to the centre of the Dead Flat	31		8
From the Aftermost Timber to the After Perpendicular.	4		0
Tread of the Keel – from the after side of the Sternpost to the foremost part of the Fore Foot.	60		0
Breadth			
Allowing thickness of the Bottom on each side to be added to the Moulded Breadth to compute it	25		10
Moulded.	25		5
At the after part of the Wing Transom from out to outside of the Plank.	14		0
Of the Stern at the height of the Toptimber line from out to outside at the Plank.	11		4
Height			
Of the Upper (or Main) Deck from the upper edge of the Keel to the topside of the deck planking at the middle line;			
at the Fore Perpendicular	12		8
at the Dead Flat	12		4
at the After Perpendicular	15		8
Upper side of the Wing Transom from the top edge of the Keel at the middle line	14		0
Upper Edge of Keel to the Touch of the Lower Counter at the middle line	17		4
Upper Edge of Keel to the Touch of the Upper Counter.	20		8
Platforms			
Height between the upper side of the plank of the Fore Platform and the under side of Upper Deck Plank at the centre line. (minimum)	5		4
Height between the upper side of the plank of the After Platform and etc., (minimum).	6		4
Plank thickness	0		2
Height of the Port from Waterline at the Midships	5		3
Upper Deck			
Beams to round	0		7
Plank – thick			2½
Bollard Timbers			
The bollard or knighted timbers to be sided at the heads	0		10
And at the heels	0		6½
Hawse pieces			
Hawse pieces on each side in number		2	
Sided at their heads	0		10½
Sided at their heels	0		9

	Ft		In
Hawse holes			
The hawse holes in diameter	0		7½
Lower part from the deck	2		3
Their counters to come exactly on the joints of the hawsepieces and their insides lined with lead, in thickness	0		0¼
Stem			
The stem to be moulded	2		0
Number of pieces		2	
Scarphs in length	2		10
And bolted with bolts in number		5	
in diameter	0		0¾
Two of the middle bolts to go through the false stem and the line of the Scarphs to be in diameter	0		1
To be thwartships at the head	1		2
And at the end of the keel to be.	0		8
Apron			
The false stem or apron to be thick	0		9
And in breadth	1		4
The scarphs to be long	2		3
Main Post			
Length	17		2
Moulded at the head, (fore and aft)	1		2
For and aft at the Keel (the False Post included)	2		10
Athwartships at the Head	1		1
Athwartships at the Keel	0		8
The after side of it abaft the after part of the Rabbet of the Wing Transom.	1		0
Inner post			
Moulded	1		0
Sided at its Head	1		0
Sided at its Heel	0		8
Wing Transom			
Sided	0		11
Moulded at the ends	0		10
In length on the after side	13		0
To be bolted with Bolts, in diameter	0		1
Main keel			
Square in the midships	0		11
Square afore	0		8
Sided at the rabbet of the post	0		8
Number of pieces		3	
Scarphs in length	3		0
Lips of the scarphs in thickness	0		3
And bolted with Bolts, in number		6	
in diameter	0		0¾

	Ft		In
Dead Wood			
To have a sufficient number of pieces of dead or rising wood on the keel in midships thick	0		9
Broad	1		1
And the dead wood afore and abaft for the security of the half timbers, to be of a proper height to answer the run of the keelson, and to give proper shifts to the scarphs of the keel, and to each other; the lower piece of dead wood on the keel abaft to tenon into inner post with two tenons in the after end.			
Keelson			
The keelson square	0		11
Scored down on the floor timbers	0		0½
Number of pieces		3	
The scarphs in length	4		3
And so disposed that the middle of each scarph is over a floor timber that is not bolted, that a keelson bolt may go through the middle of the scarph; the scarphs, hook and butt, and the lips of the scarphs in thickness.	0		3
And bolted with bolts, in number		2	
in diameter	0		0½
The keelson to be bolted through every other floor timber and the main keel with bolts in diameter	0		1
Room and Space			
The room and space of the timbers to be	2		2
Number of rooms in the after body		18	
Ditto in the fore body		13	
Frame			
It being of the utmost consequences to the strength of a ship that timbers of the frame should as much as possible be prevented from being cut by the ports on each deck, a disposition for that purpose is generally made on a draught, and the timbers appointed to make the sides of ports are or should be continued up to the top of the side and framed in bends, by fastening the first and second futtocks, top-timbers and lengthening pieces together, letting every scarph be bolted with bolts in number.		2	
In diameter	0		0½
The stations of the frames so distinguished should be preferred with great exactness on the ship, and the lower futtock of every bend should be bolted to the floors with bolts, in number		2	
In diameter	0		0½
Floors			
The floor timbers in the bearing of the ship, Sided	0		9¼
And from thence forward and aft	0		9¼
In length in the midships	11		0
To be moulded at heads	0		9
Square timbers to be continued from		H	
To (inclusive aft)		12	
Every other floor timber to be bolted through the main keel with bolts in diameter	0		1
First Futtocks; To be sided in the midships	0		8½
Afore and abaft	0		8½
And in wake of the Half Timbers, according to the Room and Space the Cant Timbers will allow			

	Ft		In
To have chocks accross on the heels of them to supply the wood that may be wenting from thence to the cutting down.			
To scarph on the Second Futtocks in the midships	5		0
Moulded at the Heads	0		7
Second Futtocks; in the midships, sided	0		8
Afore and abaft. sided	0		8
To scarph to the Toptimbers in the midships	4		6
Moulded at the heads	0		6
Toptimbers; Sided at their Heels	0		8½
Moulded at the Waist at the top of the side	0		5½
Bottom planking: Thick	0		2½
to have 3 strakes between every 2 butts on the same timber scarph to be no less than 6 feet.			
Main Wales			
Height of the lower edge at the forward Perpendicular,	11		8
Ditto at the Dead Flat	10		1
Ditto at the After Perpendicular	13		7
in breadth from the upper to the lower edge,	1		3
Thickness	0		4
No. of Strakes		1	
Strakes of plank upon the Main Wale, in number		2	
to be , thick	0		2¼
and each to be in breadth	0		10
Rails, etc			
Upper edge of the drift rail above the upper edge of the sheer rail.	0		10
Drift rail in breadth	0		7½
Ditto, in thickness	0		2½
Upper edge of the sheer rail agreeable to toptimber line;			
Sheer rail in breadth	1		0
Ditto, in thickness	0		3
Channels			
The main channel in length	12		6
Thick at the inner edge	0		6
Ditto at the outer edge	0		2½
Foremost end afore the center of the mast	1		3
Bolted with bolts in number		5	
in diameter	0		1
Upper edge below the upper edge of sheer rail	0		10
Dead eyes			
To have on the main channel dead eyes, in number		5	
in diameter	0		11
in thickness	0		6½

Within board	**Ft**		**In**
Limber Boards: in thickness	0		2
Strake next to the limbers; thick	0		4
Broad	1		0
And distant from the side of the keelson between the foremast bulkhead of the Hold and the aftermost Magazine bulkhead	0		9
And from thence forward and aft to diminish to	0		4 ½
The next strake to that to be thick	0		3
Broad	0		9
Which two may be reduced to half its breadth afore and abaft, and in thickness	0		2½
Stuff at the Floor heads			
Strakes of thickstuff at the floor heads, in number		3	
The middle strake to be wrought on the joints of the timbers at the floorhead, and in thickness	0		4
Broad	0		11
And the strakes above and below it thick	0		3
Broad	0		9
Which three strakes are to be reduced afore and abaft to strakes in number		2	
And in thickness	0		2½
Stuff at first futtock heads			
Strakes of thickstuff at the first futtock heads, in number		3	
The middle strake wrought on the joints of the timbers at the first futtock head, and in thickness	0		4
Broad	0		11
And the strake above and below it thick	0		3
Broad	0		9
Which three strakes are to be reduced afore and abaft to strakes in number		2	
And in thickness	0		2½
Footwaling			
The common footwaling, (or Ceiling) laid between the thickstuff next to the limbers and floor heads, and also between the floor and lower futtock heads, and likewise between the lower futtock heads and platform clamps, to be in thickness.	0		2
Reduced afore and abaft to	0		1½
Crutches, in number		1	
Sided	0		9
Athwartships Length	6		6
To be bolted with six bolts, in diameter	0		1
Main Step			
The main step sided	2		2
Deep on the keelson	1		5
Breast hooks			
To have breast hooks below the Upper (or Main) Deck breast hook, in number		3	
The upper one in length	9		6
The lower one ditto	6		6
Each of them sided	0		7½
And bolted with bolts, in number		7	
in diameter	0		1

	Ft		**In**
Pillars			
The pillars in the hold under the lower deck beams, to be square at the lower end.	0		5
Ditto at the upper end	0		3½
Pump Well. The well to be fore and aft	2		10
Thwartships, in the clear.	4		0
Plank thick	0		1½
Shot Locker			
Thwartships: as the well			
to be Fore and Aft in the clear	1		6
Plank thick, the same as the well			
Magazine			
Plank, Thickness	0		2
Stanchions, square	0		3½
In the clear asunder	2		2
Magazine – fore and aft in the clear	13		4
Height from the upper side of the Magazine platform to the under side of deck above	3		0
Standards to the Pawl bitts			
The Standards sided	0		6
To run forward to the beam afore with the carling below, and bolted through both the beam and carling with bolts, in diameter	0		0¾
Hatchways			
The main hatch fore and aft.	5		0
Thwartships	3		5
The fore hatch fore and aft	2		8
Thwartships	2		8
The after companionway hatch, fore and aft	6		2
Thwartships	2		4
Fore side of it abaft the aft side of main hatch	5		6
Scuttle to be Breadroom, fore and aft	3		2
Thwartships	2		3
Tiller			
The tiller to be square in the biggest place	0		6
In length	10		0
Square at the foremost end	0		4
Centre of the Mast			
The centre of the main mast abaft the foremost perpendicular on the upper deck	29		4
Rake aft in a yard	0		1½
Upper deck clamps			
The upper deck clamps thick at the upper edge	0		3½
Bearded at the lower edge to	0		3
The Scarphs in length	3		0
Wrought with hook and butt, and bolted up and down through the lips of the scarphs with bolts, in number		2	
in diameter	0		0½

	Ft		In
Beams			
The upper deck beams to be sided	0		9
to be moulded	0		7
In number		13	
Knees			
The upper deck beams knee'd at each end with one hanging and one lodging knee.			
The hanging knees sided	0		5½
The up and down arm to be in length.	2		6
The thwartship arm long	2		10
The lodging knees sided	0		5
Thwartship arm long	3		0
Both lodging and hanging knees to be bolted with bolts, in number		5	
in diameter	0		0½
Transom			
The upper deck transom deep	0		7
Scored and bolted to the counter timbers with bolts, in diameter	0		0½
Breast hook			
The upper deck breasthook to be sided	0		7
in length	9		4
Bolted with bolts, in number		8	
in diameter	0		1
Carlings and Ledges			
To have on the upper deck from the foremost deck beam aft, carlings and ledges, number of tier		2	
And from thence forward		1	
The carlings broad	0		6
Deep	0		4½
The ledges broad	0		3
Deep	0		2½
Waterways			
The upper deck waterways thick	0		3½
Main Partners			
The partners of the main mast on upper deck in thickness	0		10
Deep	0		6
Spirketting			
The upper deck spirketting to be strakes in number		2	
in thickness	0		3
(If wrought Top and butt, to be strakes in number)		(1)	
Quickwork			
The quickwork (where fitted) between the spirketting and the Drift rail in the waist, in thickness	0		2

	Ft		In
Transom			
To have a transom across the stern at the height of the chase port sills in thickness	0		4
Scored and bolted to the stern timbers, and knee'd at each end with one iron knee, continued long enough to receive three bolts afore it, the thwartship arm in length.	2		6
Bolted with bolts in diameter	0		¼
Scuppers			
To have on the upper deck on each side lead scuppers in number		4	
in diameter	0		2½
Ring and eye bolts			
To have two ring and two eye bolts to each upper deck port, the bolts in diameter	0		1
The rings diameter in the clear	0		4
The ring bolts on the deck in diameter	0		0¾
The rings diameter in the clear	0		3¼
Main Jeer and Topsail Sheet Bitts			
Pins, to be square	0		9
Crosspiece, to be square	0		7
Counter Timbers			
To have in the stern counter timbers to form the stern and chase ports, in number		4	
Sided	0		5
To run down to the upper side of the wing transom and bolted with two bolts, in diameter	0		⅝
Rother			
The rother head to be made long enough to receive a tiller above the upper deck, and to be thwartships at the head.	0		11
Fore and aft at its head	1		0
In breadth at the lower end	2		11
Ditto at the hance	2		0
The back (if fitted) to be in thickness	0		2
Rother Irons			
To have rother irons, number of pairs		4	
The upper brace to have straps sufficient in length so as to turn and meet round the standard against the post.			
The lower one in length, from the back of the post	2		7
The pintles in diameter	0		2½
And in length	0		11
The straps of the braces and pintles broad	0		3½
And thick in the shoulder at the return	0		1¼

BIBLIOGRAPHY

Chapelle, Howard I *The Search for Speed Under Sail*, Conway Maritime Press, 1983

Clowes, W Laird *The Royal Navy*, (6 Vols), Low Marston, 1899

Colledge, J J *Ships of the Royal Navy*, (Vol 1), David and Charles, 1969

Hough, R *Fighting Ships*, Michael Joseph, 1969

Goodwin, P *The Construction and Fitting of The Sailing Man of War, 1650–1850*, Conway Maritime Press, 1987

Goodwin, P *The 20-Gun Ship Blandford*, Conway Maritime Press, 1988

Goodwin, P *The Bomb Vessel Granado, 1742*, Conway Maritime Press, 1989

Goss, J *Portsmouth-built Warships, 1497–1967*, Kenneth Mason, 1984

Landstrom, B *The Ship*, Allen and Unwin, 1961

Lavery, B *The Arming and Fitting of English Ships of War, 1600–1815*, Conway Maritime Press, 1987

Lees, J *The Masting and Rigging of English Ships of War, 1625–1860*, Conway Maritime Press, 1979

Lever, Darcy *The Young Officers Sheet Anchor*, 1819

Lewis, M *The Navy of Britain*, Allen and Unwin, 1949

May, Cdr W E *Boats of Men of War*, NMM Monograph, No 15, 1974

Munday, J *Naval Cannon*, Shire Publications

MacDougall, P *The Chatham Dockyard Story*, Meresborough Books, 1987

Ranft, B Mcl *The Vernon Papers*, Navy Records Society, Vol 99

Smith R D *British Naval Armaments*, The Trustees of the Royal Armouries, 1989

Steel, D *The Elements of Mastmaking, Sailmaking and Rigging*, 1794

Upham, N E *Anchors*, Shire Publications

Wilkinson-Lathan, R *British Artillery on Land and Sea 1790–1820*, David and Charles, 1973

Smugglers and Revenue Officers in the Portsmouth Area in the Eighteenth Century, The Portsmouth Papers, No 22, Portsmouth City Council, 1974

Articles from *Model Shipwright* (Conway Maritime Press)

'Fittings for Wooden Warships' Part 2, by Robert Gardiner, MS 19.

'An early 19th Century Naval Cutter' Parts 1 and 2, by W H Shoulder, MS 1 and 2

PRO References

ADM 51/51 – Captain's Log of *Alert* July, 1777 to May,1778.

ADM 52/1558 – Master's Log of *Alert* 8 July 1777 to October 1777.

ADM 36 Series – Ship's Muster Books.

ADM 95/64 – Letter 79, *Alert* Cutter.

ADM 95/64 – Letter 85, *Sprightly* Cutter.

ADM 95/77 – Letter 26, *Pheasant* Cutter – Mast & Yard Dimensions.

ADM 95/77 – Letter 27, *Expedition* and *Sprightly* Cutters.

ADM 95/77 – Letter 97, *Alert* Cutter.

ADM 95/83 – Men, Ballast and Provisions.

ADM 95/84 – Ships built/repaired 1771–1783.

ADM 106/2509 – ships' boats

ADM 180/12 – 6th Rates and below.

NMM References

SPB/15; Miscellaneous documents concerning mast, yards, rigging, sails, armaments and provisions and other various details.

ADM/B/173 – ships' boats

Draughts used (NMM)

Rattlesnake (1777); Profile, Half Breadth & Body Plan (No 6994 Box 65)

Expedition/Sprightly (1778) Upper Deck Plan (No 6492 Box 65)

True Briton (1778) Upper Deck Plan (No 6655 Box 65)

Speedy (1821) Disposition of Frame for Cutters of 122 tons (No 6488A Box 65).

The Photographs

2. The painting of the *Alert* cutter model showing the starboard quarter view painted by Joseph Marshall. This painting also formed part of the George III Collection of ship model paintings. It is believed that the model was originally based on a design by Sir J Ackworth.
(Courtesy of the Science Museum)

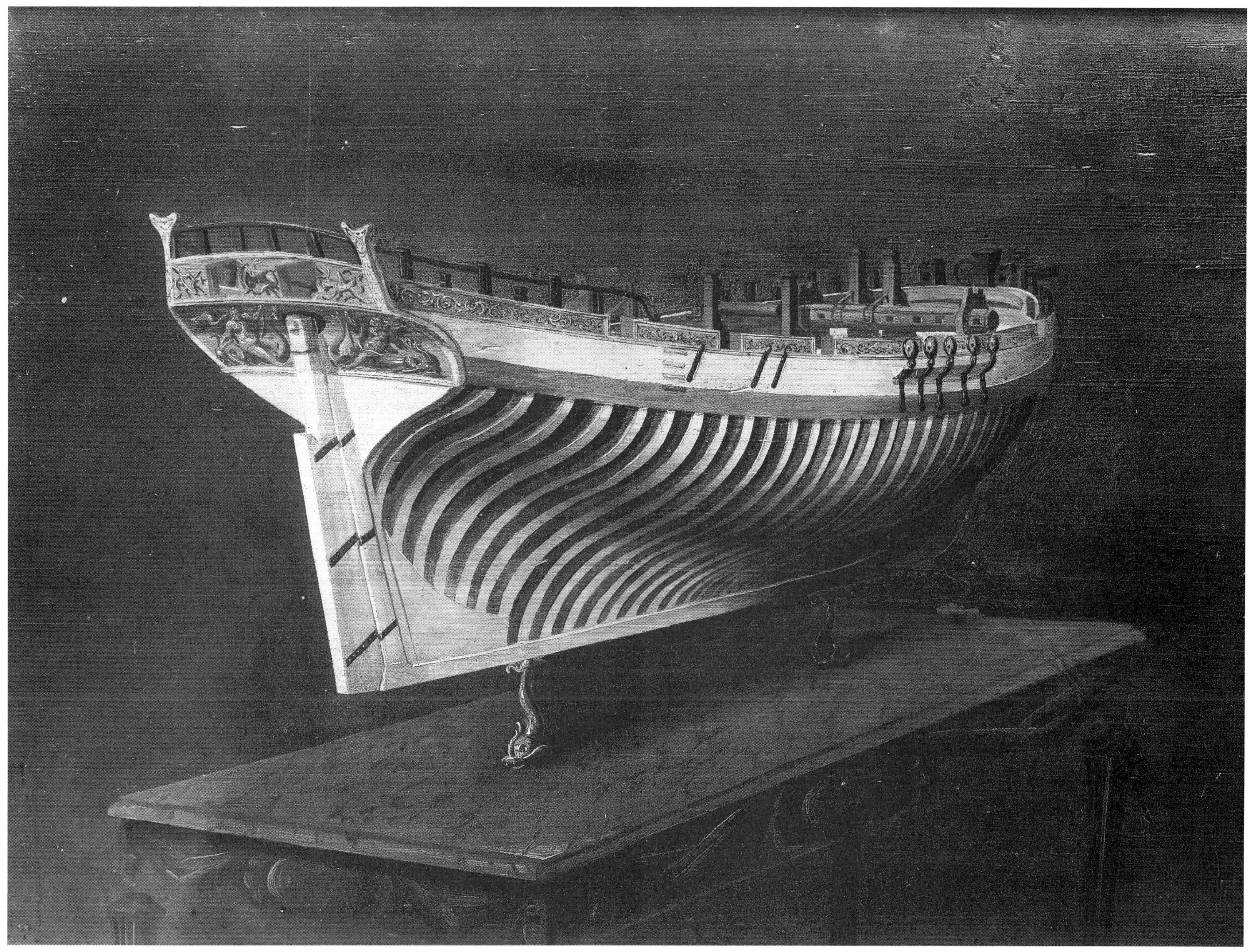

3. The naval cutter *Hawke* of around 1777.
(NMM)

4. The port bow view of the *Hawke* which shows clearly the arrangement of foresail and jib and the details of the shrouds and backstays.
(NMM)

5. The starboard bow view of the *Hawke* which shows the arrangement of the main square sail, topsail and topgallant, foresail and jib. Note that the topsail braces run to the outer end of the bowsprit.
(NMM)

6. The port quarter of the *Hawke* which shows the mainsail, the main shrouds and the backstays. The topgallant mast, stepped abaft the lower mast is also clearly visible.
(NMM)

7. The starboard quarter of the *Hawke* clearly showing the square sail sheets and tack. The topsail yard brace running aft to the quarter is of particular interest. This brace, which does not conform to the standard rig at that period, appears to be an addition which could have been used in the event of loss or damage to the bowsprit which carried the common brace running forward.
(NMM)

8. The stern view of the *Hawke* showing the arrangement of the spread-yard for the topsail and its position with the square sail yard.
(NMM)

9. The port bow view shows the bowsprit retaining hoop, bowsprit shroud tackle and out-haul block on the stempost. On this particular model the outhaul is rigged on the port side as opposed to the common practice of being rigged to starboard. The jib inhaul can be seen secured to the bollard timber head.
(NMM)

10. Detail of the forestay with its deadeye and lanyard, preventer stay and the square heel of the bowsprit. The windlass on this particular model is unconventional for, having no carrick bitts, the spindle ends are supported directly on the bulwarks.
(NMM)

11. The view of the forecastle showing the arrangement of the cathead, windlass and bowsprit step. The iron horse employed for the foresail sheet shown on the extreme right was not a common feature. The armament shown comprises both swivel and carriage guns.
(NMM)

12. The starboard quarter which clearly shows the square tuck and counter. Also shown are the spread-yard brace (secured at the quarter) and the entry port hand ropes.
(NMM)

13. A general view of the upper deck which shows the ship's boat, shroud and backstay details, main armament and swivel guns.
(NMM)

14. The jeer and topsail bitts and their associated windlass. The anchor cables can be seen passing through the main hatchway.
(NMM)

15. The upper deck. Of particular note is the mainsheet a little afore the tafferal and a seat of ease.
(NMM)

16. General view of upper deck of the *Hawke* showing the rudder housing platform and tiller. On this particular model only four shrouds were employed whereas five were fitted on the *Alert*. *(NMM)*

17. The upper deck looking forward. *(NMM)*

18. Mainmast details showing the tie blocks and halliards for the spread-yard, square sail yard and topgallant yard.
(NMM)

19. Detail of the mainmast head and gaff showing arrangement of the topping lift and jeer tackle.
(NMM)

20. A cutter, *circa* 1750, rigged with a spread-yard for the topsail. The square sail itself is not rigged. The ship is a detail from *Shipping in Light Airs in the Thames Estuary* by Charles Brooking 1723–56. *(Author)*

21. A small cutter of *circa* 1750 carrying a large mainsail, a topsail with its spread-yard, the topgallant sail set flying, and a foresail and jib. The detail is taken from *Shipping in Light Airs in the Thames Estuary* by Charles Brooking. *(Author)*

22. A port bow view of a naval cutter of around 1785 showing an improved and standardised rig. The spread-yard by this period had been omitted and the foot of the topsail spread on the square sail yard. The longer topgallant mast was stepped afore the lower mast head and supported by shrouds rigged through rigging spreaders. *(Courtesy of the Science Museum)*

23. A port side view of the same naval cutter showing built up bulwarks with gun port lids and the simplified improved rig.
(Courtesy of the Science Museum)

24. Starboard quarter view of the cutter showing the general arrangement of deck fittings, the closed transom and chase ports.
(Courtesy of the Science Museum)

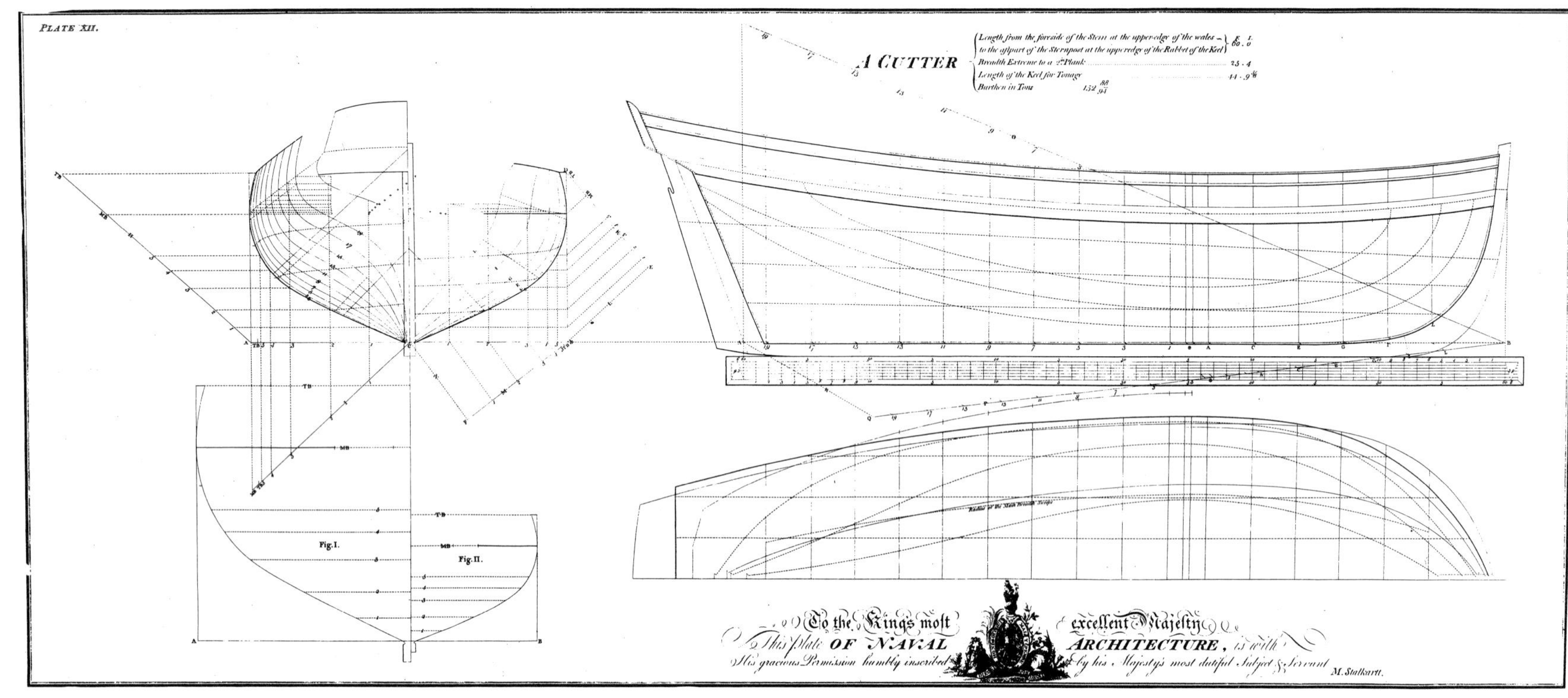

25. Draught of a 60ft naval cutter from Stalkartt's *Naval Architecture* (1781). *(Courtesy of the Science Museum)*

The Drawings

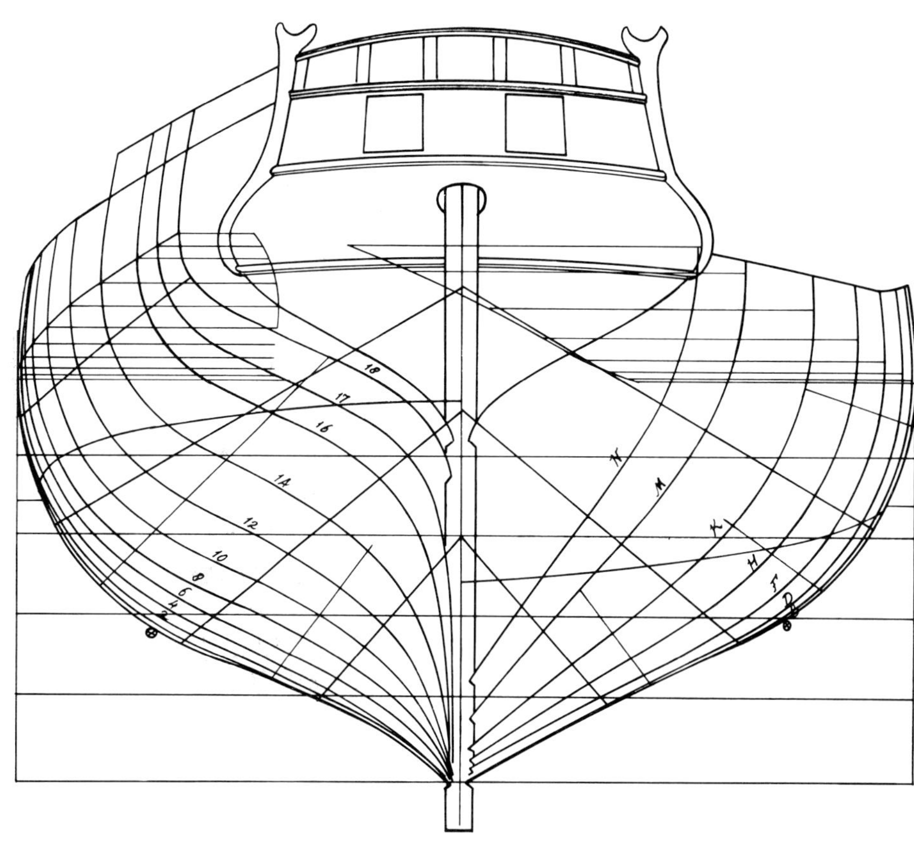

	Length.		Diam^r
	F^t	Ins	Ins
Main Mast,	80 .	0	21.
Bowspreet	58 .	0	19.
Boom.	62	0	13½
Gaff.	37 .	0	9½
Storm Gaff.	18 .	0	7
Top Gallant Mast, (Short)	36 . (28)	0 (0)	9 (9)
Square Sail Yard	54 .	0	9¼
Topsail Yard	41 .	0	7¼
Mizen Mast	40 .	0	9¼
Out Rigger	34 .	0	8½
Yard	33 .	0	6½
Jibb Boom	52 .	0	9.
Driver Boom	40	0	7

A1 ALERT (1/64 scale)

A1/1 Body plan

A1/1

A Lines and general arrangement

A1/2 Sheer and profile

A1/3 Half-breadth plan

NB This draught is based on the *Rattlesnake* (1777) a sister vessel to the *Alert*. Of particular note are the modifications which are indicated by the ticked lines. These improvements included the addition of a fifth deadeye and a longer channel. Other modifications entailed moving the third gunport further forward and making all gunports square.

A1/2

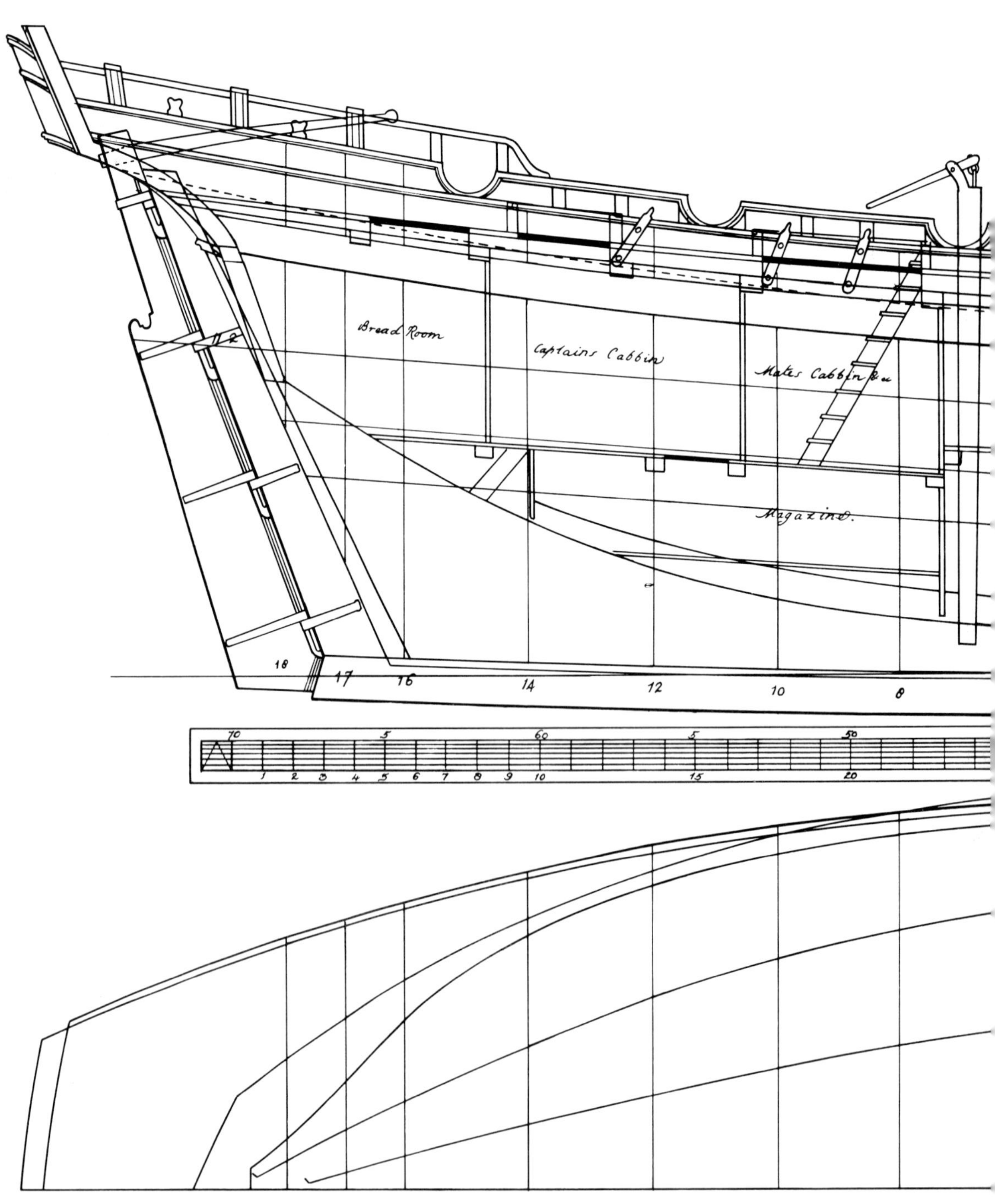

A1/3

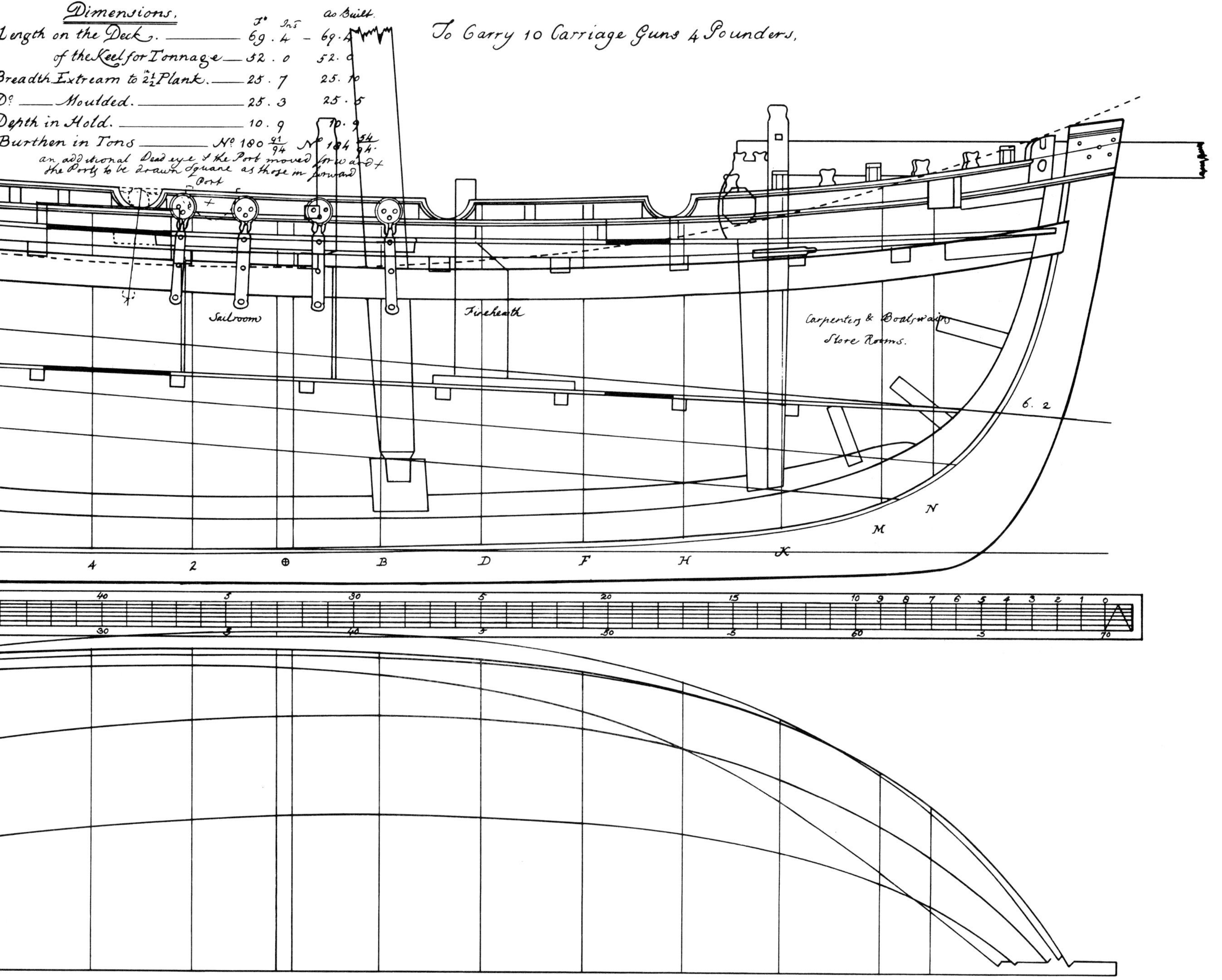

Dimensions.
Fᵒ Ins
as Built.
Length on the Deck. 69 . 4 – 69 . 4
of the Keel for Tonnage 52 . 0 52 . 0
Breadth Extream to 2½ in Plank. 25 . 7 25 . 10
Dº Moulded. 25 . 3 25 . 5
Depth in Hold. 10 . 9 10 . 9
Burthen in Tons Nº 180 41/94 Nº 184 54/94.
an additional Dead eye & the Port moved forward + the Ports to be drawn Square as those in forward Port
To Carry 10 Carriage Guns 4 Pounders,
Sailroom
Fireheath
Carpenters & Boatswains Store Rooms.
6. 2
N
M
K
4
2
⊕
B
D
F
H

A Lines and general arrangement

A2 SPRIGHTLY (1/64 scale)

A2/1 Body plan

A2/2 Sheer and profile

A2/3 Half-breadth plan

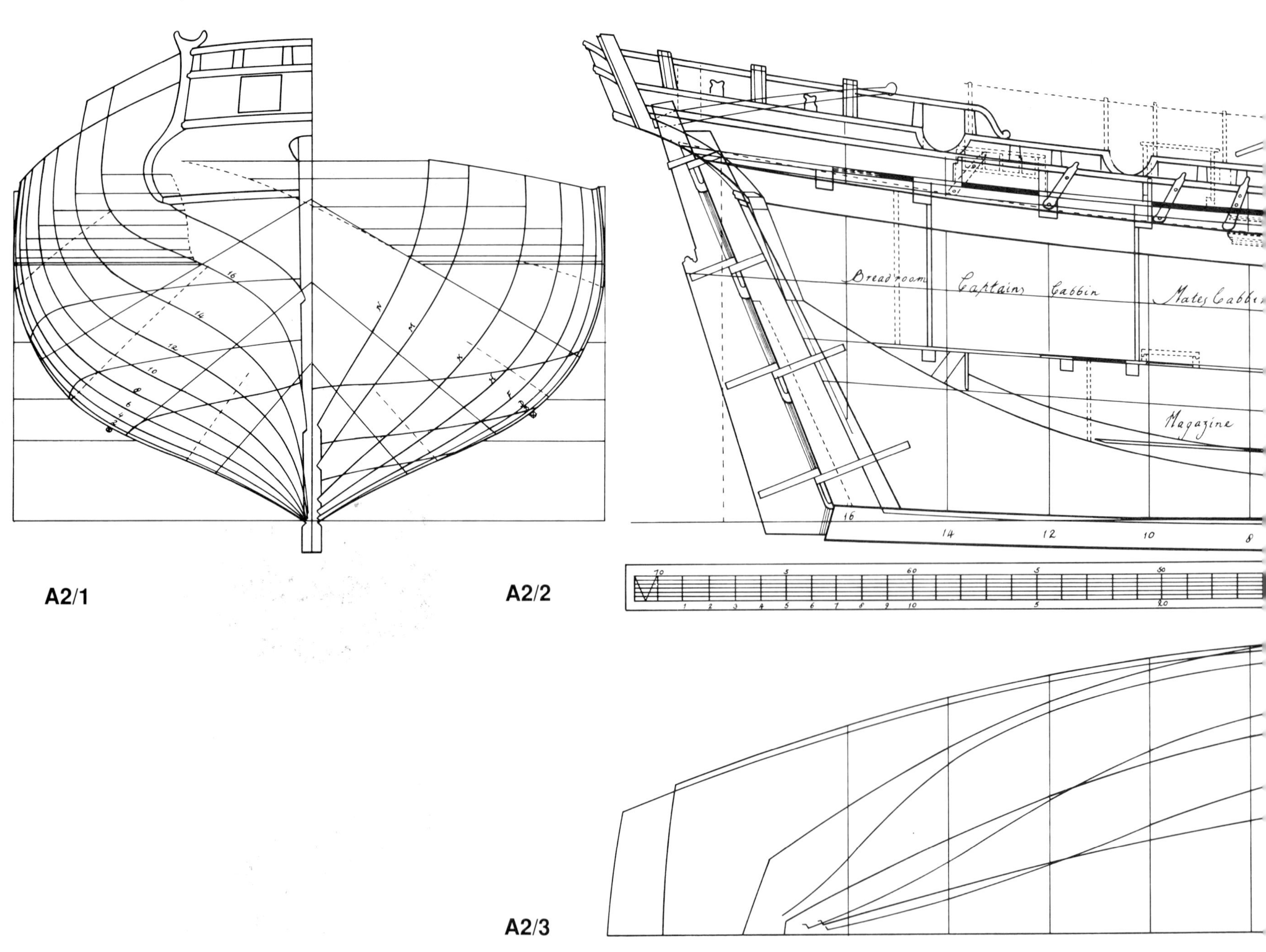

A2/1

A2/2

A2/3

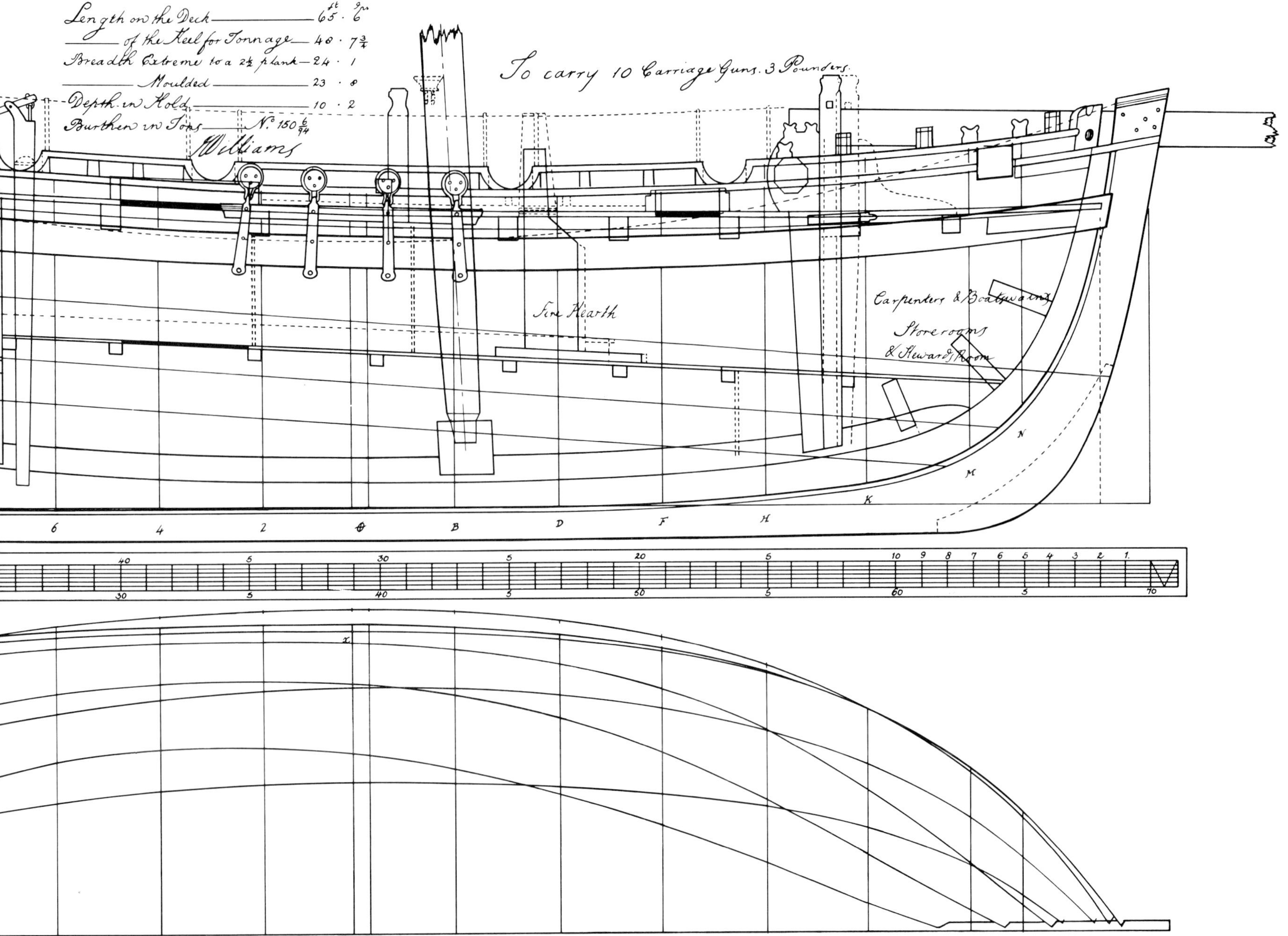

Length on the Deck 65 ft 6 in
of the Keel for Tonnage 48 · 7¾
Breadth Extreme to a 2½ plank 24 · 1
Moulded 23 · 8
Depth in Hold 10 · 2
Burthen in Tons No. 150 6/94
Williams
To carry 10 Carriage Guns. 3 Pounders.
Fire Hearth
Carpenters & Boatswains
Storerooms
& Stewards Room

A2/4 Upper deck plan

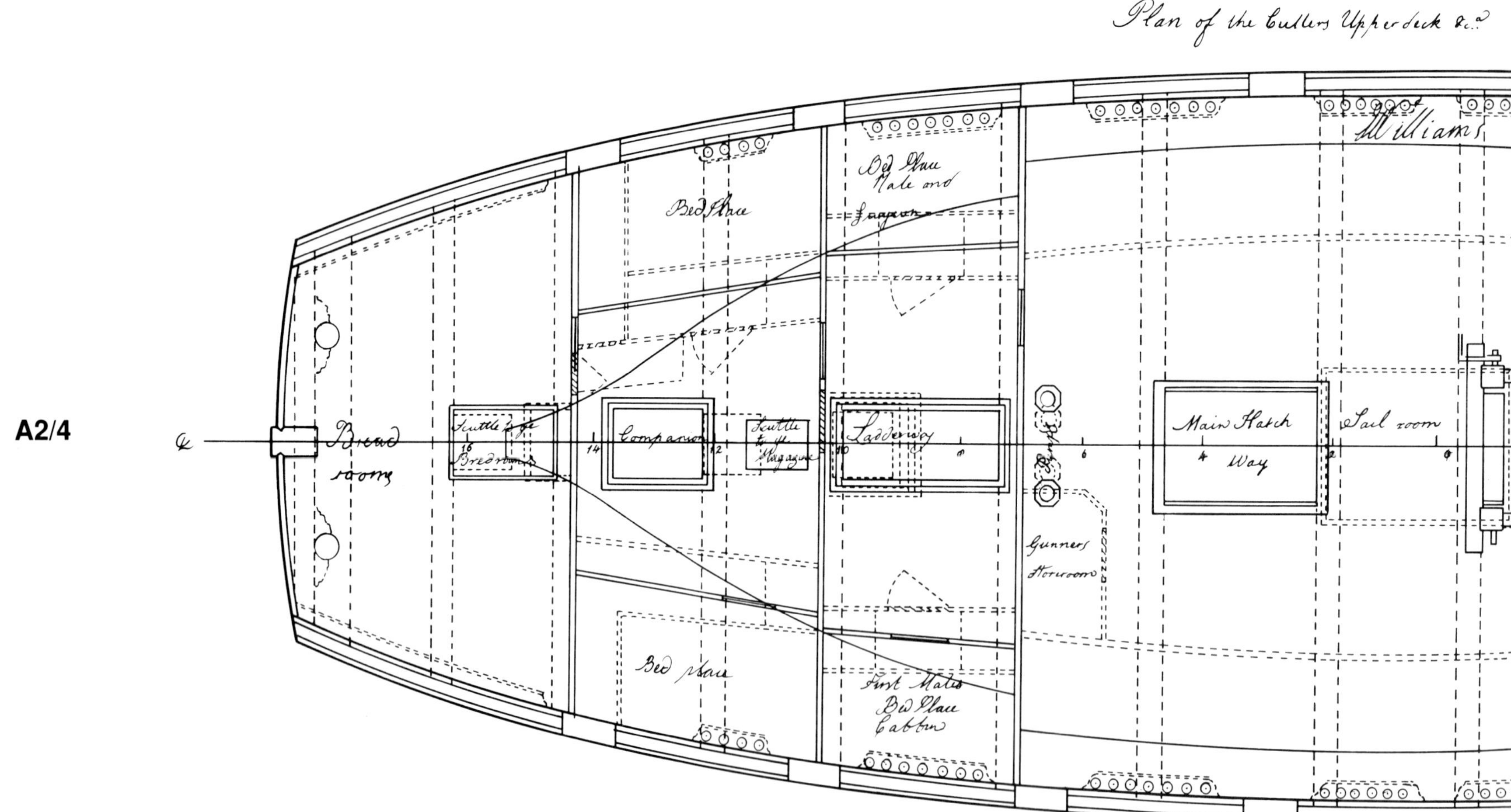

A2/4

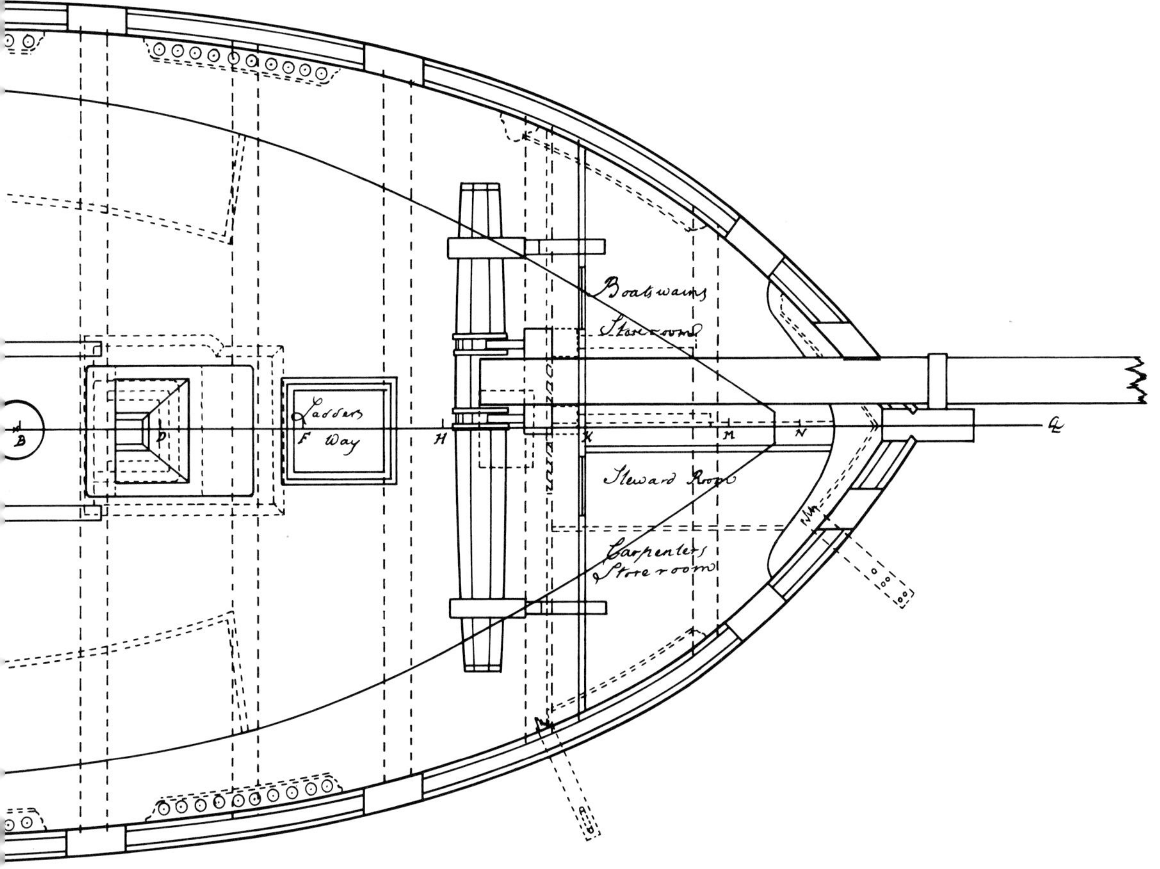
Boatswains
Storeroom
Ladders
Way
Steward Room
Carpenters
Store room

A2/5 External hull profile

A2/5

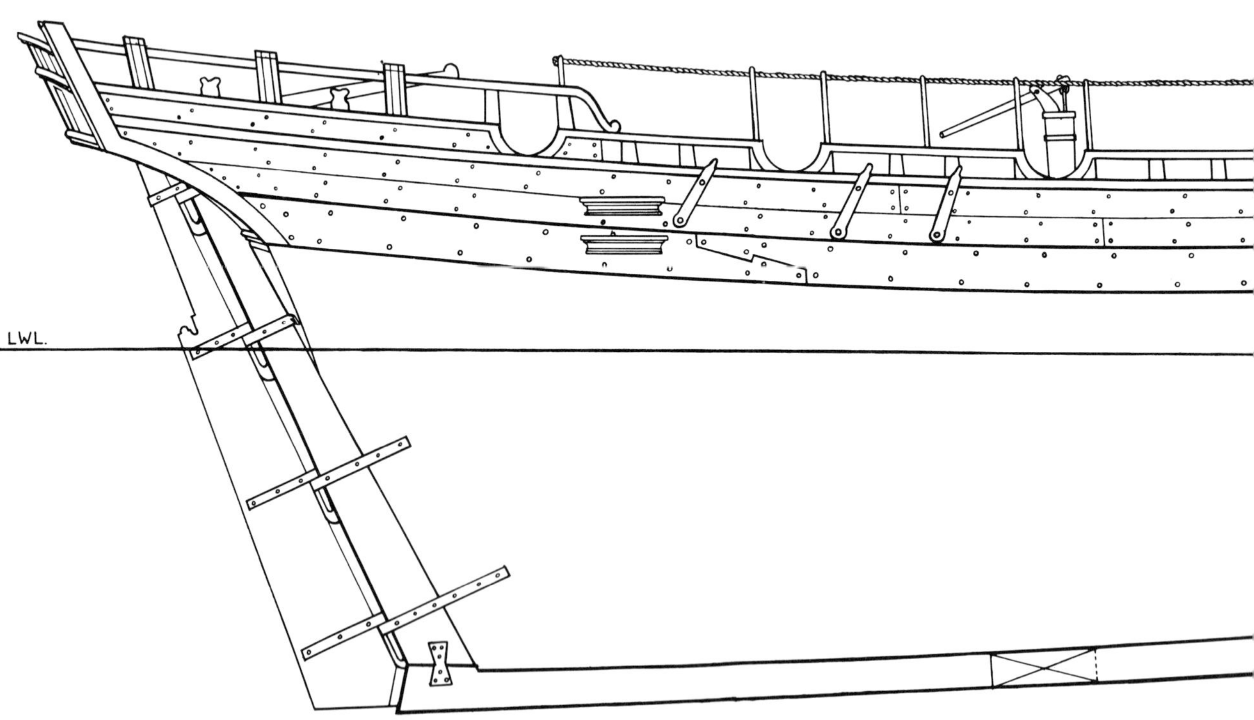

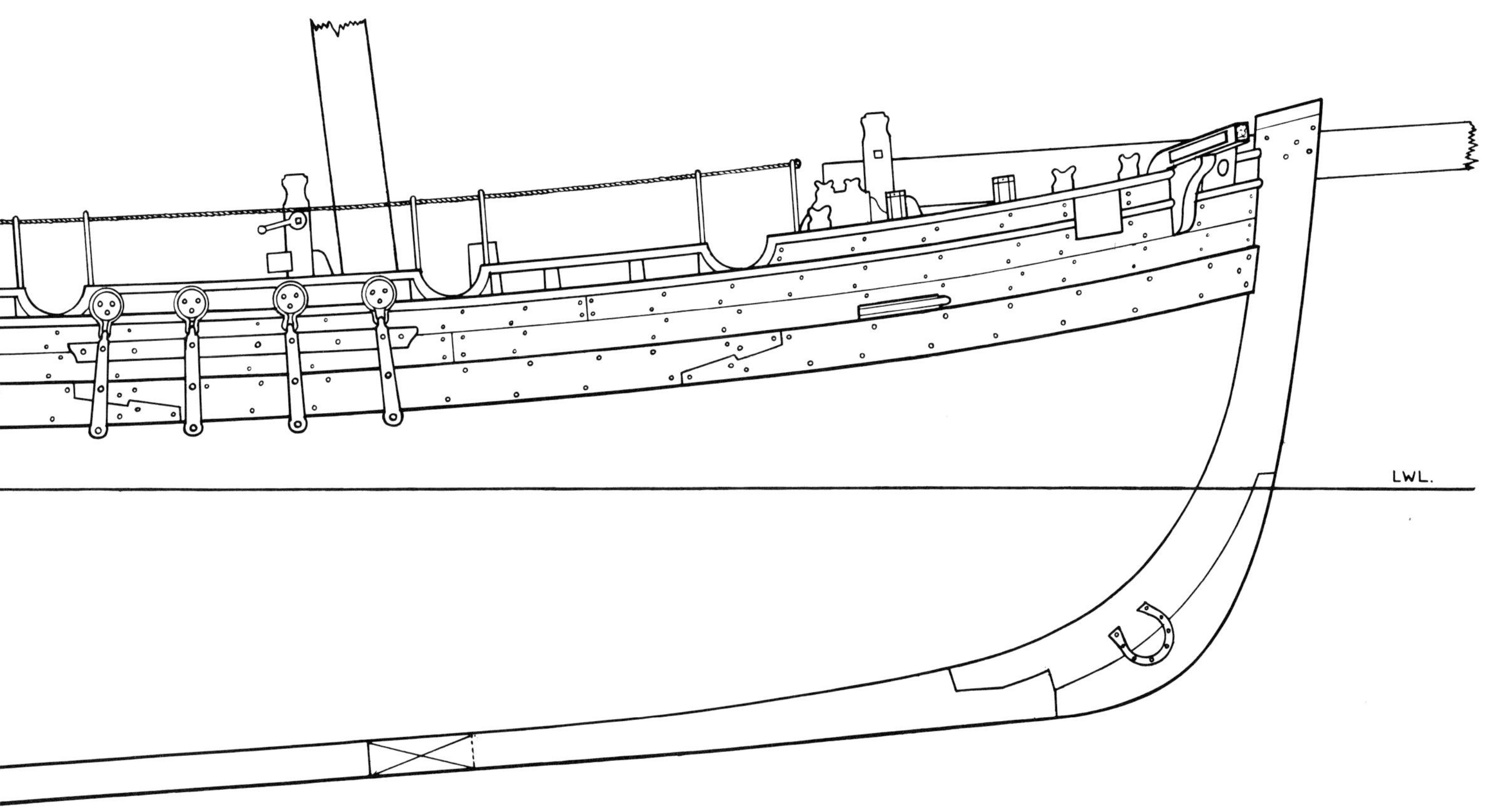
LWL.

B Hull construction

B1 BOW (1/64 scale)

B1/1 Stempost, apron and associated timbers – profile

1 Upper deck planking
2 Deck hook
3 Stem head
4 Stempost – upper section
5 Upper deck beam
6 Apron (or false post)
7 Breast hooks
8 Stem scarph
9 Bolts
10 Stempost – lower section
11 Fore foot
12 Boxing
13 Deadwood
14 Void space between frames for ventilation
15 Scarph of the hog (or rising wood) to the deadwood
16 Fore section of keel
17 Hog (or rising wood)
18 Keel scarph
19 Middle section of keel
20 Single frame at the dead flat
21 Cross chock of single frame
22 Cross chock of double frame
23 Section of keelson
24 Main or double frame
25 Keelson scarph
26 Floor of double frame
27 Floor of single frame
28 Foremost square frame
29 Fore section of keelson
30 Lower section of apron

B1/2 Disposition of the head timbers

1 Stempost
2 Section of bowsprit
3 Hawse hole
4 Fore Chase port lintel
5 Finger and thumb fashioned timberhead
6 Fore chase port
7 Fore chase port sill
8 Toptimber
9 Foremost cant frame
10 Hawse pieces
11 Bollard timber
12 First futtocks
13 Stempost heel
14 Breast hooks
15 Deck hook
16 Apron or false post

B1/3 Boxing – stem post to keel scarph (1/32 scale)

1 Fore end of keel
2 Tabled faces
3 Heel of stem post
4 Bolt
5 Bolt holes
6 Portion of stem post tabling

B1/4 Stempost scarph (1/32 scale)

1 Upper section of stempost
2 Lip of scarph
3 Bolt
4 Bolt holes
5 Tabling of scarph
6 Lower section of stempost
7 Rabbet to receive hood ends of hull planking

B1/1

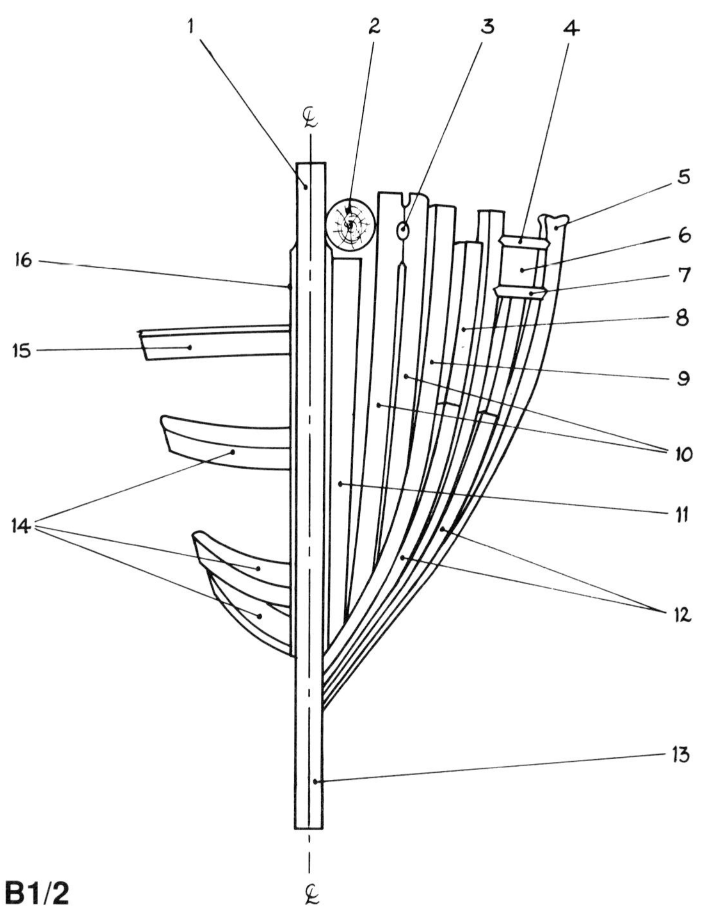

B1/2

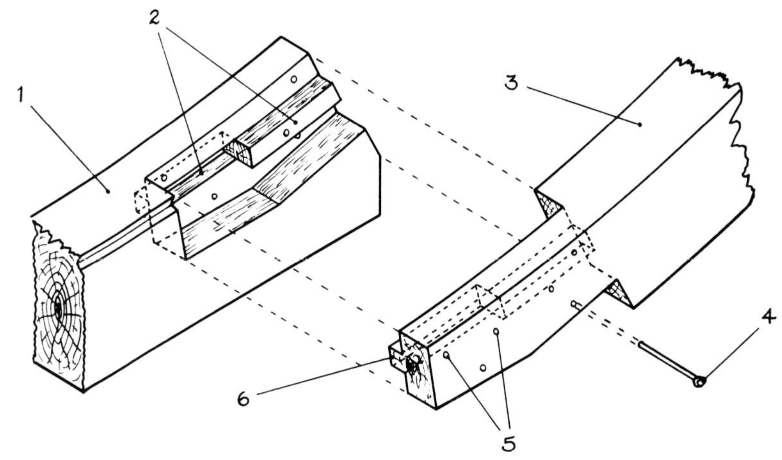

B1/3

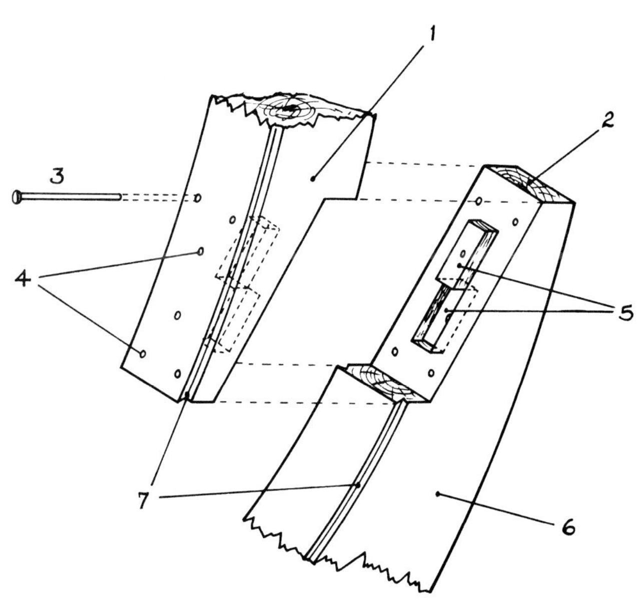

B1/4

B2 STERN (1/64 scale)

B2/1 Sternpost deadwood and associated timbers – profile

1 Deck transom
2 Wing transom
3 Upper deck planking
4 Upper deck beam
5 Scuttle to breadroom
6 Sternpost head
7 Inner post
8 Sternson knee
9 Scarph
10 Crutch
11 Bolts
12 Bolts
13 After section of keelson
14 Aftermost square frame
15 Single frames
16 Keelson scarph
17 Single frame cross chock
18 Single frame floor timber
19 Middle section of keelson
20 Void space between frames for ventilation
21 Floor timbers of main (or double) frames
22 Cross chocks of main (or double) frames
23 Deadwood
24 Sternpost
25 Sternpost heel
26 Tenon of sternpost
27 Tenon of inner post
28 After section of keel
29 Main or double frame
30 Keel scarph
31 Middle section of keel
32 Scarph of the hog (or rising wood) to the deadwood
33 Hog or (rising wood)

B2/2 Disposition of the stern timbers

1 Crutch to support boom
2 Counter timbers
3 Tafferal
4 Transom beam
5 Side counter timber
6 Stern chase port
7 Helm port transom
8 Helm port
9 Deck transom
10 Wind transom
11 Fashion piece
12 Keel
13 Sternpost
14 Transom beam
15 Sternpost head

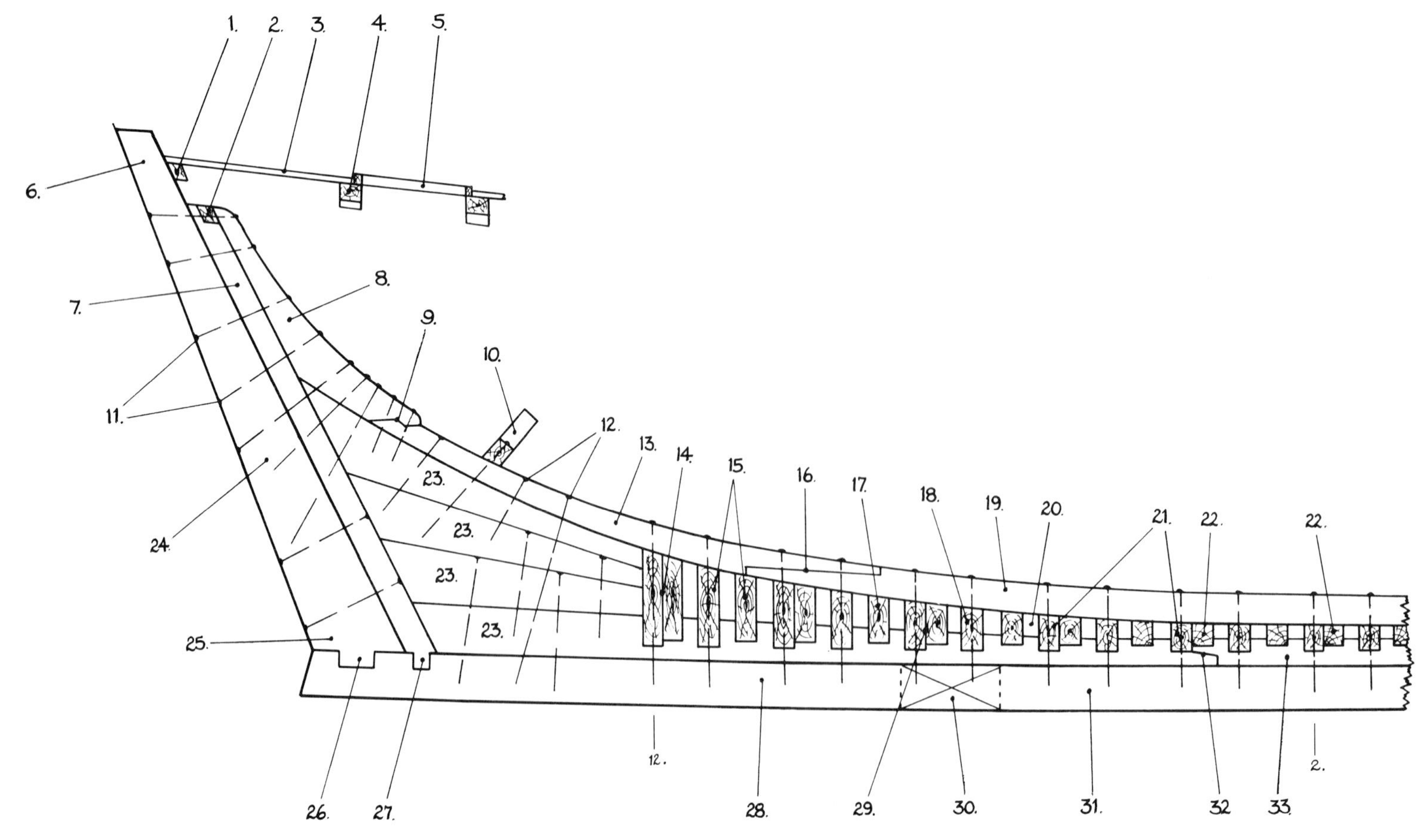

B2/1

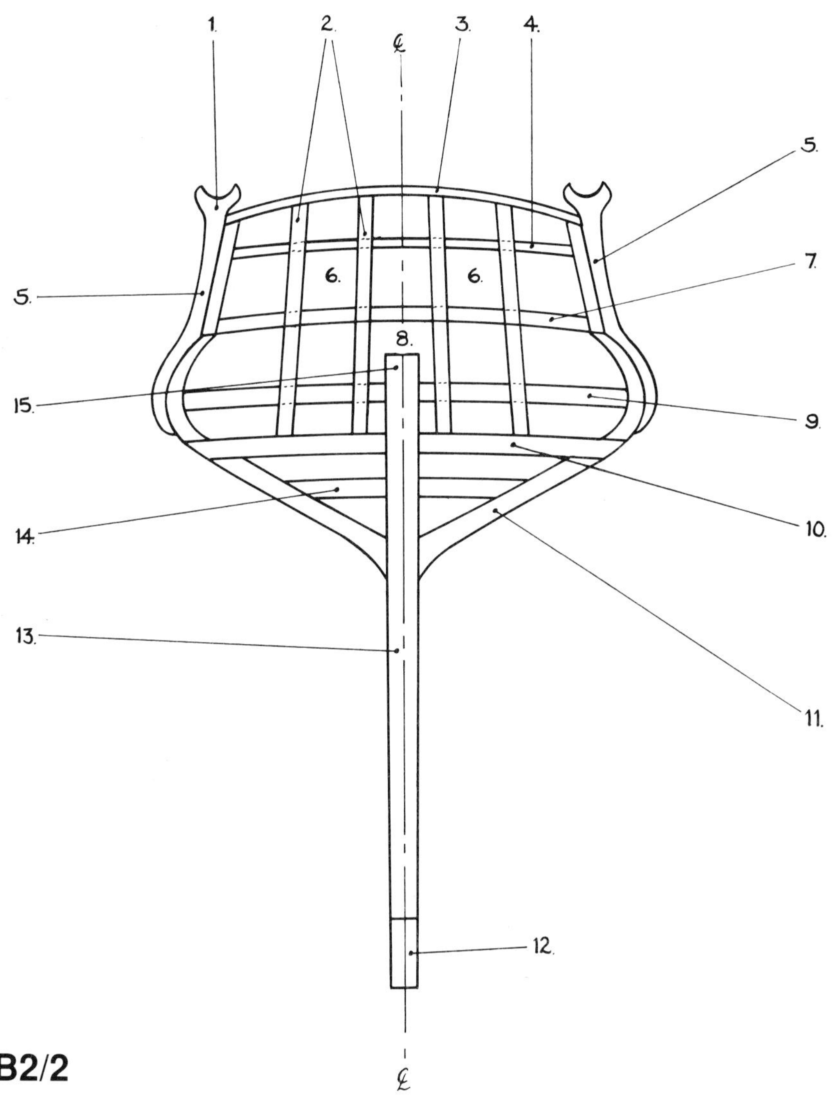

B2/2

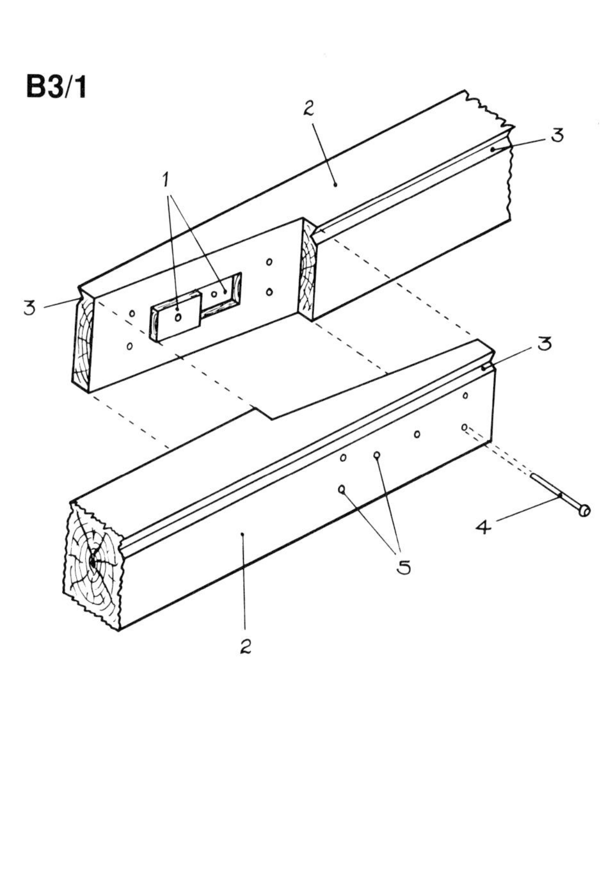
B3/1

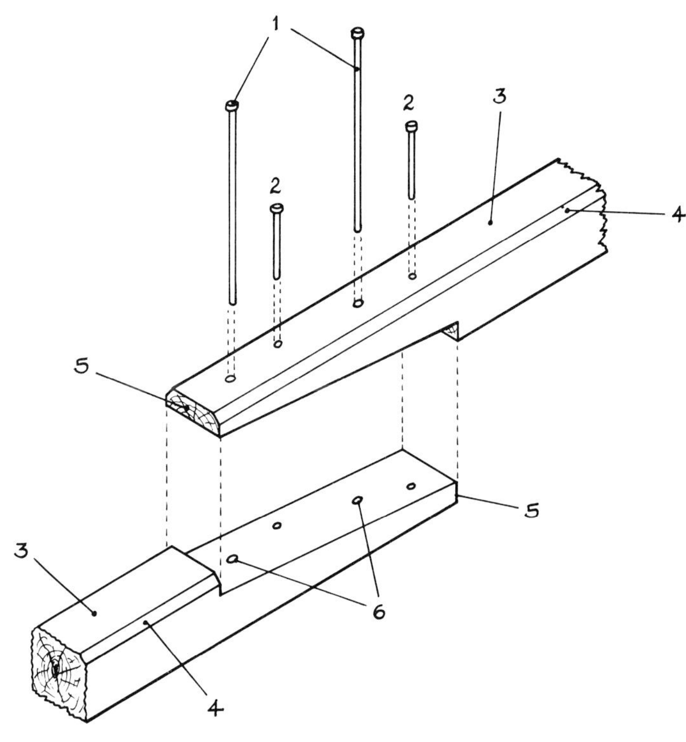

B3/2

B/3 KEEL DETAILS (1/32 scale)

B3/1 Keel scarph

1 Tabled faces
2 Section of keel
3 Rabbet
4 Bolt
5 Bolt holes

B3/2 Keelson scarph

1 Long bolts, driven through frames and keel
2 Short bolt driven through keelson only
3 Section of keelson
4 Bearding
5 Lip of scarph
6 Bolt holes

B Hull construction

B4 FRAMING (1/64 scale)

B4/1 Framing elevation

B4/2 Framing plan

As designed with semi circular gun ports. For 'as built' refer drawings B4/3 & B4/4.

1 Top timbers (forming swivel gun pedestal)
2 Finger and thumb timberhead
3 Short toptimbers
4 Gun port sill
5 Second futtocks of cant frames
6 Toptimber
7 Filling lengthening piece
8 Side cast lengthening piece
9 Lengthening piece
10 Second futtocks of square frames
11 Line of the first futtock heads
12 Side cast lengthening piece forming timberhead
13 Fore chase port sill
14 Fore chase port
15 Fore chase port lintel
16 Second futtock of foremost cant frame
17 Hawse hole
18 Stempost
19 Hawse pieces
20 Bollard piece
21 Rabbet
22 Cant frame floor (or long timber)
23 Cant frame first futtock
24 Foremost cant frame (N)
25 First futtocks of main cant frames
26 First futtocks of single cant frames
27 Line of the floor timber heads
28 Floor of main frame
29 First futtock of single frame
30 Joint line of square frame
31 Floor of single frame
32 Frame bend at the dead flat
33 First futtocks of main frame
34 Aftermost square frame (12)
35 Rabbet of keel
36 Keel
37 Filling timbers
38 Sternpost
39 Deadwood
40 Inner post
41 Rabbet
42 Joint line of double cant frame
43 Single cant frames
44 Fashion piece – aftermost cant frame
45 Wing transom
46 Side counter timber
47 Counter timbers
48 Fashion piece – supporting wing transom
49 Continuation of fashion piece framing to toptimber line
50 First futtock timbers
51 Foremost square frame (H)
52 Fore deadwood and keelson
53 Apron or false post
54 Bollard timber
55 Station lines – denoted by letters in fore body, and by numerals in after body

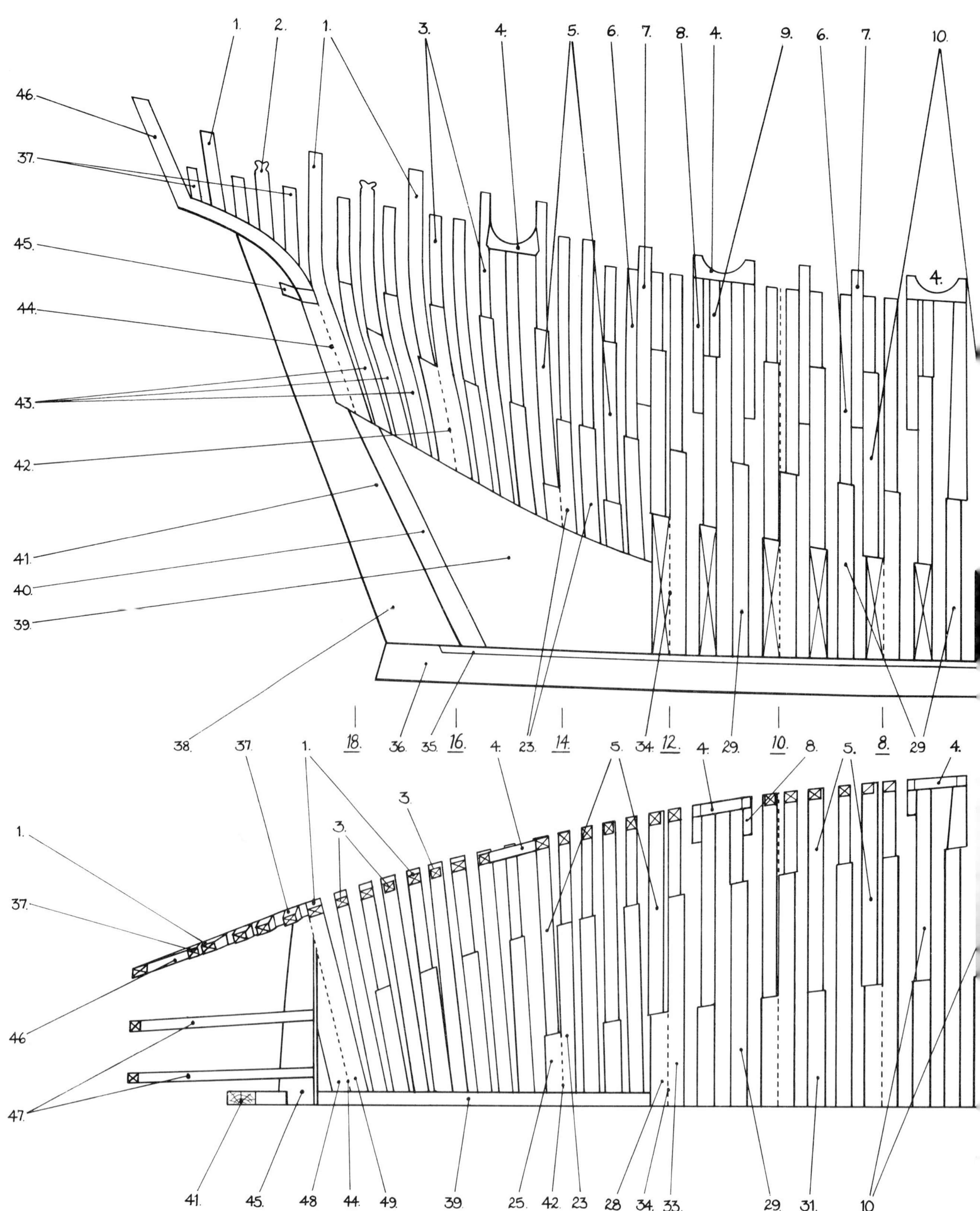

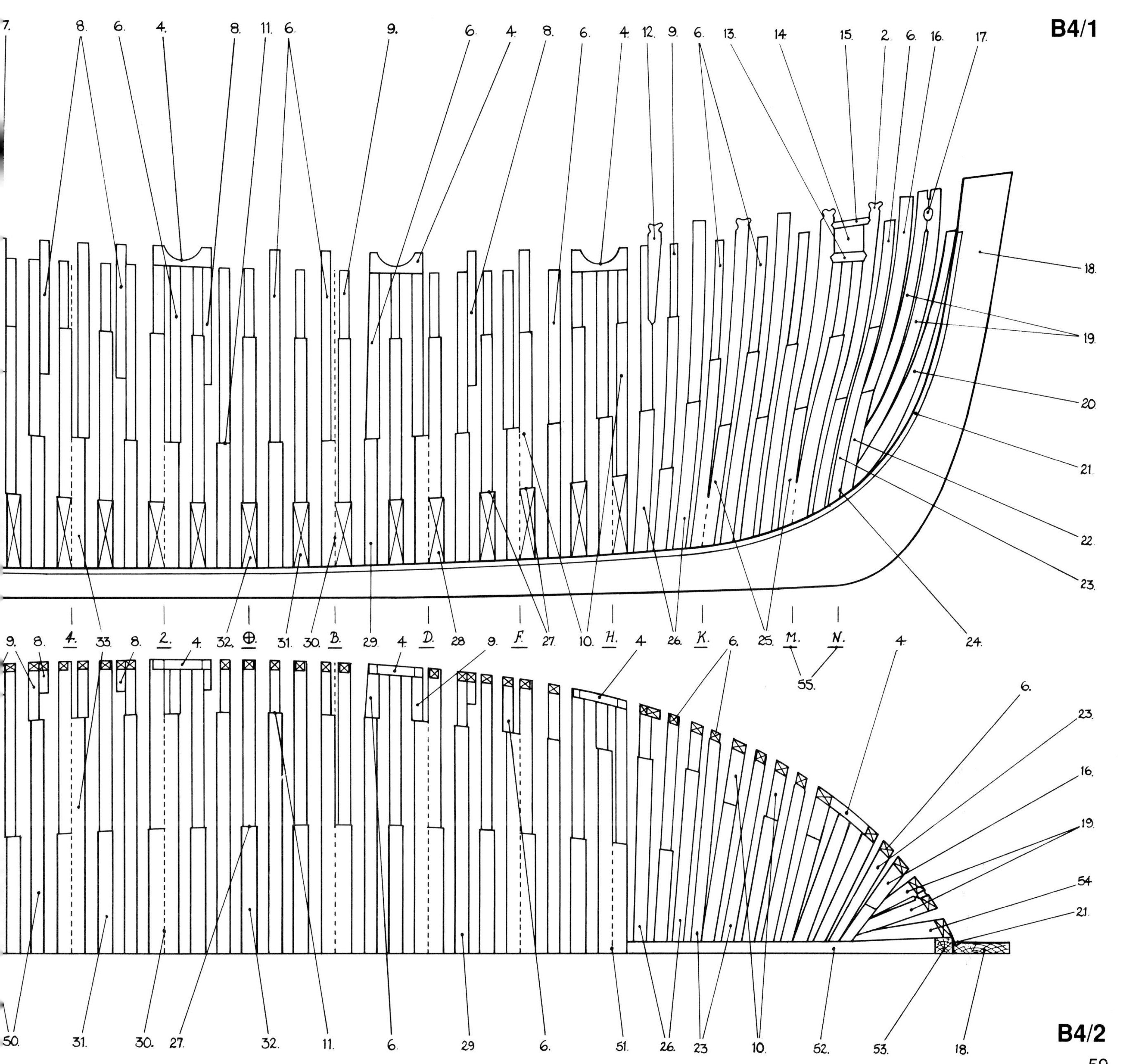
B4/1
B4/2

B4/3 Disposition of framing 'as built' with square gun ports and open drift

1 Square gun ports
2 Filling lengthening piece
3 Toptimber
4 Lengthening piece
5 Joint line
6 Second futtock
7 Side cast lengthening piece
8 Port sill
9 Side cast lengthening piece forming timberhead

B4/4 Disposition of framing 'as built' with square gun ports and closed drift

1 Square gun port
2 Seccond futtock
3 Side cast lengthening piece
4 Lengthening pieces
5 Toptimber
6 Port sill
7 Side cast lengthening piece forming timberhead

B4/3

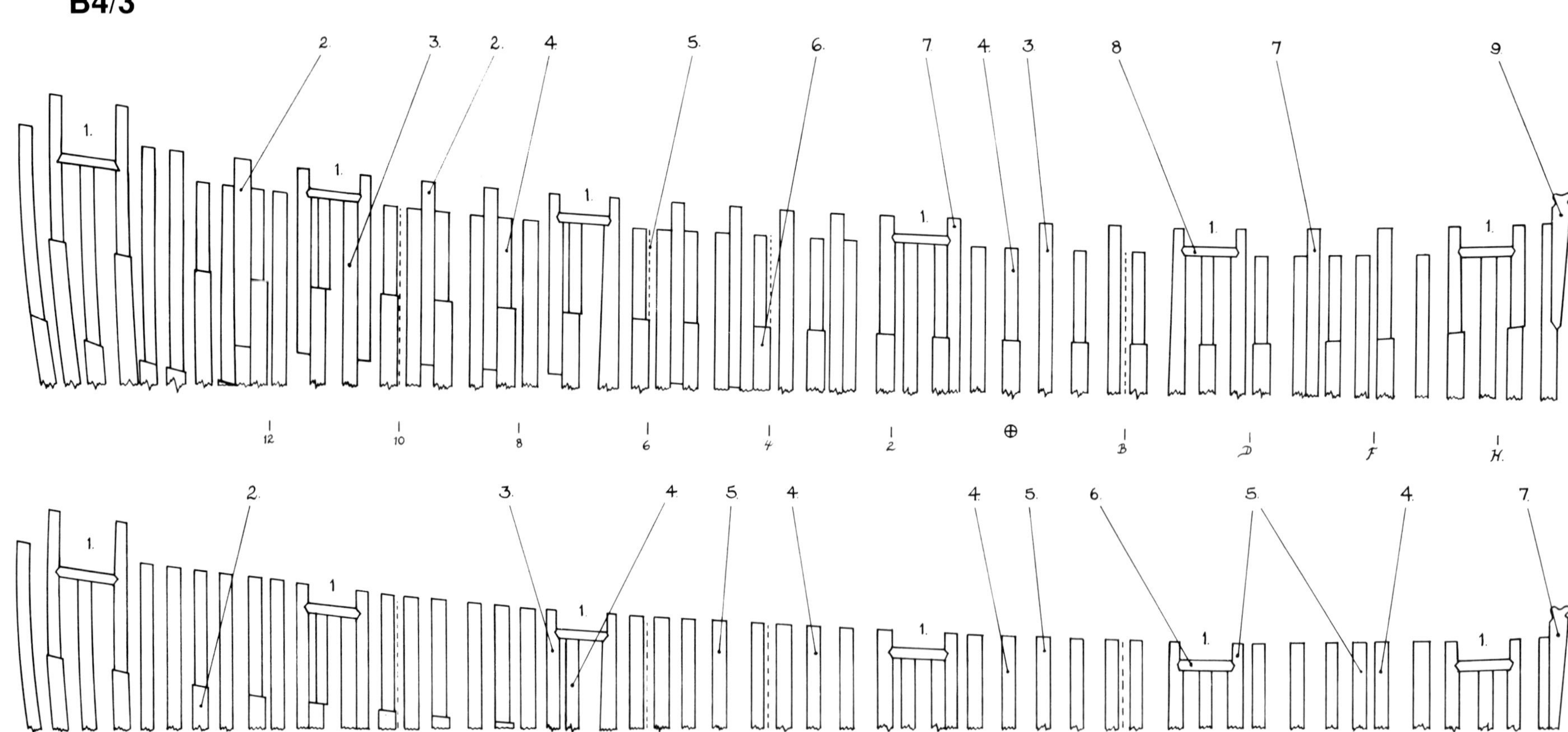

B4/4

B4/5 Disposition of the midship timbers, isometric projection (no scale)

1 Bolt
2 Cross chock
3 Lengthening piece
4 Toptimber
5 Planksheer
6 Gunport sill
7 Recess to receive beam end
8 Side cast lengthening piece
9 Second futtock
10 Lower deck (or fore platform) deck clamp
11 Toptimber
12 Chock or anchor piece
13 First futtock
14 Land for chock
15 Chock
16 Floor timber
17 Recess to set floor across hog
18 Recess to receive cross chock
19 Hog or rising wood
20 Recess to receive floor timber
21 First futtock
22 Rabbet of keel
23 Keel
24 Centreline stanchion
25 Keelson
26 Limber board
27 Limber strake
28 Footwaling
29 Lower strake of thickstuff footwaling
30 Thickstuff over the floor heads
31 Upper strake of thickstuff footwaling
32 Single frame, first futtock
33 Double frame, first futtock
34 Lower deck (or fore platform) beam
35 Thickstuff over first futtock heads
36 Upper deck beam
37 Beam shelf
38 Deck clamp

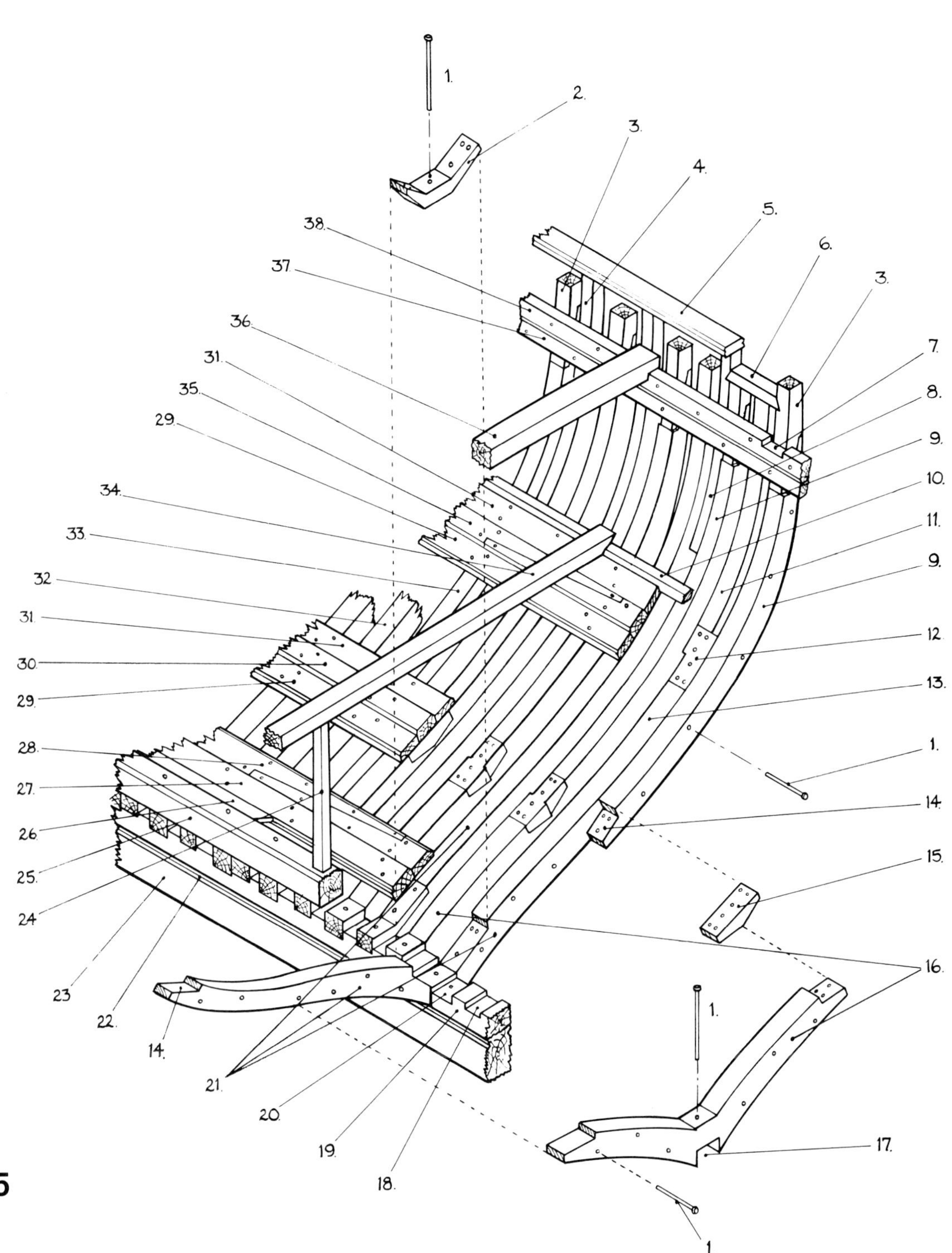

B4/5

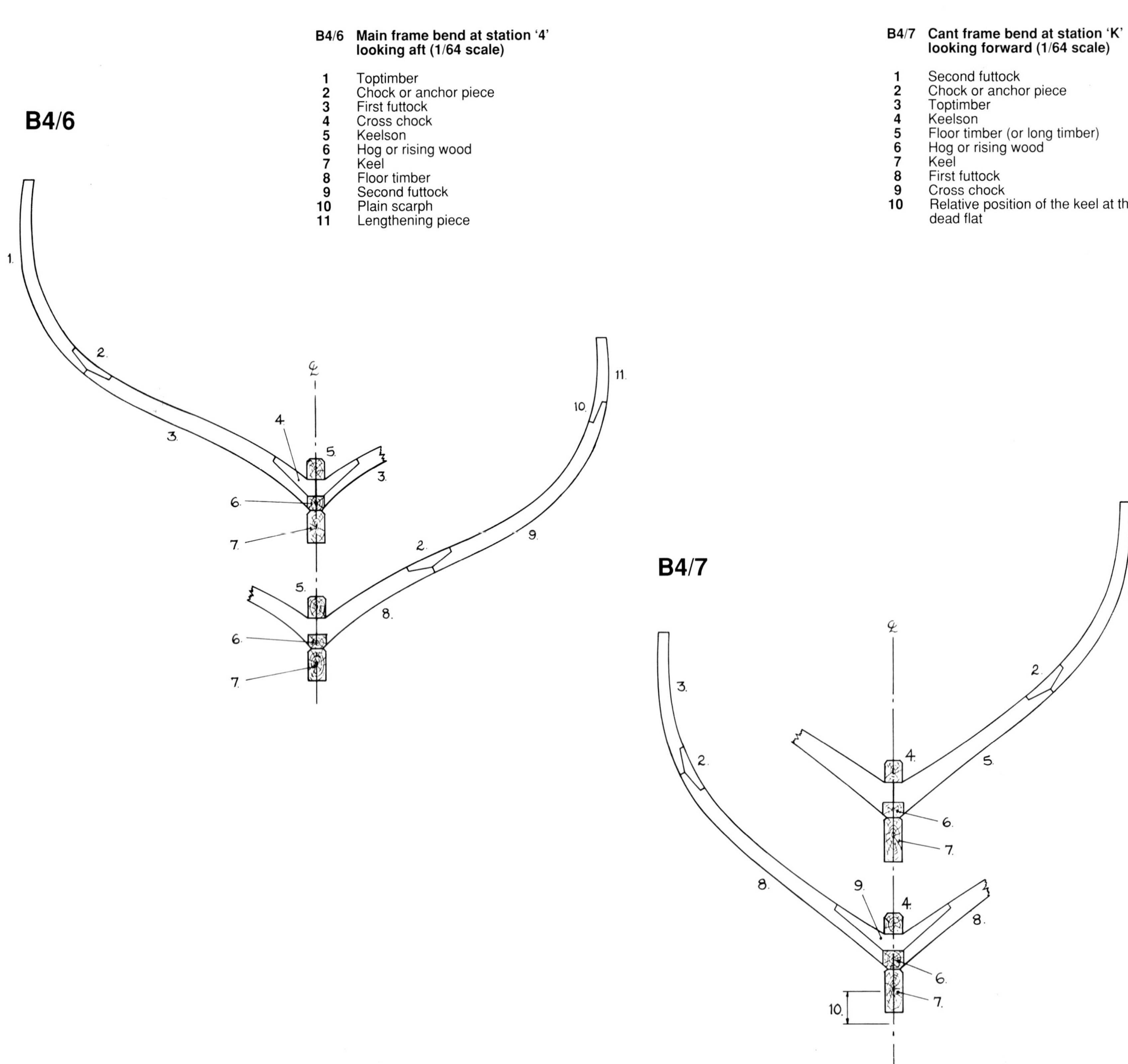

B4/6 Main frame bend at station '4' looking aft (1/64 scale)

1 Toptimber
2 Chock or anchor piece
3 First futtock
4 Cross chock
5 Keelson
6 Hog or rising wood
7 Keel
8 Floor timber
9 Second futtock
10 Plain scarph
11 Lengthening piece

B4/7 Cant frame bend at station 'K' looking forward (1/64 scale)

1 Second futtock
2 Chock or anchor piece
3 Toptimber
4 Keelson
5 Floor timber (or long timber)
6 Hog or rising wood
7 Keel
8 First futtock
9 Cross chock
10 Relative position of the keel at the dead flat

B5 BEAMS

B5/1 Construction of the upper deck beams, knees, carlings, ledges and mast partners (1/48 scale)

1 Recess to receive partner
2 Upper deck beam
3 After partner chock
4 Mast partner
5 Section of jeer bitt pin
6 Filling chock
7 Ledge
8 Carling, midship tier
9 Fore partner chock
10 Recess to receive ledge
11 Carling, side tier
12 Lodging knee
13 Hanging knee
14 Beam shelf
15 Deck clamp
16 Frame timber
17 Lining
18 Score in beam end for ventilation
19 Double lodging knee
20 Side and midship tiers of carlings

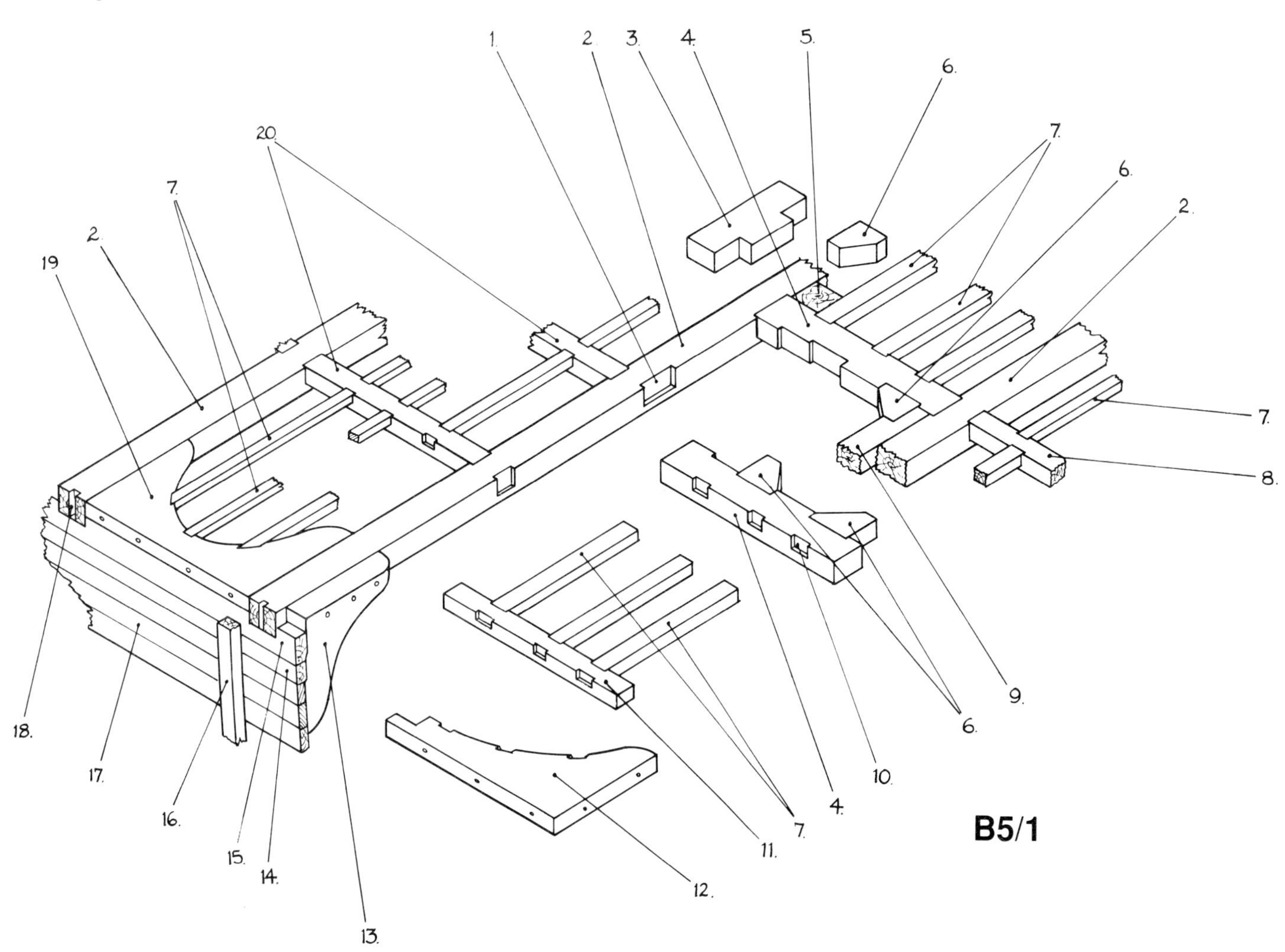

B5/1

B6 CLINKER HULL PLANKING

B6/1 Midship section at the dead flat, looking forward (1/64 scale)

1 Spirketting
2 Waterway
3 Deck clamp and beam shelf
4 Lodging knee
5 Carling, outer tier
6 Jeer bitt pin
7 Windlass for halliards
8 Bitt crosspiece
9 Upper deck planking
10 Upper deck beam
11 Sailroom transverse bulkhead
12 Lower deck (or fore platform) planking
13 Lower deck beam
14 Centreline stanchion
15 Keelson
16 Hog or rising wood
17 Keel
18 Garboard strake
19 Limber strake
20 Footwaling
21 Ceiling
22 Footwaling (lower strake)
23 Thickstuff over the first futtock heads
24 Footwaling (upper strake)
25 Frame
26 Hold
27 Footwaling (lower strake)
28 Thickstuff over the second futtock heads
29 Footwaling (upper strake)
30 Bottom planking, clinker or lap strake fashion
31 Accommodation area, lower deck
32 Lining
33 Hanging knee
34 Main wale
35 Upperwork planking, carvel fashion
36 Channel
37 Sheer rail
38 Rough tree rail

B6/2 Side elevation (1/24 scale)

B6/3 Sectional elevation (1/24 scale)

1 Double frame
2 Single frame
3 Rabbet to receive plank strake above
4 Upper edge of plank
5 Ticked line denotes upper edges of plank strakes
6 Rabbet edge
7 Bolt and trennal holes
8 Lower edges of plank strakes
9 Plank strakes
10 Single plank strake width
11 Bolt head
12 Trennals
13 Ventilation space between frames
14 Rove
15 Copper bolt
16 Frame
17 Bolt end rivetted over internal rove

B6/1

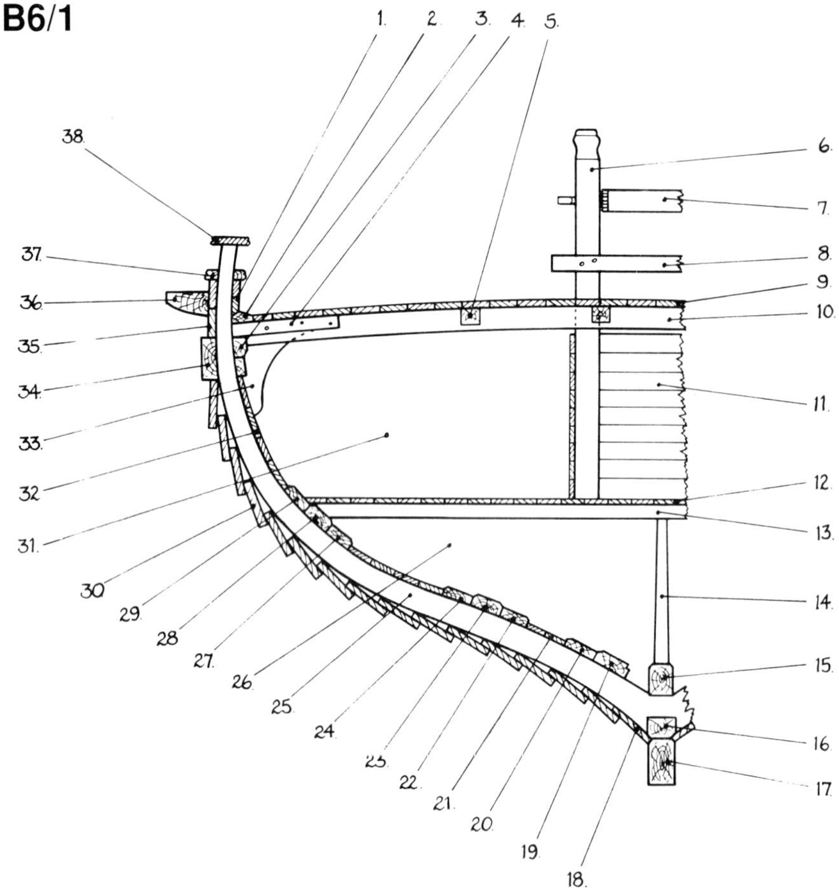

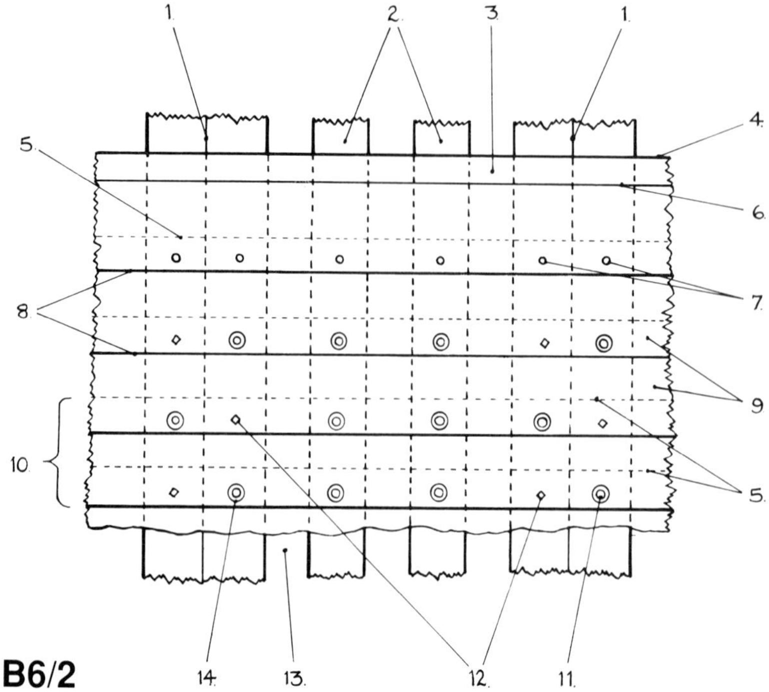

B6/2

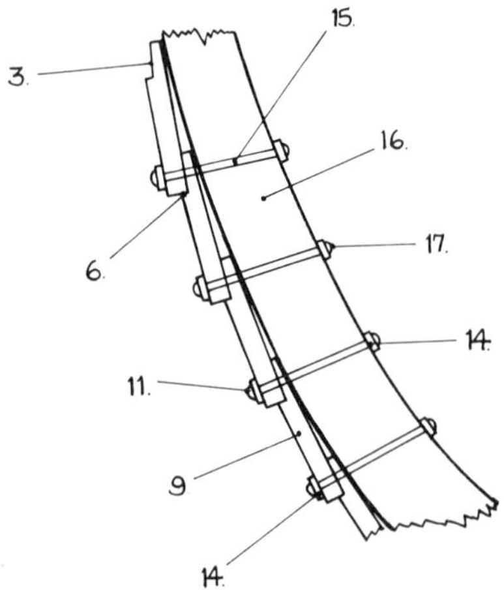

B6/3

B6/4 Carvel laid straight butt planking, main wale and ship's side planking (1/48 scale)

1 Butt joint
2 Single frames
3 Main or double frame
4 Hook and butt scarph
5 Treenails
6 Main wale
7 Bolts
8 Topside planking

B6/5 Top and butt planking employed for spirketting, bands of thickstuff or alternative method for main wales (1/48 scale)

1 Main frame
2 'Touch' of the plank
3 Butt joint
4 Single baulk of top and butt planking
5 Single frames
6 'Top' end of plank
7 'Butt' end of plank
8 Upper strake
9 Lower strake

B6/6 Hook and butt planking, usually employed for solid-built main wales (1/48 scale)

1 Single frames
2 Butt joint
3 Hook of scarph
4 Single baulk of top and butt planking
5 'Touch' of the plank
6 Main or double frame
7 Upper strake
8 Lower strake

B6/7 Standard planking technique employed for deck clamps (1/48 scale)

1 Upper deck beam
2 Plain scarph
3 Main or double frame (single frames omitted for clarity)
4 Bearding
5 Recess to receive beam end
6 Plain scarph
7 Deck clamp
8 Beam shelf
9 Frame

B6/8 Anchor stock, alternative planking technique employed for deck clamps (1/48 scale)

1 Upper deck beam
2 Recess to receive beam end
3 Anchor stock fashioned plank
4 Main or double frames (single frames omitted for clarity)
5 Bearding
6 Upper strake
7 Lower strake
8 Frame

B6/4

B6/5

B6/6

B6/7

B6/8

C Internal hull

C1 GENERAL ARRANGEMENT

C1/1 Longitudinal cross section (1/64 scale)

1 Rudder head housing platform
2 Tiller
3 Breadroom scuttle
4 Breadroom transverse bulkhead
5 Captain's day cabin
6 Companionway to captain's quarters
7 Upper deck planking
8 Companionway to ward room
9 Ladder
10 Scuttle to light room
11 Elm tree pump
12 Dry provision room
13 Main hatchway
14 Deck clamp
15 Beam shelf
16 Sailroom
17 Upper deck beam
18 Jeer and topsail sheet bitt pin
19 Mainmast
20 Galley flue
21 Hanging knee
22 Fore hatchway
23 Windlass
24 Pawl bitt pin
25 Bowsprit heel
26 Fore chase port
27 Inboard part of cathead
28 Stempost
29 Deck hook
30 Apron (or false post)
31 Steward's room
32 Carrick bitt pin
33 Fore accommodation space
34 Iron fire hearth
35 Sailroom access door
36 After accommodation space
37 Door to master's bed place
38 Ward room
39 Door to captain's bed place
40 Bread room
41 Upper deck transom knee
42 Wing transom
43 Inner post
44 Sleeper
45 Filling room
46 Powder room
47 After hold
48 Fore hold
49 Breasthooks
50 Fore peak (pitch room)
51 Fore transverse bulkhead
52 Transverse bulkhead
53 Spirit room
54 Transverse bulkhead
55 Access hatch to hold
56 Centreline stanchion
57 Centreline carling supporting fire hearth
58 Mast step
59 Lower deck (or fore platform)
60 Keelson
61 Hatchway to hold
62 Shot locker
63 Pump well
64 Main transverse bulkhead
65 Void space below lamp shelf
66 Light room
67 Light room window
68 Magazine platform
69 After cabin deck planking
70 Magazine access lobby
71 Magazine access scuttle
72 Crutch
73 Deadwood
74 Rudder
75 Sternpost

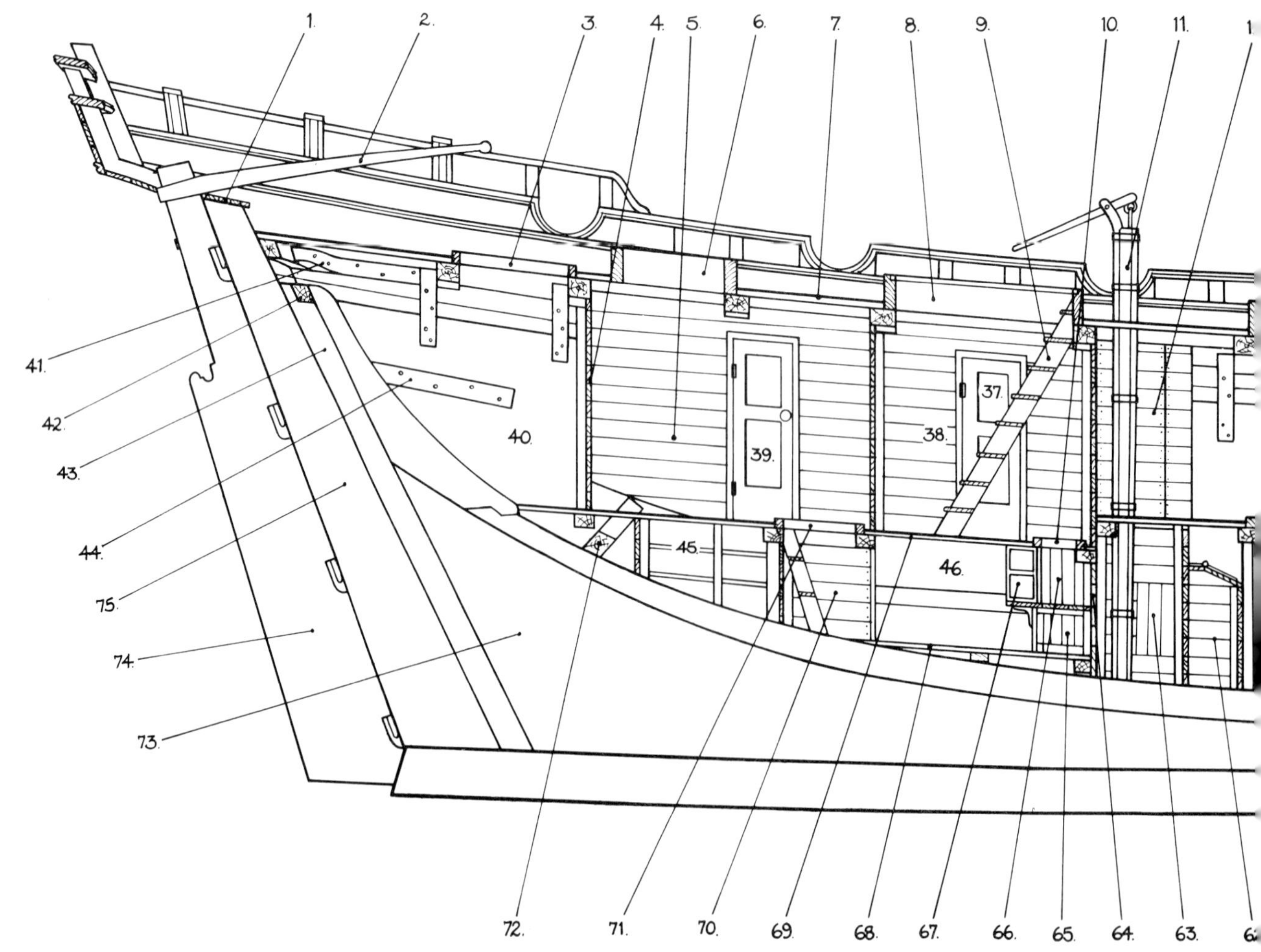

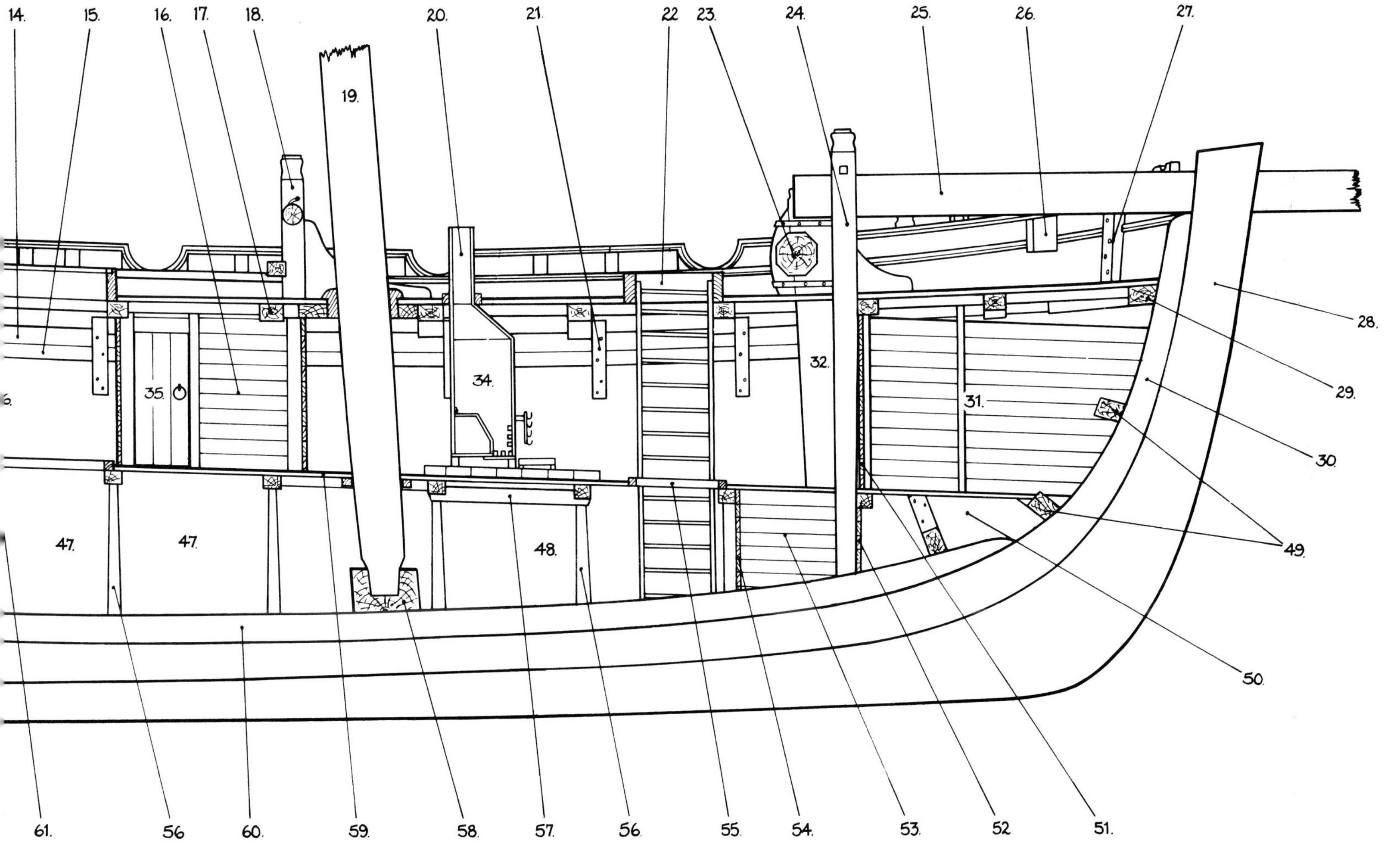
14.
15.
16.
17.
18.
19.
20.
21.
22
23.
24.
25.
26.
27.
28.
29.
30.
31.
32.
34.
35.
47.
47.
48.
49.
50.
51.
52
53.
54.
55.
56.
57.
58.
59.
60.
56
61.

C1/1

C Internal hull

C2 DECK PLANS

C2/1 Main or upper deck plan (1/64 scale)

1 Transom knee
2 Swivel gun pedestal
3 Platform deck over counter (housing for rudder head)
4 Tiller
5 Rough tree rail
6 Breadroom scuttle coaming
7 Flat of the deck
8 Gunport
9 Companionway coaming
10 Rail hance
11 Shot rack
12 After companionway coaming
13 Binding strake (oak)
14 Drift rail
15 Elm tree pump
16 Main hatchway coaming
17 Channel
18 Topsail and jeer bit crosspiece
19 Jeer topsail and jeer bitt pin
20 Mainmast
21 Galley flue
22 Fore companionway coaming
23 Timberhead (finger and thumb fashion)
24 Windlass spindle
25 Carrick bitt
26 Carrick bitt standard
27 Pawl bitt
28 Pawl bitt standard (not initially fitted)
29 Cathead
30 Hawse hole
31 Bowsprit retention hoop (iron)
32 Bowsprit
33 Stempost
34 Apron (or false post)
35 Centreline carling
36 Deck hook
37 Half beam
38 Ekeing
39 Upper deck beam
40 Lodging knee
41 Hanging knee
42 Section of carrick bitt pin
43 Carling, midship tier
44 Fore companionway
45 Ledges
46 Fore partner chock
47 Filling chock
48 Mast partner
49 After partner chock
50 Section of topsail and jeer bitt pin
51 Double lodging knee
52 Main hatchway
53 Elm tree pump casing
54 Carlings, side tier
55 After companionway to ward room
56 Companionway to captain's cabin
57 Breadroom scuttle
58 Deck transom knee
59 Deck transom
60 Head of sternpost
61 Rudder head
62 Stern chase port
63 Transom beam
64 Counter timbers
65 Tafferal
66 Side counter timber

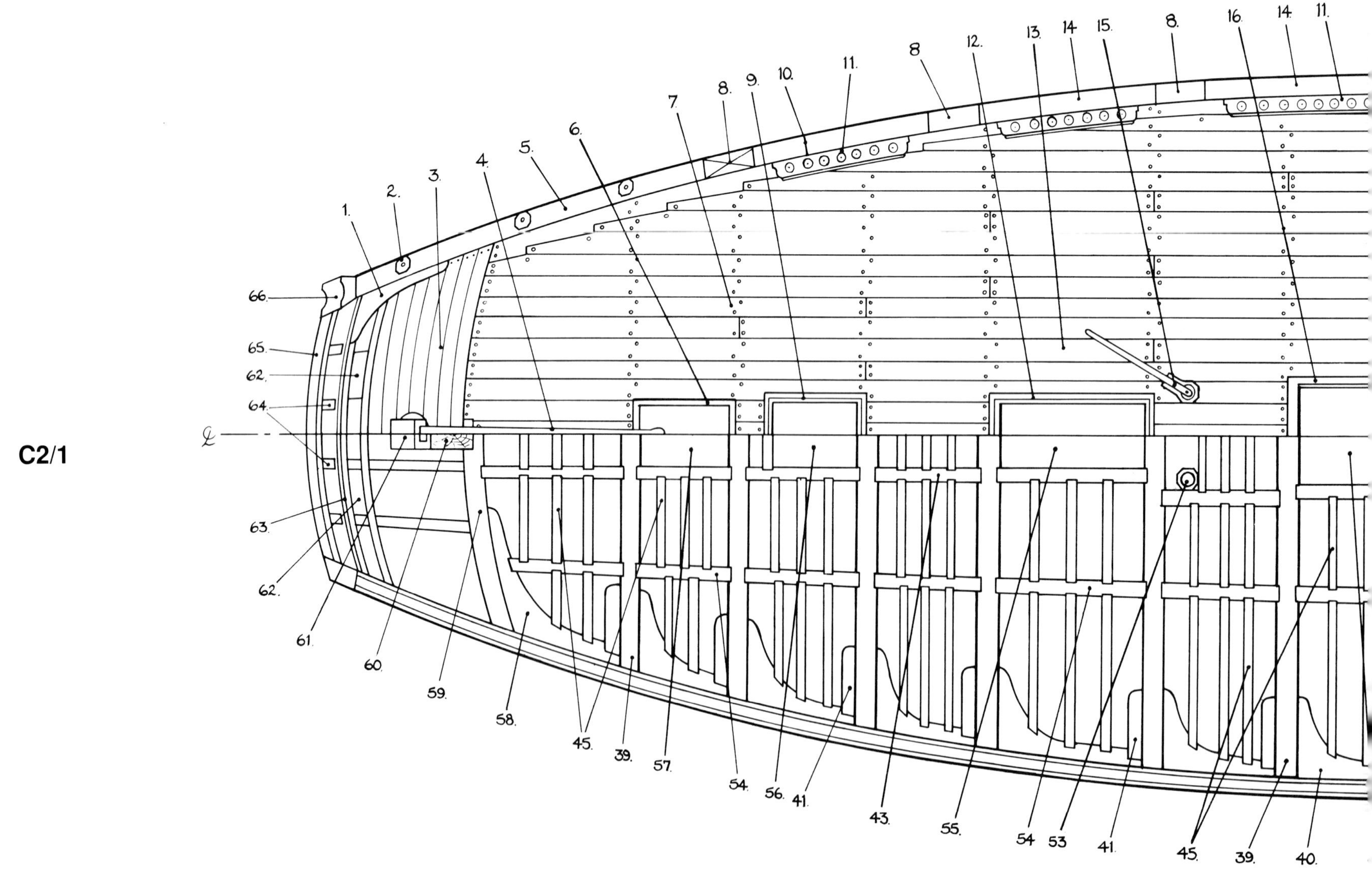

C2/1

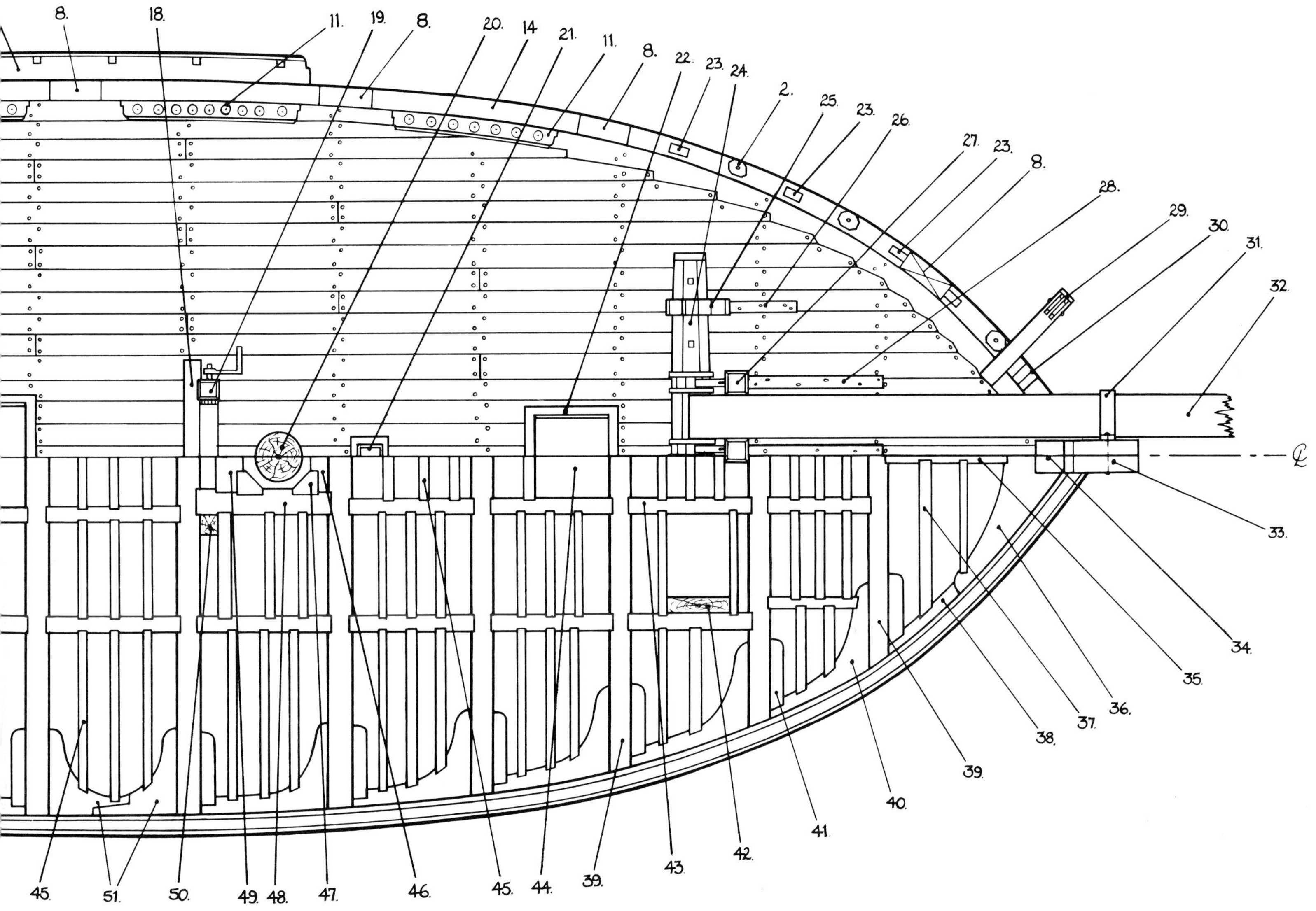
8.
18.
11.
19.
8.
20.
14
21.
11.
8.
22.
23.
24.
2.
25.
23.
26.
27.
23.
8.
28.
29.
30.
31.
32.
33.
34.
35.
36.
37.
38.
39.
40.
41.
42.
43.
39.
44.
45.
46.
47.
48.
49.
50.
51.
45.

C2/2 Plan of lower deck (or fore platform) (1/64 scale)

1 Moulding line
2 Main hatchway coaming
3 Flat of the deck
4 Line denotes limitation of the flat of the deck
5 Sailroom bulkhead
6 Mainmast
7 Galley fire hearth
8 Stone plinth of galley
9 Fore hatchway coaming
10 Section of carrick bitt pin
11 Fore transverse bulkhead
12 Bulkhead stanchion
13 Section of pawl bitt pin
14 Boatswain's storeroom
15 Fore and aft division bulkhead
16 Stempost
17 Scuttle to fore peak (pitch room)
18 Access doors
19 Scuttle to coal hole
20 Fore access hatchway to hold
21 Sailroom
22 Main hatchway to hold
23 Dry provision room
24 Access door to after cabin accommodation deck
25 Elm tree pumps
26 Main transverse bulkhead sub-dividing fore platform and after cabin deck
27 Aftermost fore platform beam
28 Gunner's storeroom
29 Main hatchway carling
30 Limit line of deck
31 Lower deck (or fore platform) beams
32 Mast partner
33 Partner ledges
34 Centreline carling supporting galley fire hearth
35 Carling for headledge
36 Scuttle to spirit room
37 Carpenter's storeroom
38 Steward's room
39 Apron (or false post)

C2/2

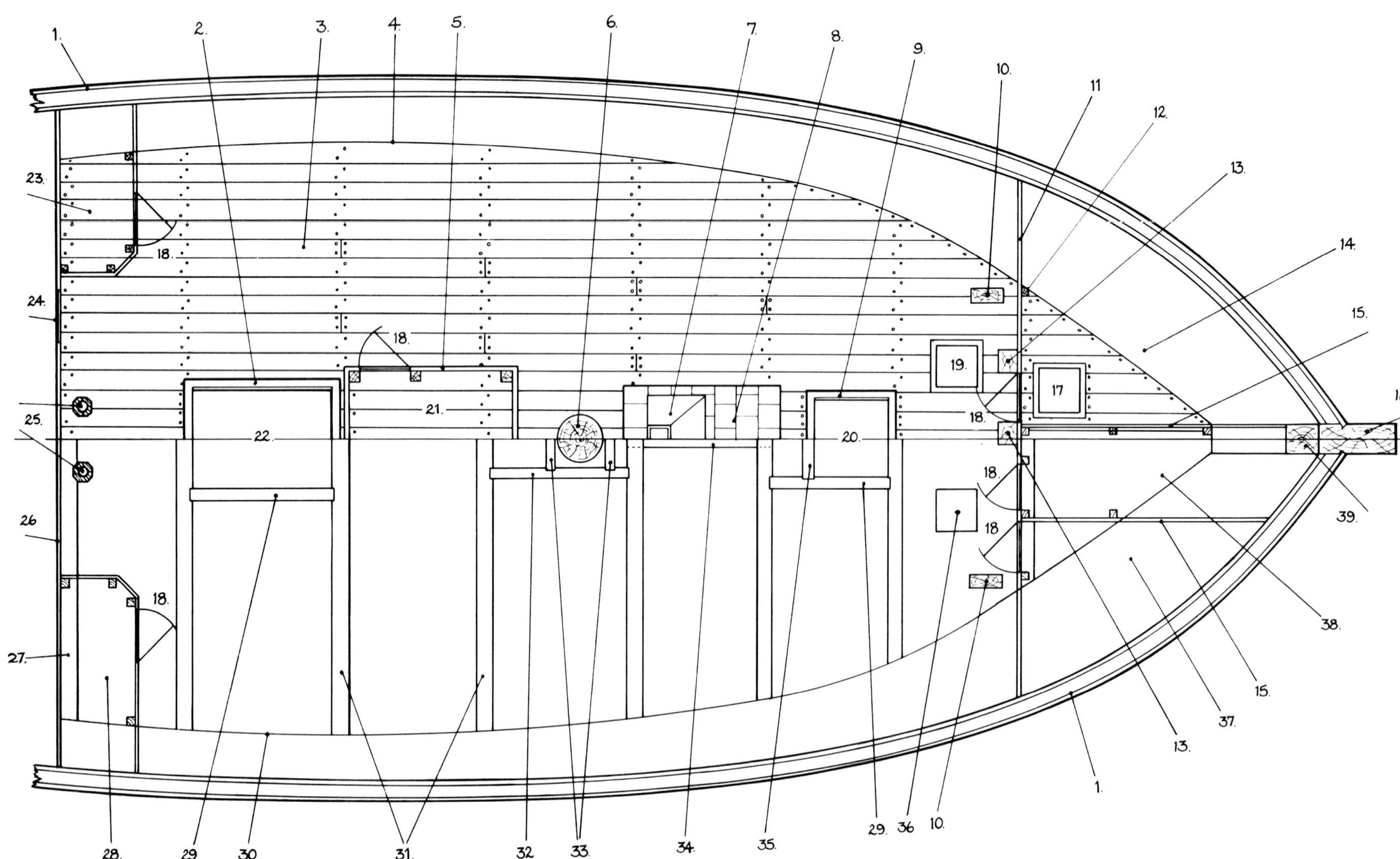

C3 COMPARTMENT BULKHEADS

C3/1 Fore bulkhead of lower deck or fore platform (view from aft) (1/48 scale)

1 Upper deck beam
2 Pawl bitt pins
3 Carling
4 Door hinges
5 Upper deck planking
6 Lodging knee
7 Bulkhead planking (6in x 2in)
8 Door to boatswain's storeroom
9 Door to steward's storeroom
10 Vertical division plank
11 Door to carpenter's storeroom
12 Lower deck (fore platform) planking

C3/2 Main transverse bulkhead and storeroom between fore platform and after cabin deck, transverse view from forward (1/48 scale)

C3/3 Side elevation (1/48 scale)

1 Upper deck planking
2 Door hinge
3 Upper deck beam
4 Side and midship tier of carlings
5 Gunner's storeroom transverse bulkhead (6in x 1¾in)
6 Door to gunner's storeroom
7 Angled panel (6in x 1¾in)
8 Main bulkhead planking (6in x 2in)
9 Lower deck (or fore platform) planking
10 Access door to after cabin deck
11 Door to dry provision room
12 Provision room transverse bulkhead (6in x 1¾in)
13 Aftermost deck beam of fore platform
14 Fore and aft bulkhead panel of provision room (gunner's storeroom identical) (6in x 1¾in)

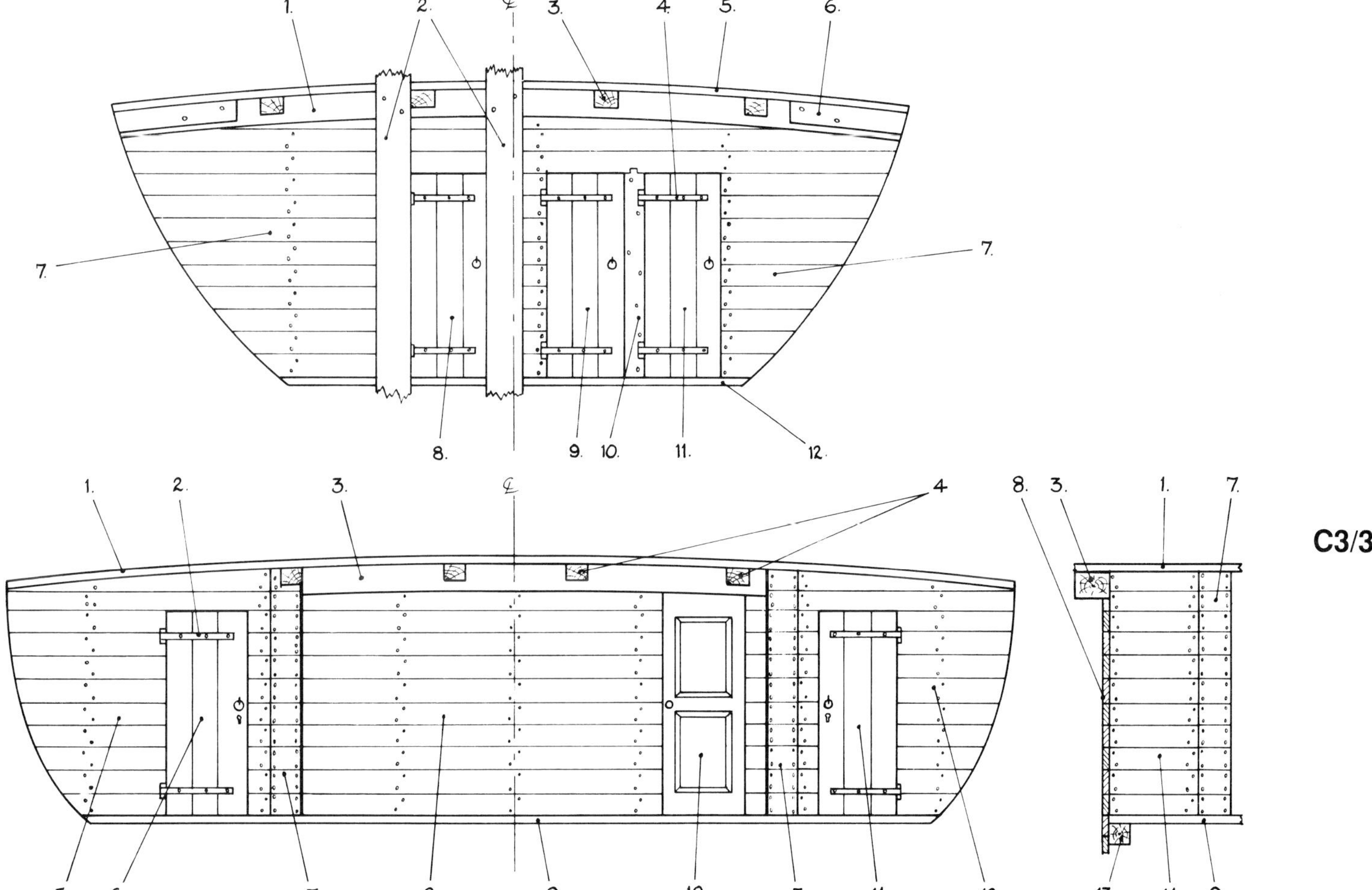

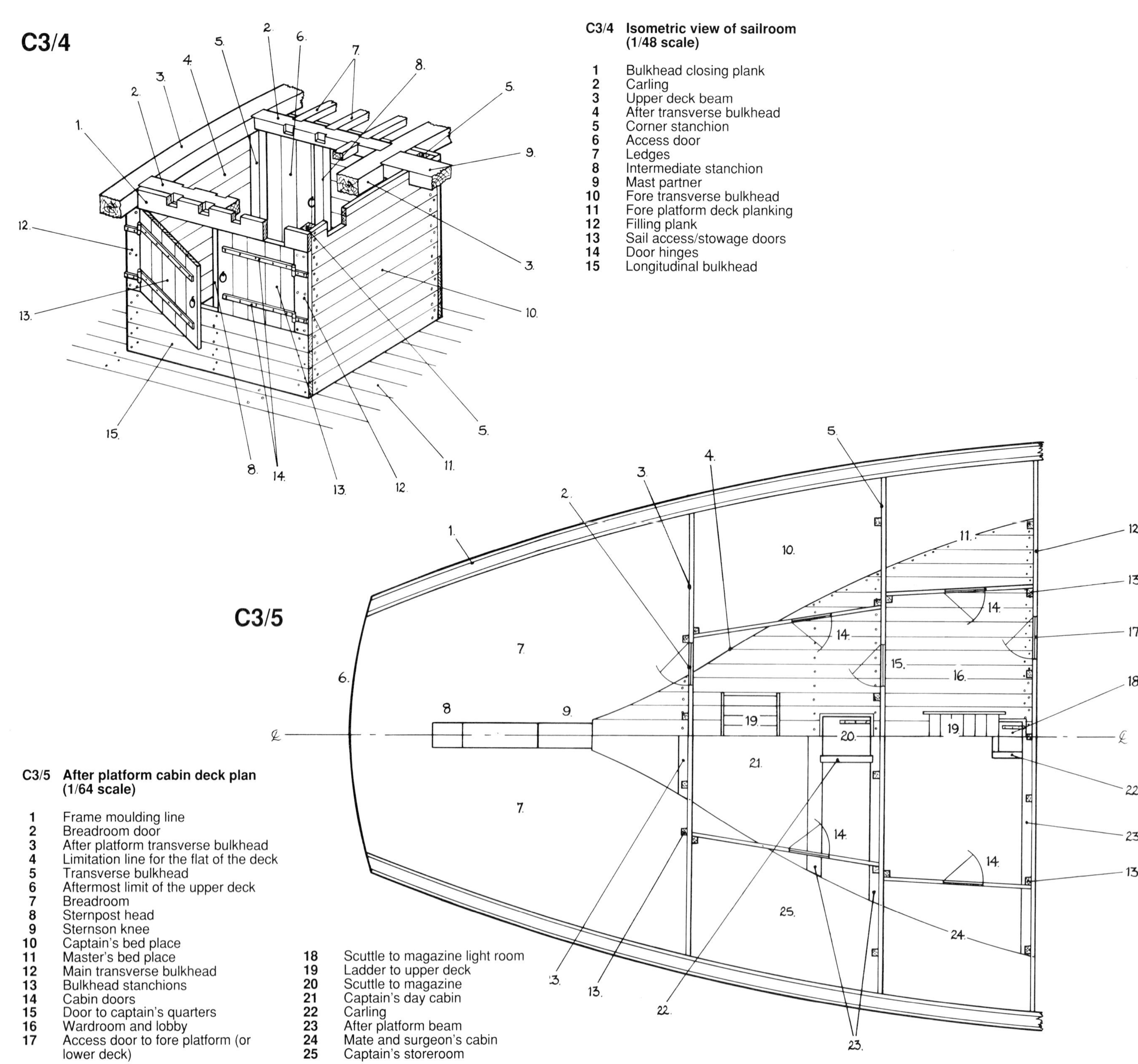

C3/4

C3/4 Isometric view of sailroom (1/48 scale)

1. Bulkhead closing plank
2. Carling
3. Upper deck beam
4. After transverse bulkhead
5. Corner stanchion
6. Access door
7. Ledges
8. Intermediate stanchion
9. Mast partner
10. Fore transverse bulkhead
11. Fore platform deck planking
12. Filling plank
13. Sail access/stowage doors
14. Door hinges
15. Longitudinal bulkhead

C3/5

C3/5 After platform cabin deck plan (1/64 scale)

1. Frame moulding line
2. Breadroom door
3. After platform transverse bulkhead
4. Limitation line for the flat of the deck
5. Transverse bulkhead
6. Aftermost limit of the upper deck
7. Breadroom
8. Sternpost head
9. Sternson knee
10. Captain's bed place
11. Master's bed place
12. Main transverse bulkhead
13. Bulkhead stanchions
14. Cabin doors
15. Door to captain's quarters
16. Wardroom and lobby
17. Access door to fore platform (or lower deck)
18. Scuttle to magazine light room
19. Ladder to upper deck
20. Scuttle to magazine
21. Captain's day cabin
22. Carling
23. After platform beam
24. Mate and surgeon's cabin
25. Captain's storeroom

C3/6 Transverse bulkhead at captain's cabin, view from forward (1/48 scale)

1 Lodging knee
2 Upper deck beam
3 Upper deck planking
4 Midship tier of carlings
5 Side tier of carlings
6 Bulkhead stanchion
7 Fore and aft cabin bulkhead (6in x 1¾in)
8 Bulkhead planking (6in x 2in)
9 After cabin deck planking
10 Access door to captain's cabin
11 Door architrave

C3/7 Aftermost transverse bulkhead, view from forward (1/48 scale)

1 Upper deck planking
2 Upper deck beam
3 Midship tier of carlings
4 Side tier of carlings
5 Lodging knee
6 Bulkhead planking (6in x 2in)
7 Bulkhead stanchion
8 Fore and aft cabin bulkhead (6in x 1¾in)
9 Aft cabin deck planking
10 Door architrave
11 Access door to breadroom

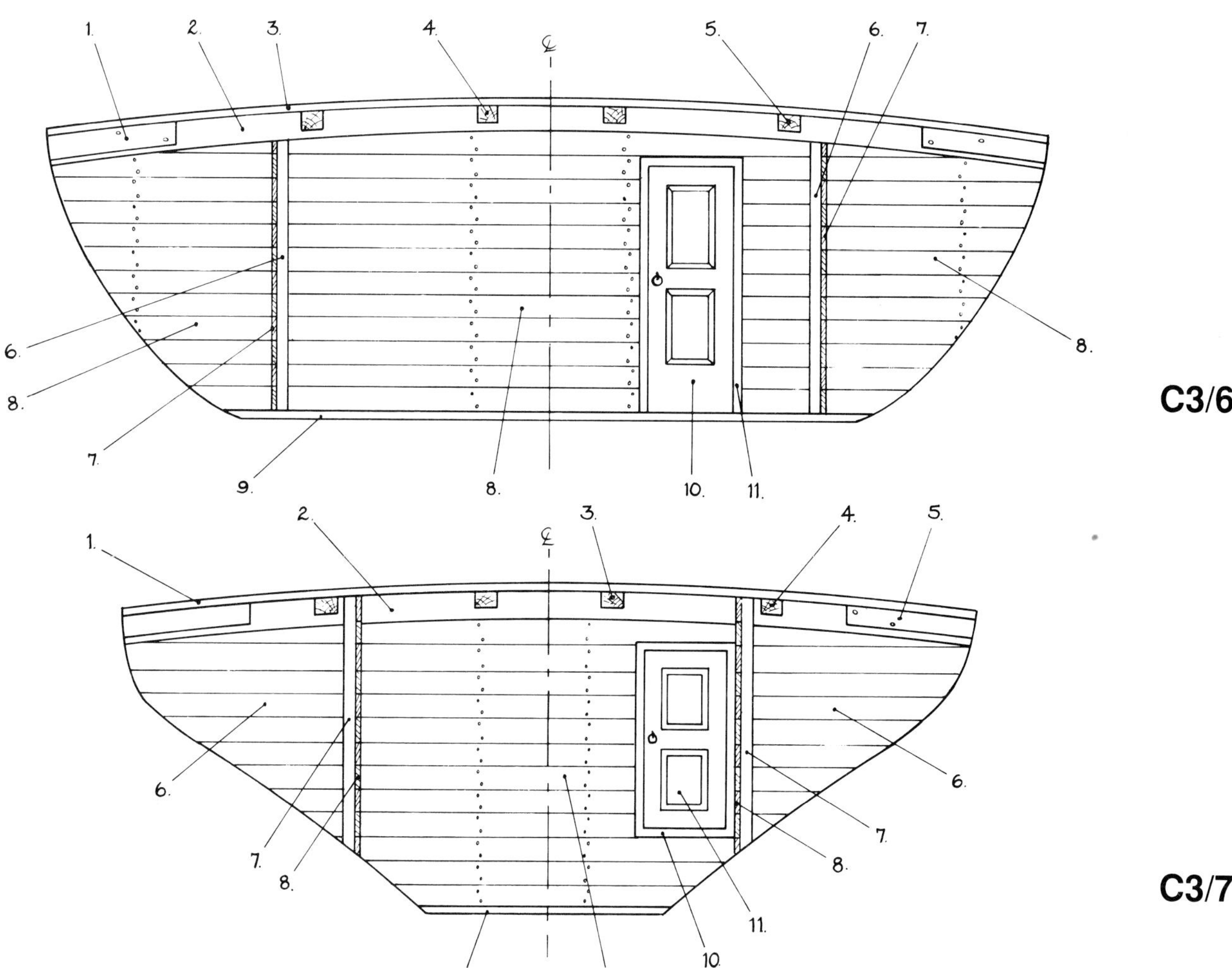

C Internal hull

C4 Plan of the hold and provision layout (1/96 scale)

1 Longitudinal bulkhead of well
2 Footwaling
3 Limber boards
4 Centreline stanchion
5 Limber passage (limber boards omitted for clarity)
6 Mainmast step
7 Limit line of hold at level of fore platform
8 Limber strake
9 Access ladder from fore platform
10 Coal hole
11 Carrick bit pin
12 Pawl bitt pins
13 Lower breasthook
14 Keelson
15 Breasthook
16 Fore peak (additional strореroom for the boatswain)
17 Scuttle from boatswain's storeroom to fore peak
18 Scuttle from fore platform to coal hole
19 Water leagers – capacity, 184 gallons
20 Half hogsheads – capacity, 28 gallons
21 Hogsheads – capacity, 54 gallons
22 Main transverse bulkhead
23 Ground tier of casks (see note above)
24 Pump well inspection door
25 Larboard elm tree pump
26 Pump well
27 Shot locker
28 Starboard elm tree pump
29 Pump well stanchion
30 Pump well inspection door
31 Ground tier of casks
32 Puncheons – capacity, 72 gallons
33 Barrel – capacity, 36 gallons
34 Scuttle
35 Apron
36 Peak bulkhead
37 Bulkhead stanchion
38 Carpenter's storeroom
39 Shot locker transverse bulkhead
40 Pump well transverse bulkhead

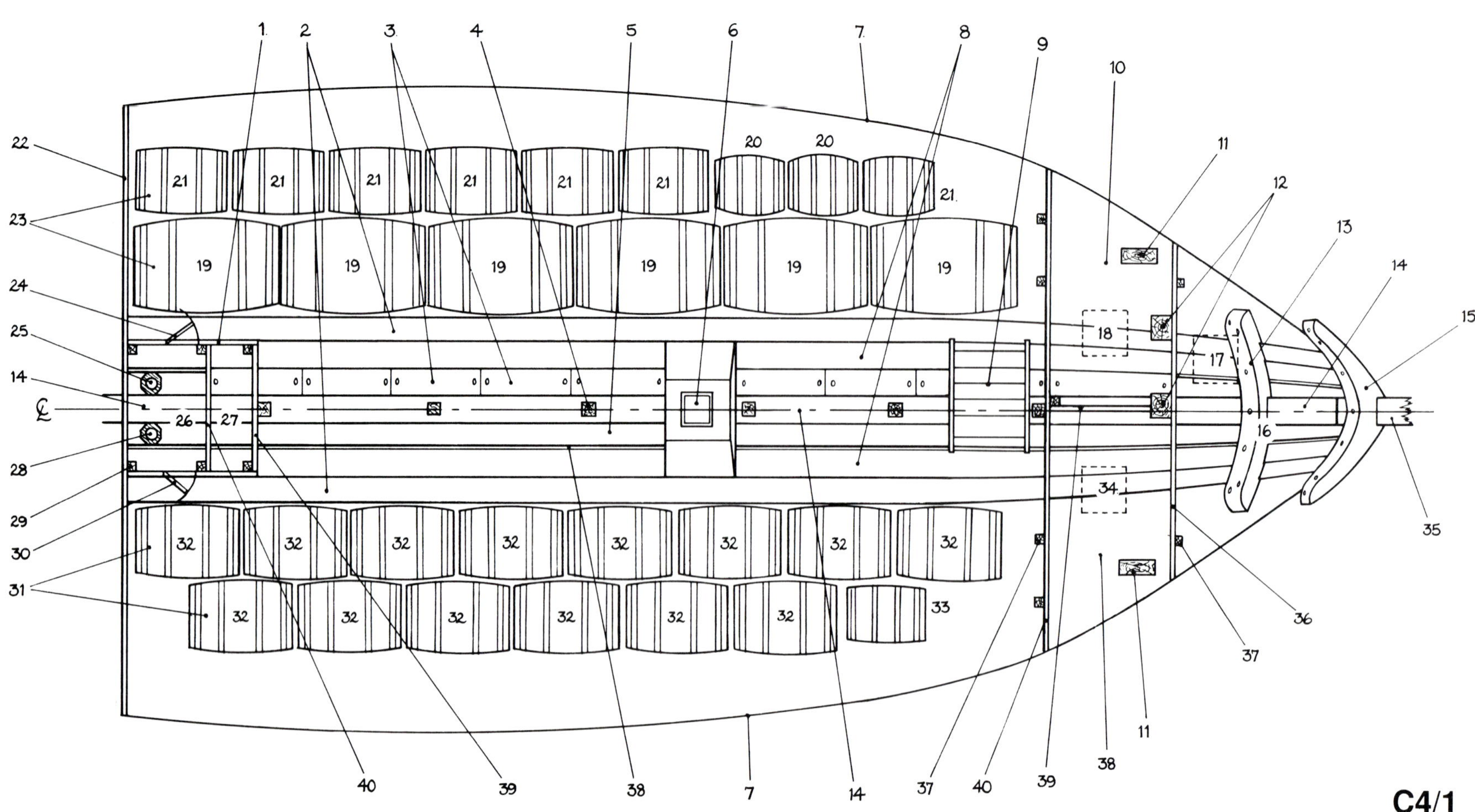

C4/1

C5 THE MAGAZINE

C5/1 Plan elevation (1/64 scale)

C5/2 Section view from forward

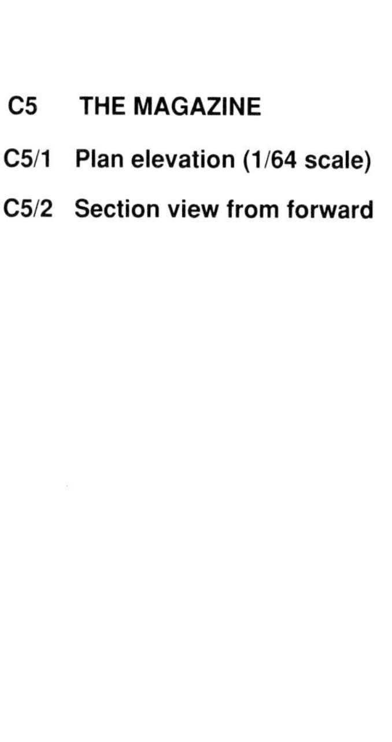

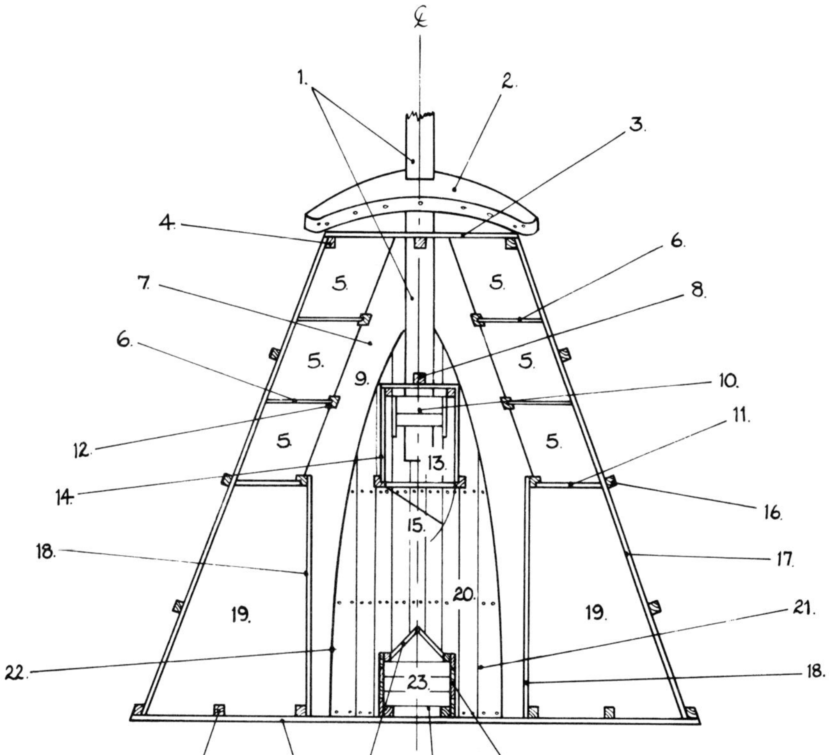

1 Keelson
2 Crutch
3 After bulkhead
4 After bulkhead stanchion
5 Cartridge racks
6 Rack division panel
7 Ceiling and internal planking
8 Centreline pillar
9 Filling room
10 Access ladder
11 Division bulkhead between powder room and filling room
12 Rack stanchion
13 Entry lobby
14 Lobby bulkhead
15 Magazine access door
16 Wing bulkhead stanchion
17 Wing bulkhead
18 Rail to retain powder kegs in the wing
19 Wing
20 Powder room
21 Magazine platform
22 Boundary line of platform planking
23 Light room
24 Main transverse bulkhead stanchion
25 After cabin deck planking
26 Main transverse bulkhead
27 Light room window – glass panels covered with copper mesh
28 Light room access scuttle
29 Lantern shelf
30 Carling
31 Light room bulkhead
32 Void space
33 Ceiling
34 Footwaling
35 Magazine platform planking
36 Magazine deck beam
37 Keel
38 Hog
39 Limber strake
40 Frame

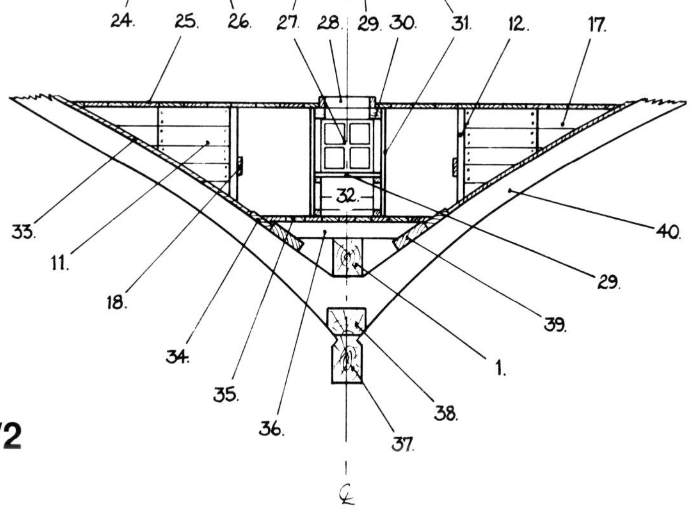

C5/3 The pump well and shot locker, isometric projection (1/48 scale)

1 Bulkhead stanchion
2 Larboard elm tree pump
3 Centreline stanchion
4 Starboard elm tree pump
5 Aftermost lower deck beam
6 Carling
7 After bulkhead planking
8 Pump well transverse bulkhead
9 Top of the shot locker
10 Lower deck beam
11 Hatchway carling
12 Lid hinge
13 Shot locker lid
14 Footwaling
15 Limber strake
16 Limber board
17 Keelson
18 Limber passage
19 Shot locker transverse bulkhead
20 Corner stanchion
21 Ceiling
22 Pump inspection door
23 Fore and aft bulkhead
24 Foremost after cabin deck beam
25 Magazine
26 Cabin deck planking

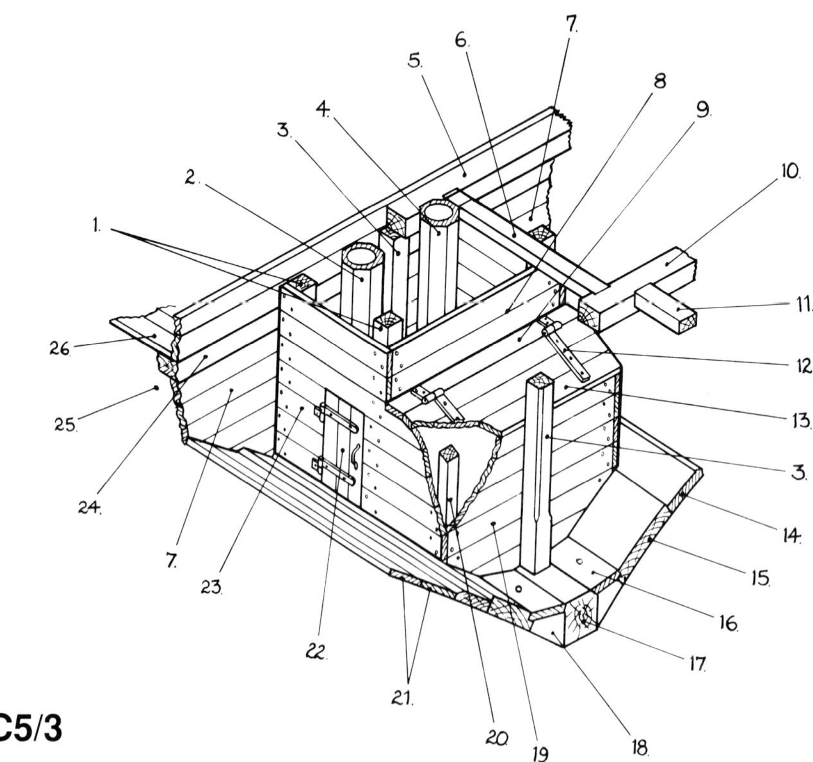

C5/3

C6 MAINMAST STEP (1/48 scale)

C6/1 Section elevation

C6/2 Side elevation

C6/3 Isometric projection

1 Limber board
2 Mast step
3 Mortice to receive mast heel tenon
4 Bolts
5 Limber strake
6 Keelson
7 Keel
8 Hog
9 Limber passage
10 Footwaling
11 Frame
12 Ceiling

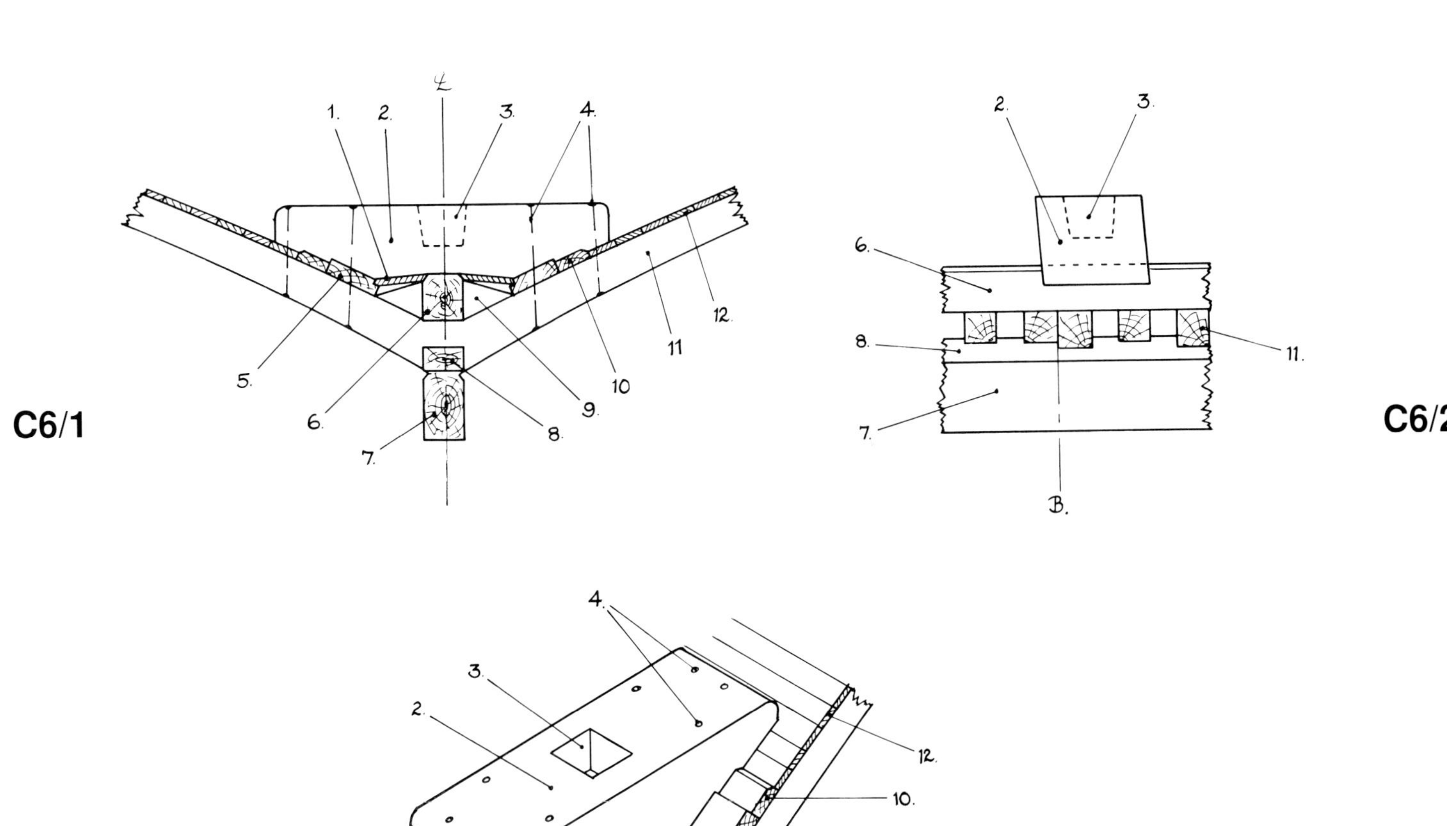

D External hull

D1 GENERAL ARRANGEMENT (1/64 scale)

D1/1 External hull features

1 Tafferal
2 Rough tree rail
3 Swivel gun pedestal
4 Timberhead (finger and thumb fashion)
5 Drift planking
6 Gunport
7 Short iron guardrail stanchion
8 Entry steps
9 Iron plate for standing end of running backstay
10 Iron guardrail stanchion
11 Iron plate for running backstay tackle
12 Head of lengthening piece
13 Drift rail
14 Iron plate for standing backstay
15 Elm pump brake handle
16 Elm tree pump
17 Sheer rail
18 Rope guardrail
19 Shroud deadeyes
20 Channel
21 Jeer bitt pin
22 Mainmast
23 Galley flue
24 Ship's side planking, carvel fashion
25 Windlass carrick bitts
26 Pawl bitt pin (also serves as bowsprit step)
27 Bowsprit heel
28 Cathead
29 Stem head
30 Holes for forestay deadeye lanyards
31 Bowsprit
32 Hawse hole
33 Cathead supporter
34 Main wale
35 Stempost
36 Draught mark, fashioned in copper
37 Fore foot
38 Copper horseshoe plate
39 Stempost heel
40 Boxing
41 Anchor chock
42 Fore section of keel
43 Keel scarph
44 Mid section of keel
45 Deadeye chain plates
46 Hook and butt scarph
47 After section of keel
48 Copper fish plate
49 Lower gudgeon and pintle braces
50 Sternpost
51 Rudder
52 Gudgeon and pintle braces
53 Square tuck transom
54 Tuck rail
55 Rudder head
56 Counter
57 Upper gudgeon and pintle braces
58 Stern side counter timber
59 Lower counter rail
60 Transom
61 Stern chase port
62 Upper counter rail

D1/1

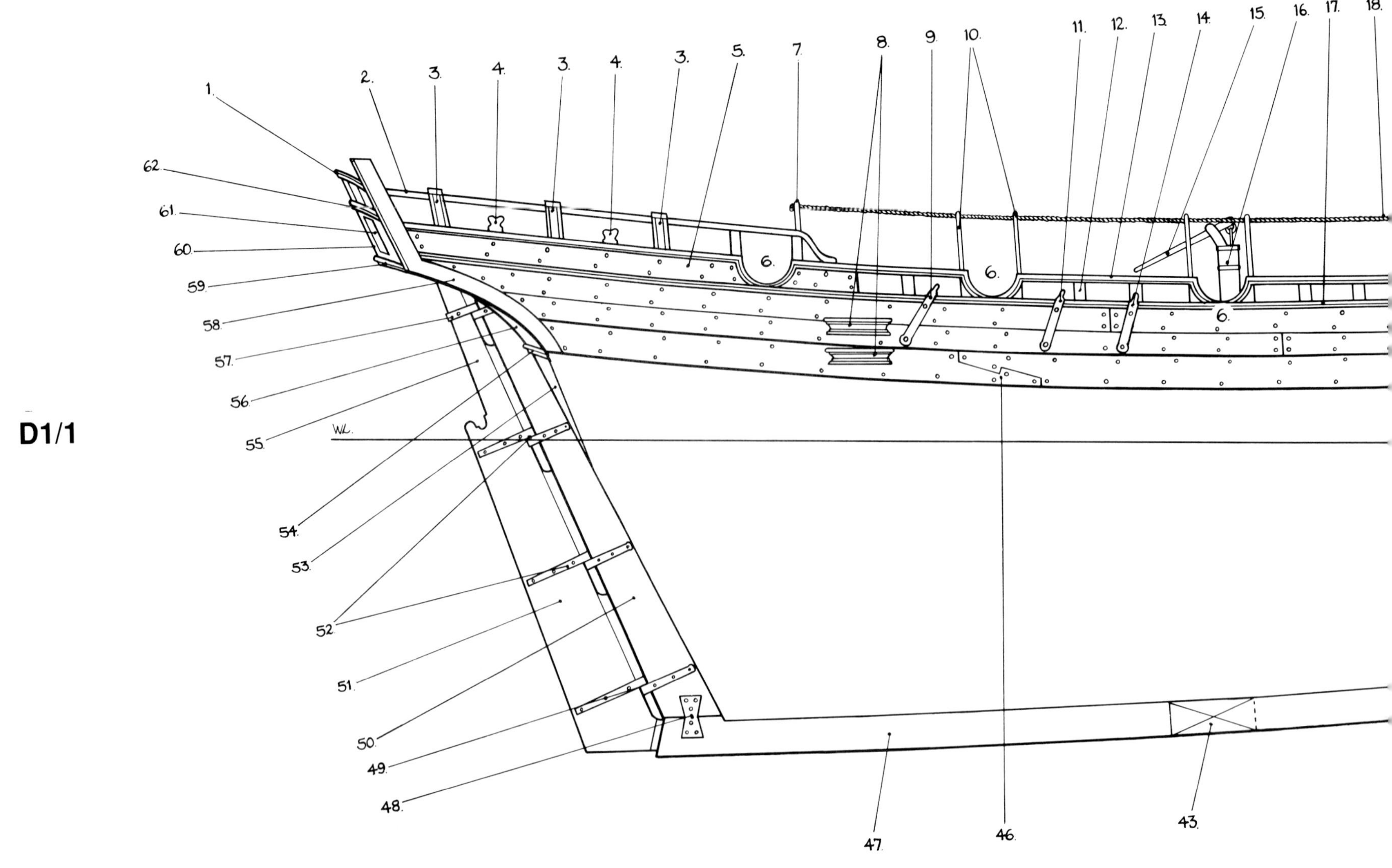

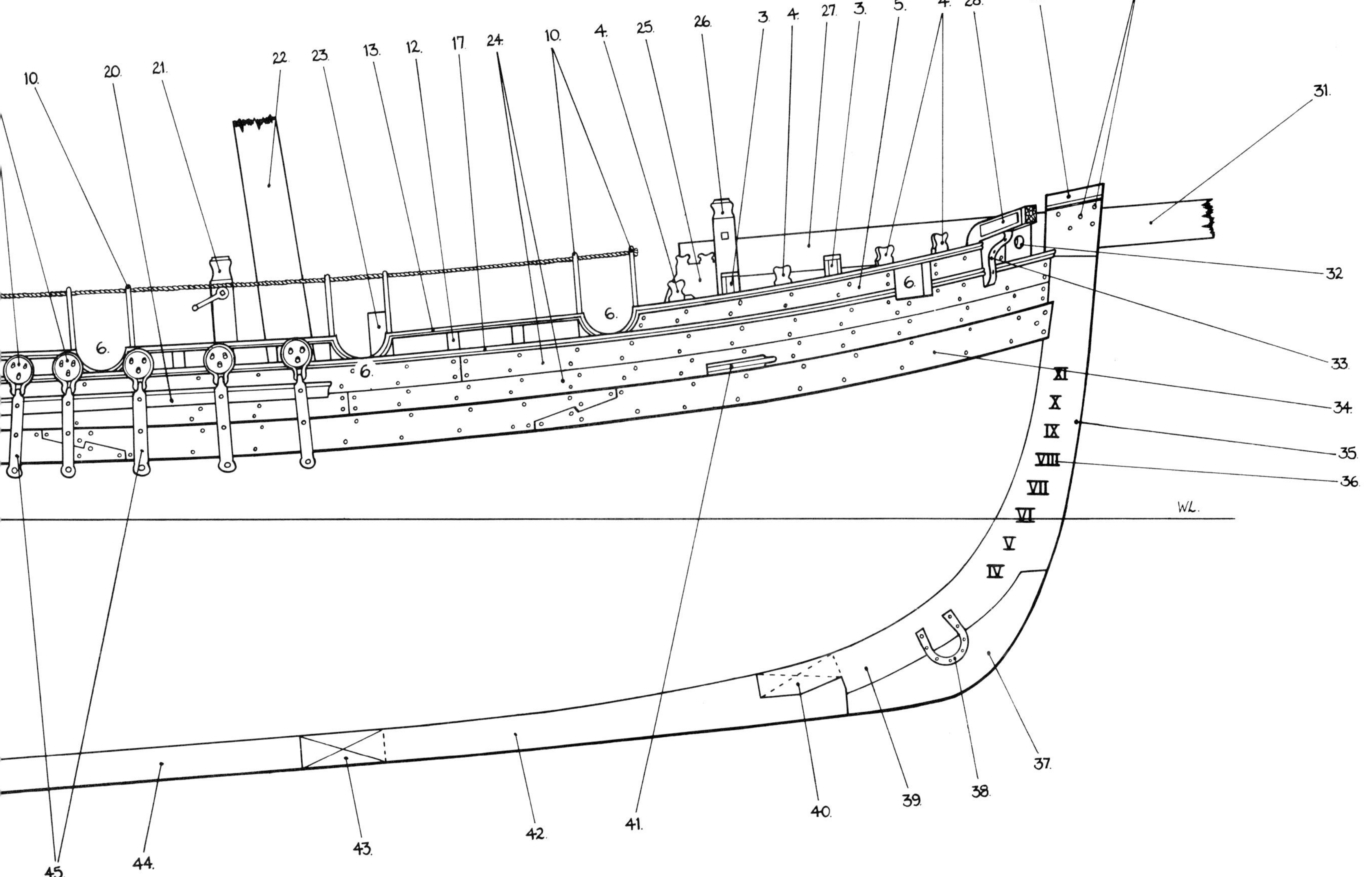
10.
20.
21.
22.
23.
13.
12.
17.
24.
10.
4.
25.
26.
3.
4.
27.
3.
5.
4.
28.
29.
30.
31.
32.
33.
34.
35.
36.
6.
6.
6.
6.
XI
X
IX
VIII
VII
VI
V
IV
WL.
45.
44.
43.
42.
41.
40.
39.
38.
37.

D1/2 External hull as fitted with square ports and open drift

1 Closed in drift planking
2 Aftermost gun port (as original draught)
3 Head of lengthening piece
4 Square gun ports (as amended on original draught)
5 Drift rail
6 Open drift
7 Sheer rail
8 Closed in drift planking
9 Foremost chase port

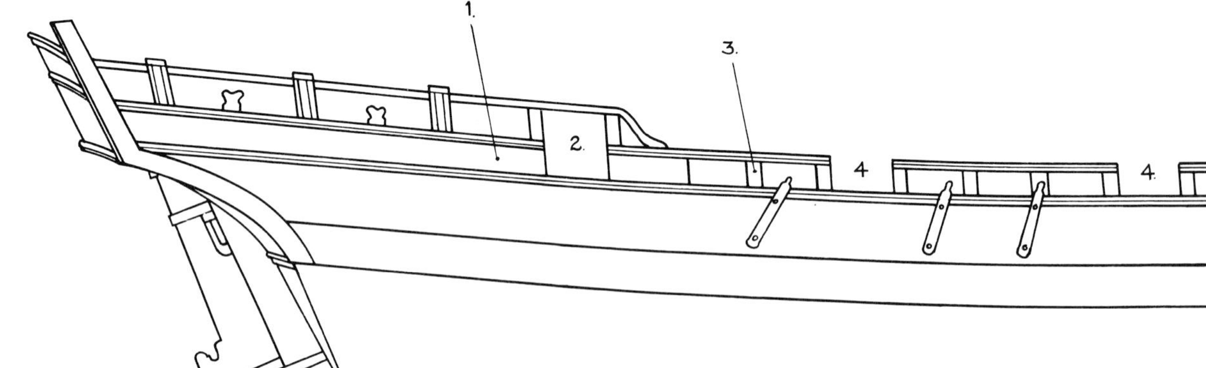

D1/3 External hull as fitted with square ports and closed drift

1 Closed in drift planking (as original)
2 Aftermost gun port (as original draught)
3 Drift rail
4 Square gun ports (as amended on original draught)
5 Closed in drift planking (modification)
6 Sheer rail
7 Closed in drift planking (as original)
8 Foremost chase port

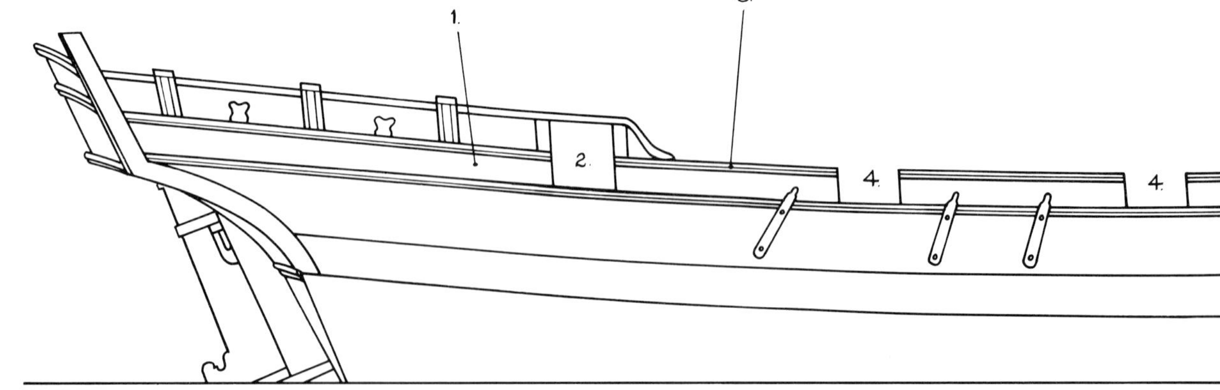

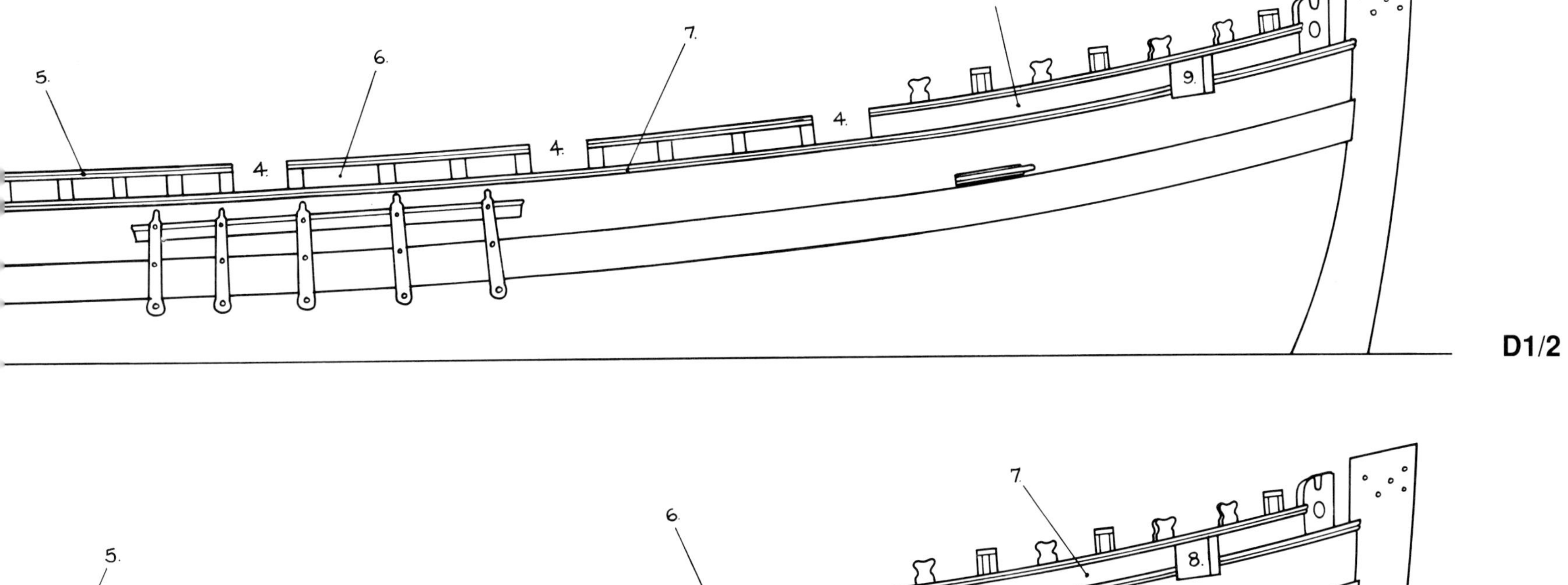

D1/3

D External hull

D2 The stern (1/64 scale)

1 Square tuck
2 Shroud deadeye
3 Tuck rail
4 Sheer rail
5 Counter
6 Counter rail
7 Helm port
8 Stern chase port
9 Stern counter timber
10 Transom rail
11 Tafferal
12 Stern transom
13 Rough tree rail
14 Drift rail
15 Entry steps
16 Main wale
17 Channel
18 Chain plate
19 Bottom planking (clinker fashion)
20 Rudder pintle braces
21 Keel
22 Rudder

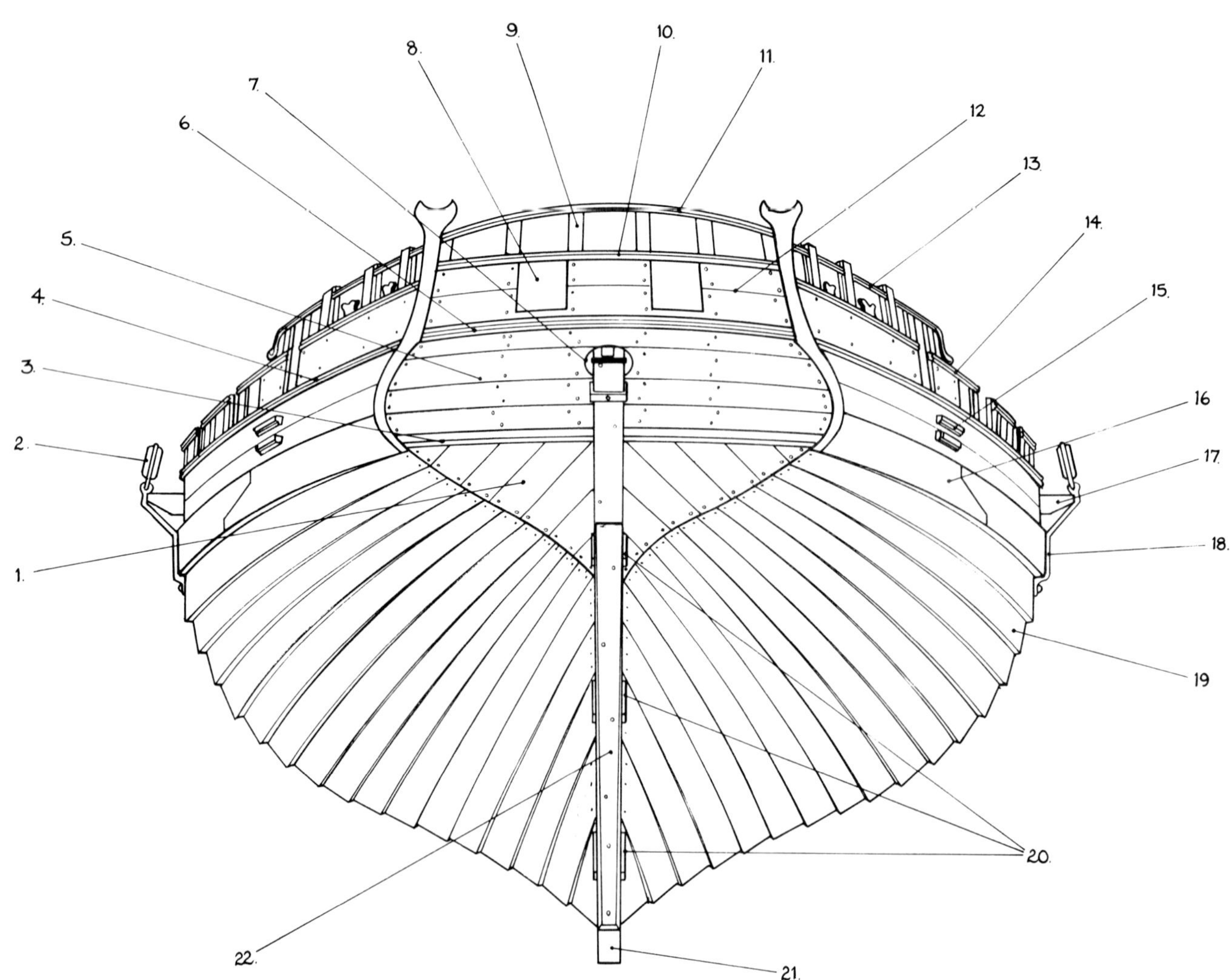

D2

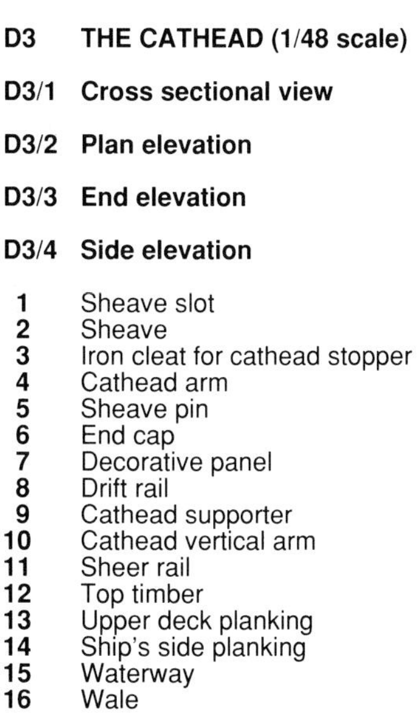

D3 THE CATHEAD (1/48 scale)

D3/1 Cross sectional view

D3/2 Plan elevation

D3/3 End elevation

D3/4 Side elevation

1 Sheave slot
2 Sheave
3 Iron cleat for cathead stopper
4 Cathead arm
5 Sheave pin
6 End cap
7 Decorative panel
8 Drift rail
9 Cathead supporter
10 Cathead vertical arm
11 Sheer rail
12 Top timber
13 Upper deck planking
14 Ship's side planking
15 Waterway
16 Wale

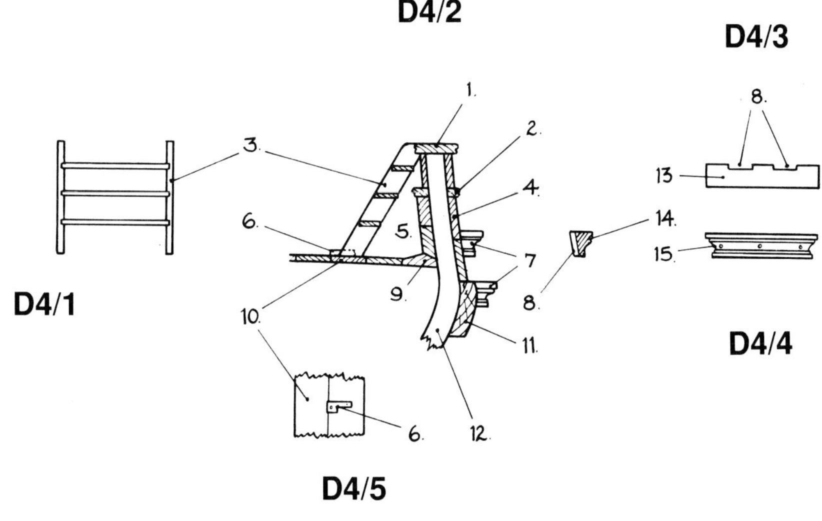

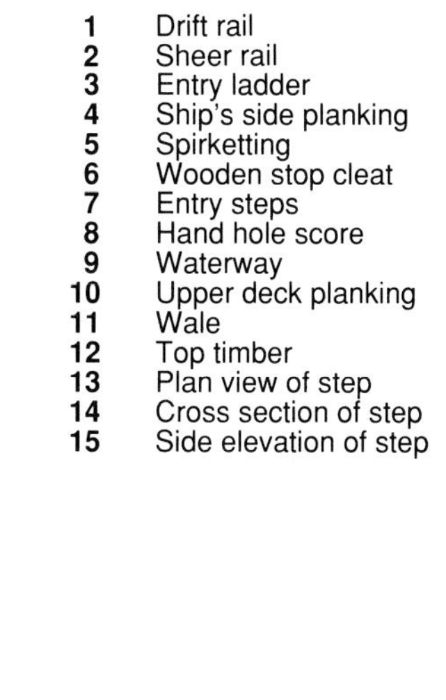

1 Drift rail
2 Sheer rail
3 Entry ladder
4 Ship's side planking
5 Spirketting
6 Wooden stop cleat
7 Entry steps
8 Hand hole score
9 Waterway
10 Upper deck planking
11 Wale
12 Top timber
13 Plan view of step
14 Cross section of step
15 Side elevation of step

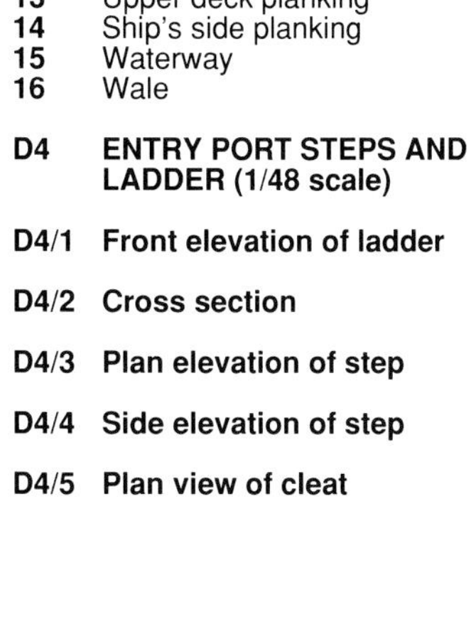

D4 ENTRY PORT STEPS AND LADDER (1/48 scale)

D4/1 Front elevation of ladder

D4/2 Cross section

D4/3 Plan elevation of step

D4/4 Side elevation of step

D4/5 Plan view of cleat

D5 DETAIL OF GUARDRAIL STANCHION (1/48 scale)

D5/1 Inboard view

D5/2 Cross section

1 Eye for hand rope
2 Iron stanchion
3 Bolt plate
4 Gun port
5 Drift rail
6 Sheer rail
7 Ship's side planking
8 Top timber
9 Spirketting

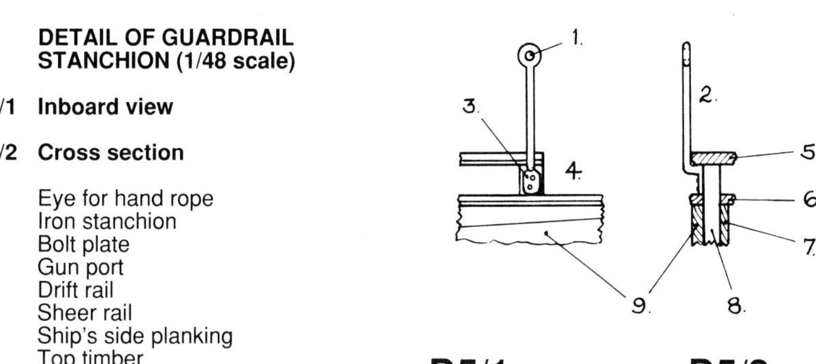

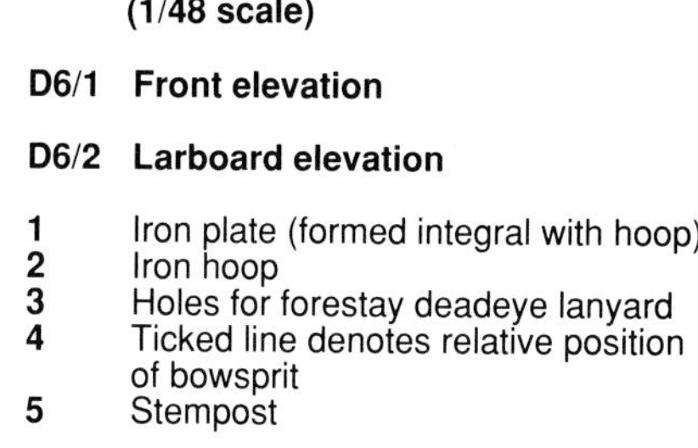

D6 IRON BOWSPRIT HOOP (1/48 scale)

D6/1 Front elevation

D6/2 Larboard elevation

1 Iron plate (formed integral with hoop)
2 Iron hoop
3 Holes for forestay deadeye lanyard
4 Ticked line denotes relative position of bowsprit
5 Stempost

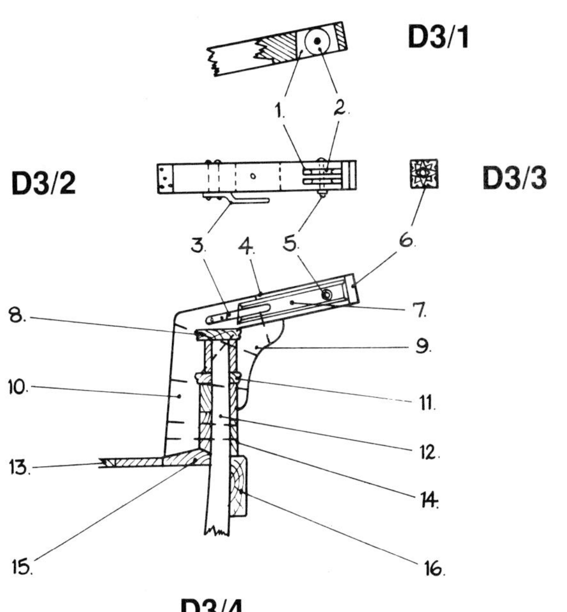

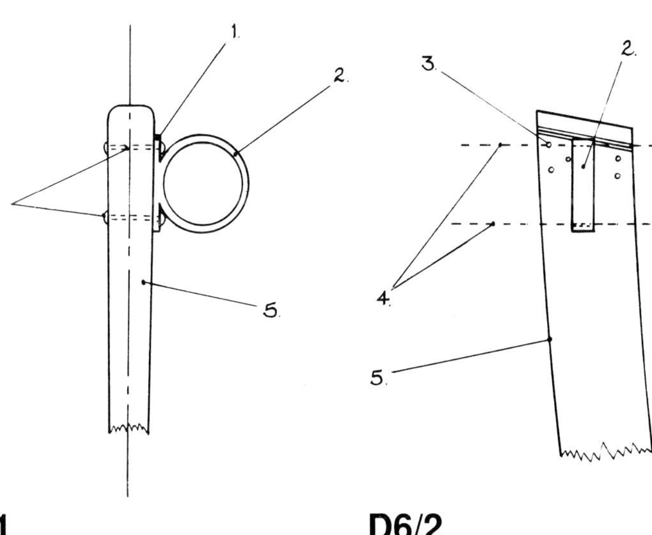

E Fittings

E1 RUDDER AND TILLER (1/48 scale)

E1/1 Rudder end view

E1/2 Rudder and sternpost side elevation

E1/3 Rudder side elevation, showing construction

1 Iron hoop
2 Mortice for tiller
3 Upper pintle brace
4 Rudder head
5 Hance
6 Bearding of rudder stock
7 The back piece (fir)
8 Lower pintle braces
9 Flat of the rudder
10 Sole (fir)
11 Bearding of sternpost
12 Gudgeon brace
13 Pintle
14 Score
15 Sternpost
16 Keel
17 Bearding of rudder heel and keel
18 Recess for iron hoops
19 Bolts
20 Tabling of the main and back pieces
21 The main piece (oak)

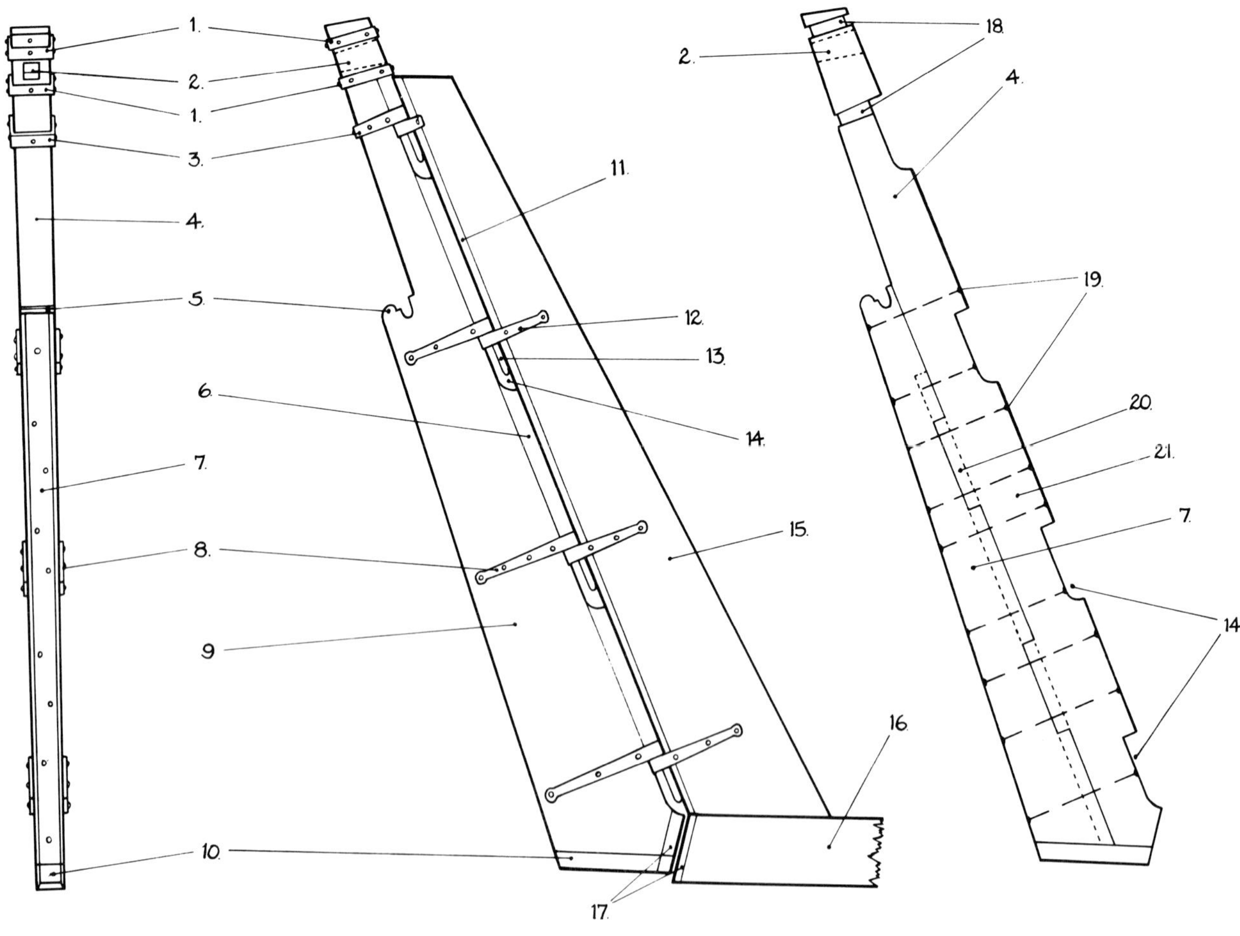

E1/4 Pintle and gudgeon brace, side and plan elevations (1/24 scale)

1 Pintle brace
2 Pintle
3 Copper washer
4 Hole for pintle
5 Gudgeon brace
6 Rove
7 Back piece of rudder
8 Main piece of rudder
9 Sternpost
10 Bolts

E1/5 Rudder hinge assembly, side elevation (1/24 scale)

1 Bearding of rudder
2 Bearding of sternpost
3 Copper washer
4 Sternpost
5 Gudgeon brace
6 Score
7 Rudder
8 Pintle
9 Pintle brace

E1/6 Tiller (1/48 scale)

1 Plan elevation
2 Side elevation
3 Tenon
4 Shaft
5 Handle

Rudder head housing platform and mizzen mast steps (1/24 scale)

E1/7 Plan elevation

E1/8 Side elevation

1 Upper helm port
2 Platform planking (2in thick)
3 Fore panel planking (2in thick)
4 Mizzen mast
5 Sternpost head
6 Iron bracket forming step
7 Hole for mast
8 Step block
9 Upper deck planking

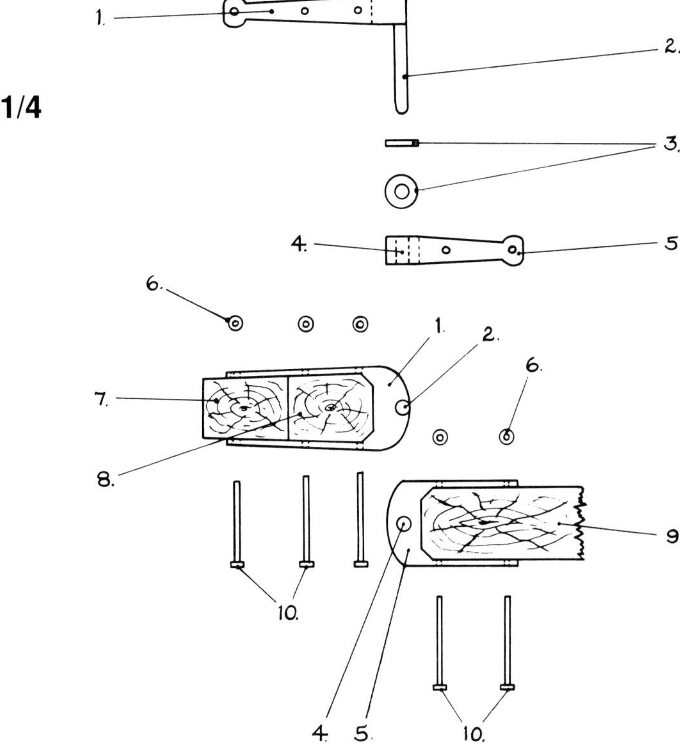

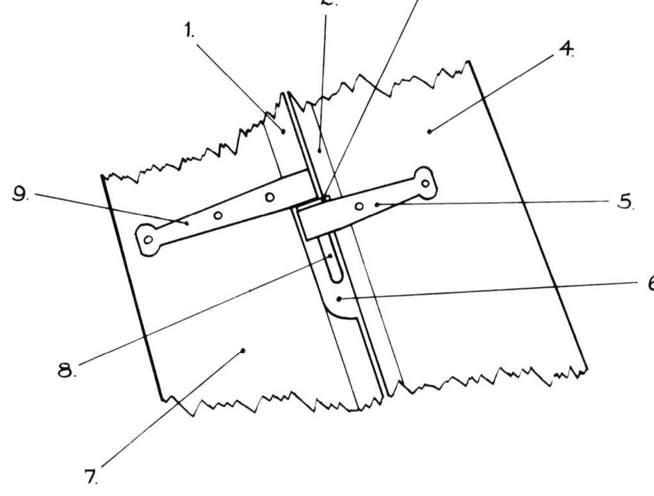

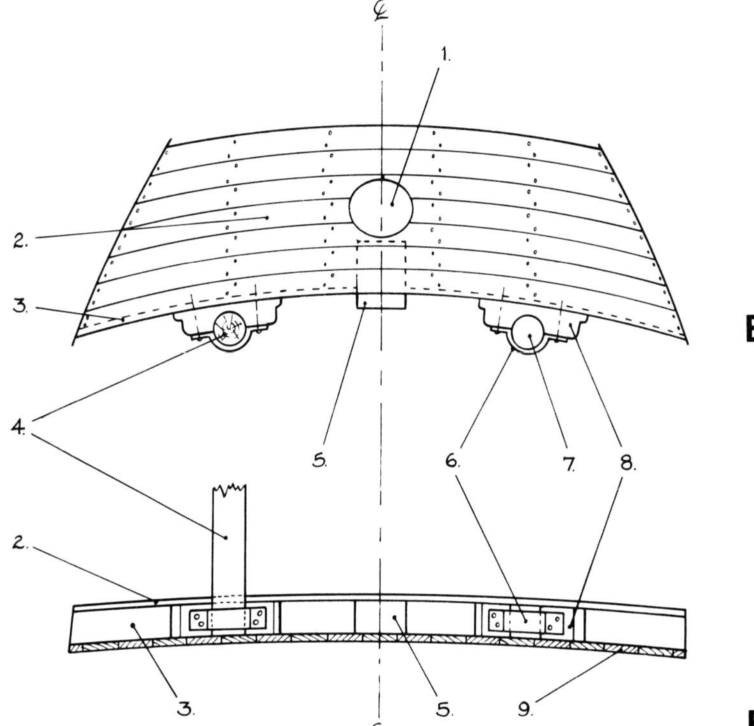

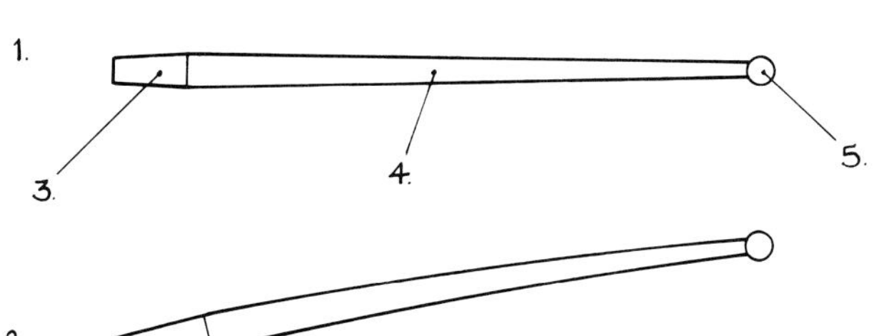

E Fittings

E2 PUMPS (1/48 scale)

E2/1 Elm tree bilge pump, cross-section from forward

E2/2 Elm tree bilge pump, side elevation

1 Brake handle
2 Eye for spear
3 Brake handle pivot pin
4 Yoke
5 Iron hoops
6 Discharge port
7 Upper deck planking
8 Upper deck beam
9 Midship tier of carlings
10 Pump case (elm)
11 Spear (connecting rod)
12 Reciprocating valve box
13 Lower deck (or fore platform) planking
14 Lower deck beam
15 Main traverse bulkhead
16 Wing space
17 Fixed valve box (could be removed for repair)
18 Centreline stanchion
19 Pump well fore and aft bulkhead
20 Ceiling
21 Pump well bulkhead stanchion
22 Frame
23 Footwaling
24 Limber strake
25 Pump suction
26 Keelson
27 Hog (or rising wood)
28 Keel
29 Limber passage
30 Ticked line denotes position of limber boards
31 Main transverse bulkhead (not fully shown in section drawing)
32 After platform deck planking
33 Canopy of shot locker
34 After platform beam
35 Pump well transverse bulkhead
36 Main frame

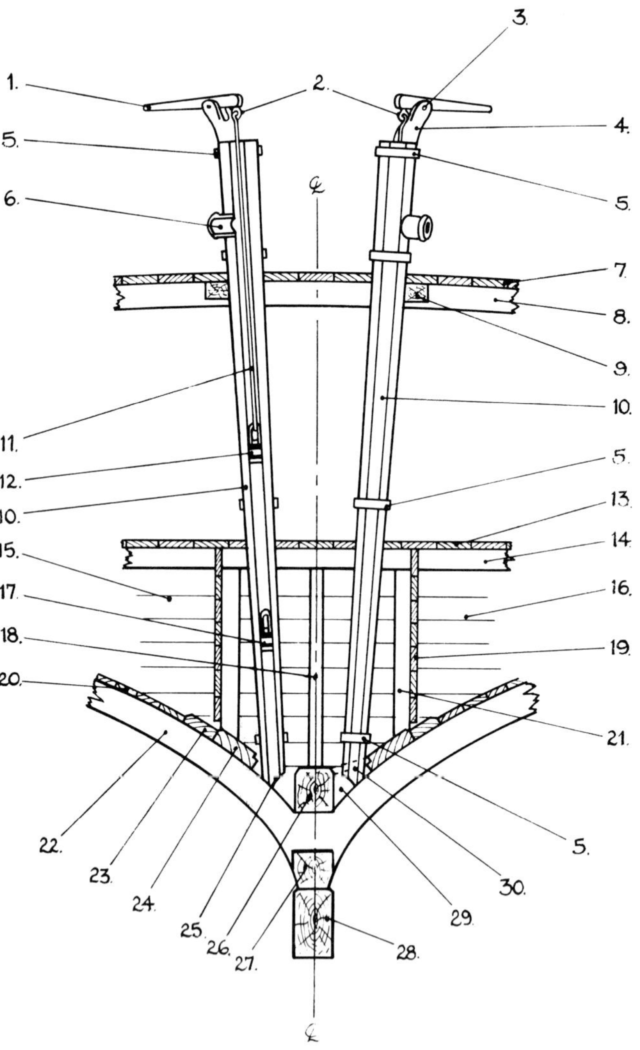

E2/1

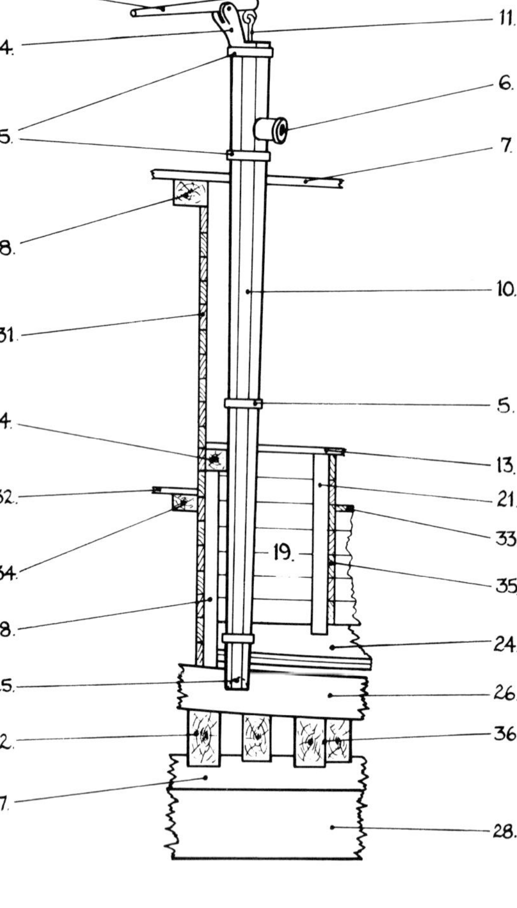

E2/2

E3 WINDLASS (as fitted) (1/48 scale)

E3/1 Elevation looking forward

E3/2 Side elevation

see page 88 for key

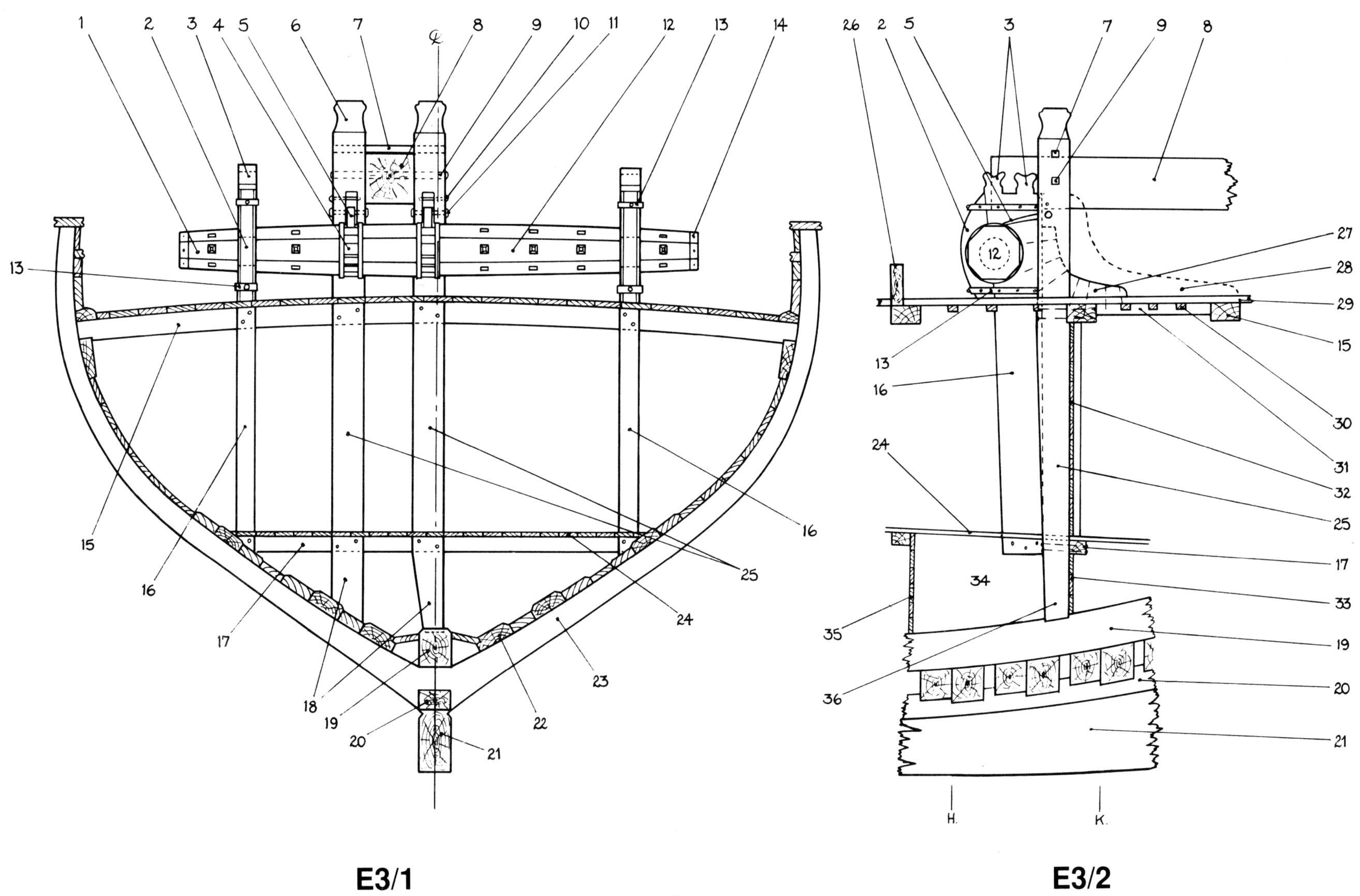

E3/1

E3/2

E3/3 Plan elevation

1	Warping head
2	Cheek (removable)
3	Carrick bitt head (double 'finger and thumb' timberhead)
4	Iron pawl ring
5	Pawl
6	Timberhead of pawl bitt pin
7	Iron strongback
8	Bowsprit
9	Iron bowsprit retaining fid
10	Locking bolt (to disengage pawl)
11	Fulcrum bolt for pawl
12	Windlass spindle
13	Iron strap (retains cheek)
14	Iron hoop
15	Upper deck beam
16	Carrick bitt pin
17	Fore platform beam
18	Pawl bitt pin heel
19	Keelson
20	Hog or rising wood
21	Keel
22	Limber strake
23	Frame
24	Platform planking
25	Pawl bitt pins
26	Fore hatchway head ledge
27	Carrick bitt standard
28	Pawl bitt standard (if fitted)
29	Upper deck planking
30	Ledge
31	Carling
32	Foremost transverse bulkhead
33	Fore peak bulkhead
34	Coal hole
35	Transverse bulkhead
36	Starboard pawl bitt pin heel (tenoned into keelson)
37	Ticked line denotes bowsprit
38	Handspike sockets
39	Handspike

E3/3

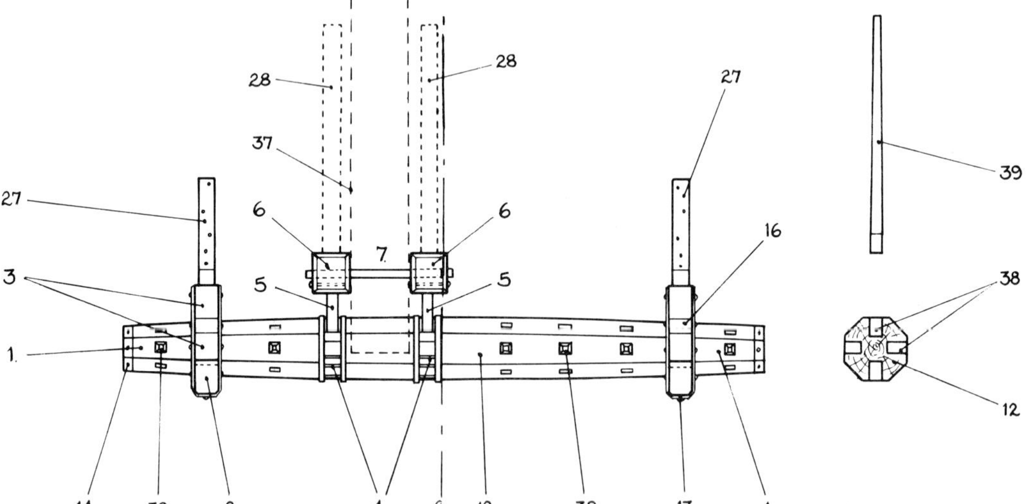

E3/4 **Modified windlass. Elevation looking forward (1/48 scale)**

E3/5 **Side elevation**

E3/6 **Plan elevation**

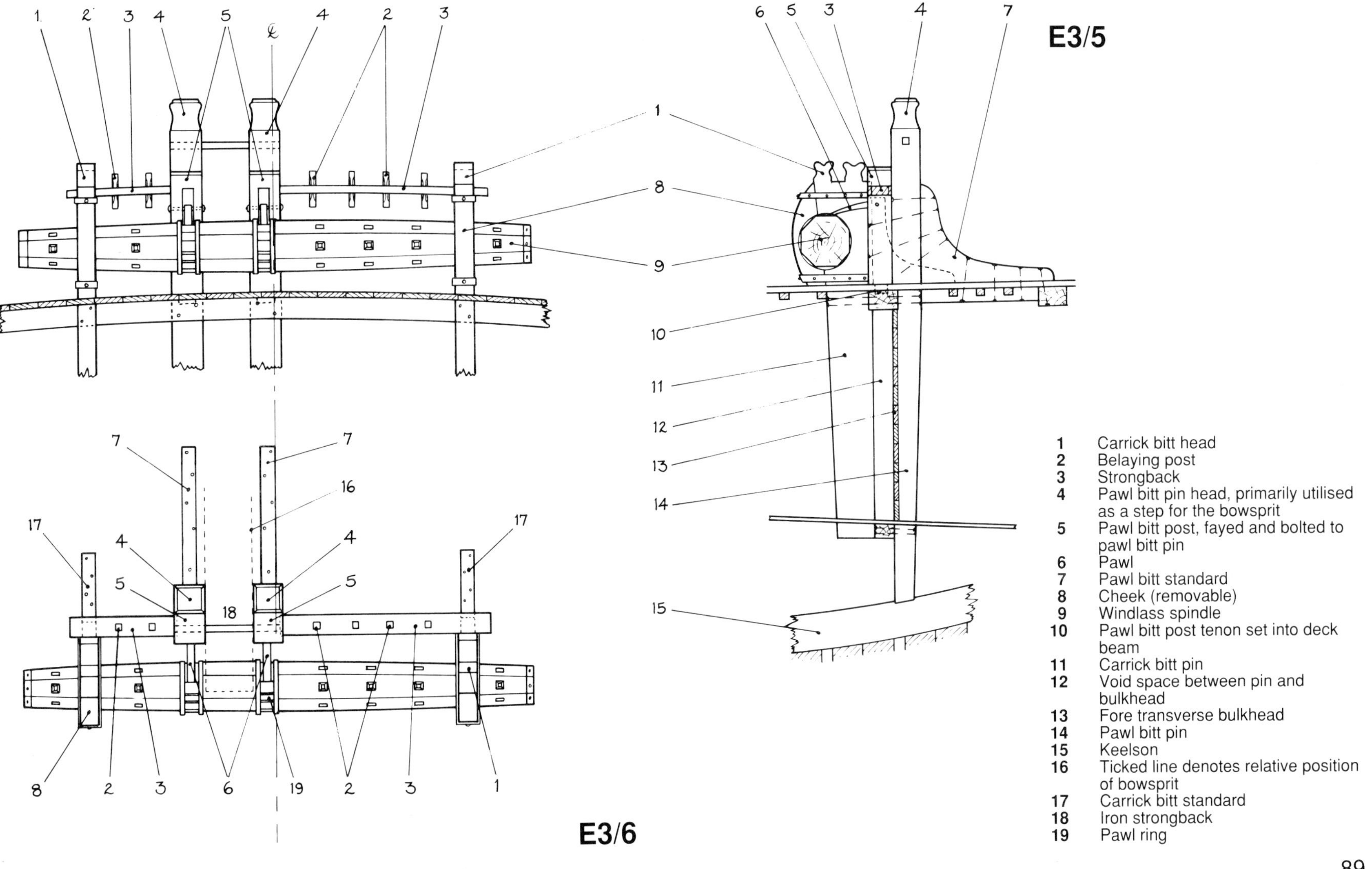

E4 Jeer and topsail bitts (1/48 scale)

E4/1 Side elevation

E4/2 End elevation

1 Bitt pin
2 Crank handle
3 Iron spindle
4 Pawl
5 Forelock pin
6 Crank handle (end view)
7 Upper deck planking
8 Pawl drum
9 Cross piece
10 Windlass
11 Upper deck beam
12 Bolts
13 Bitt pin standard
14 Bolt for pawl

E4/3 Detail of jeer and topsail bitt windlass pawl mechanism (1/24 scale)

1 Timberhead of bitt pin
2 Pawl
3 Iron spindle
4 Pawl drum
5 Bitt pin

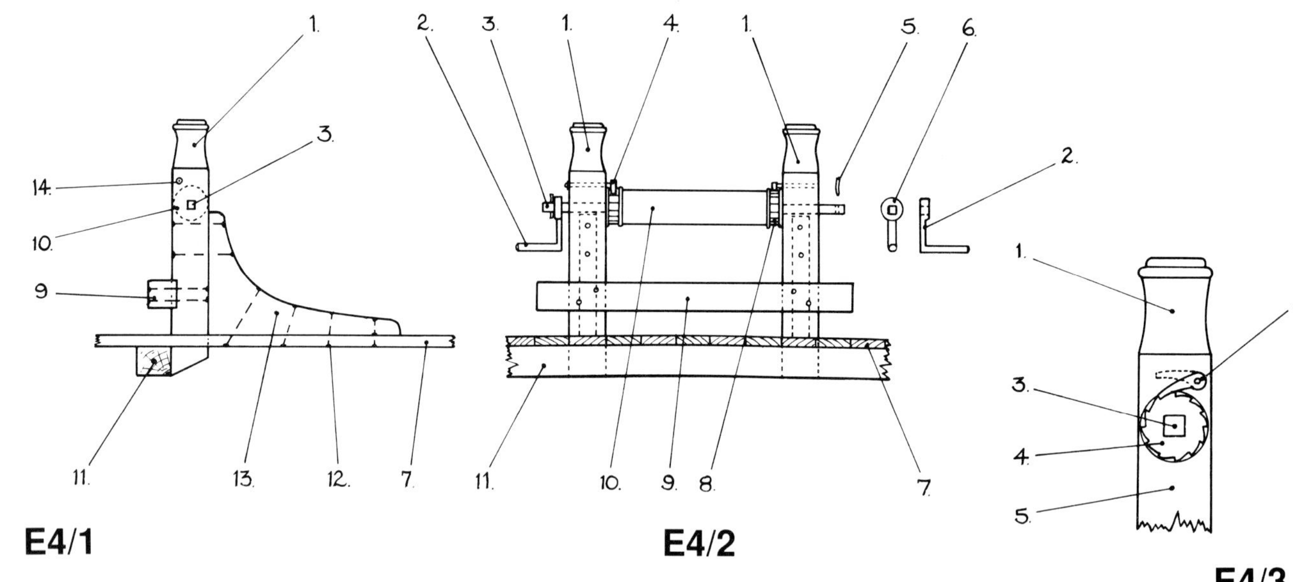

E5 GROUND TACKLE (1/48 scale)

E5/1 Sheet anchor, front elevation of the square

E5/2 Side elevation with detail of fluke

E5/3 End elevation of stock

E5/4 Plan of stock

E5/5 Front elevation

1 The square
2 Hole for anchor ring
3 Nut
4 Shank
5 Bill
6 Large round
7 Snipe
8 Palm
9 Blade
10 Arm
11 Crown
12 End elevation of stock
13 Iron hoop
14 Bolt holes
15 Hole for the square of the shank
16 Anchor ring
17 Iron hoop
18 Wooden stock
19 Small round
20 Trend (balance point)

E5/1

E5/2

E5/3

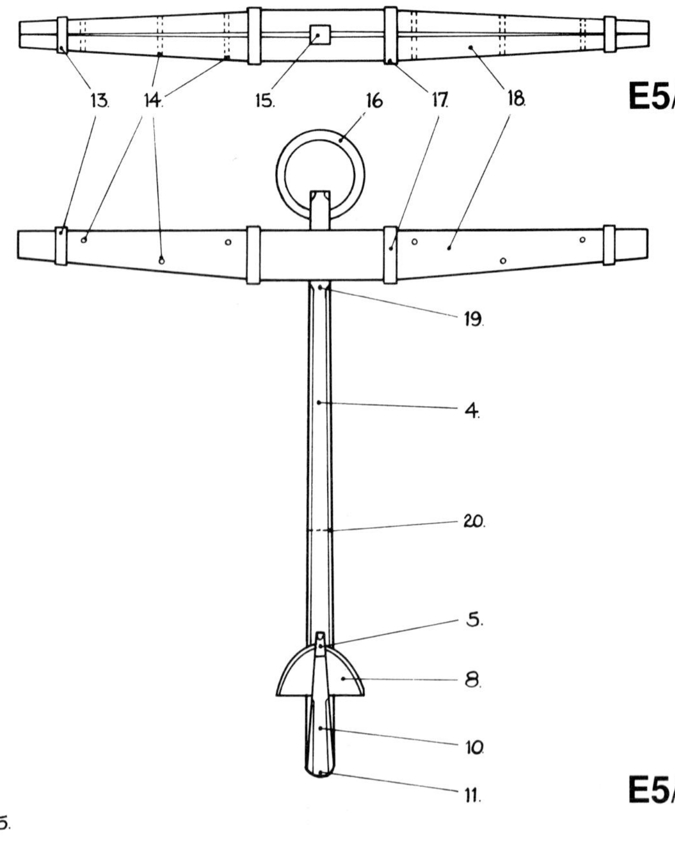

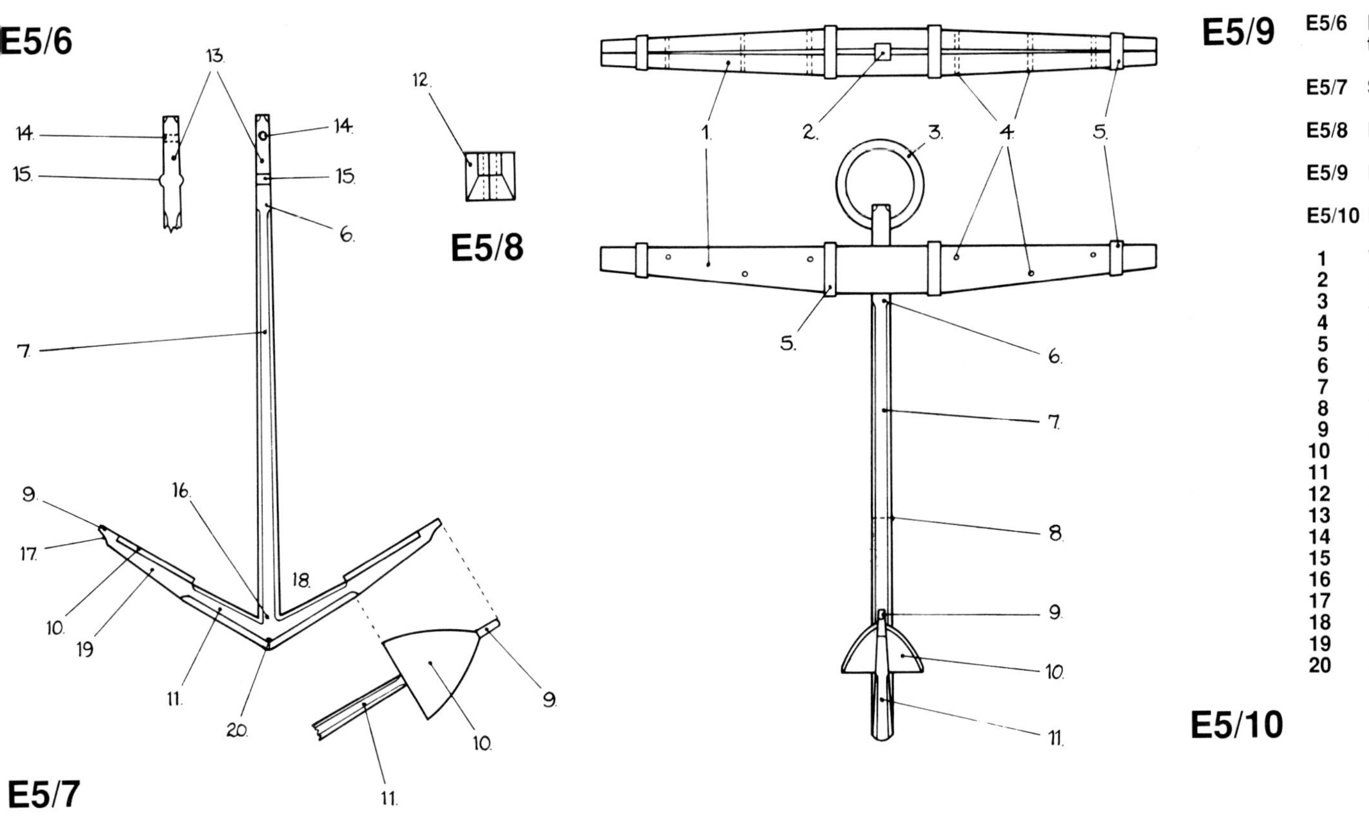

E5/6 **Bower anchor, front elevation of the square**

E5/7 **Side elevation with detail of fluke**

E5/8 **End elevation of stock**

E5/9 **Plan elevation of stock**

E5/10 **Front elevation**

1	Wooden stock
2	Hole for the square of the shank
3	Anchor ring
4	Bolt holes
5	Iron hoops
6	Small round
7	Shank
8	Trend (balance point)
9	Bill
10	Palm
11	Arm
12	End elevation of stock
13	The square
14	Hole for anchor ring
15	Nut
16	Large round
17	Snipe
18	Throat
19	Blade
20	Crown

E5/11 6cwt stream anchor

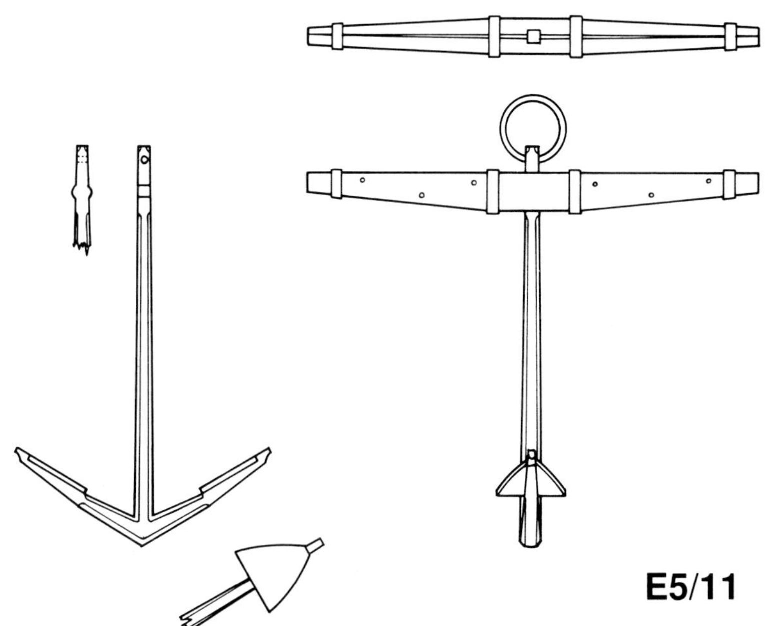

E5/12 3cwt kedge anchor

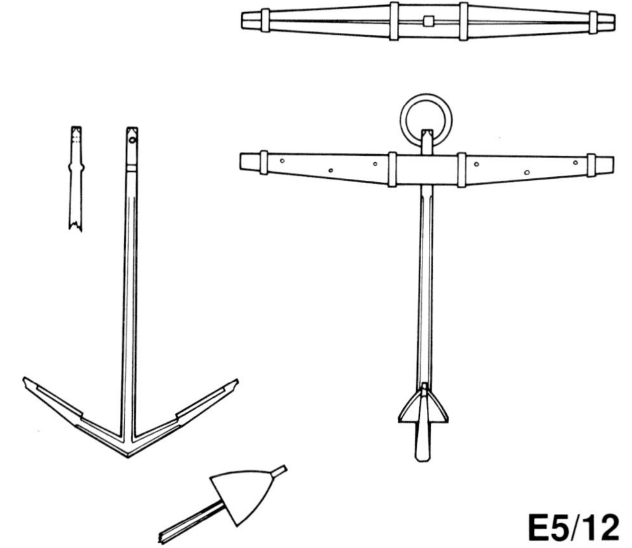

E5/13 Sheet anchor with buoy

1 Lanyard
2 Upper sling eyes
3 Tarred wicker buoy
4 Upper sling
5 Upper hoop
6 Lower sling
7 Lower hoop
8 Lower sling eyes
9 Seizing
10 Buoy rope
11 Clove hitch around anchor crown
12 Anchor
13 Seizing of buoy rope to anchor shank

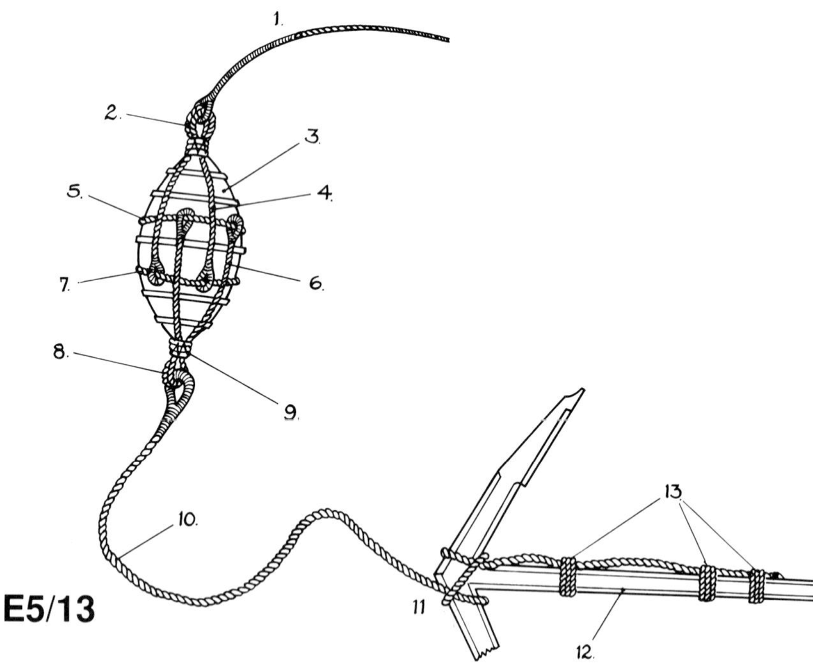

E5/14 Puddening of the anchor ring (no scale)

1 Seizing
2 Lashing
3 Anchor shank
5 Anchor ring
6 Tarred ends of puddening

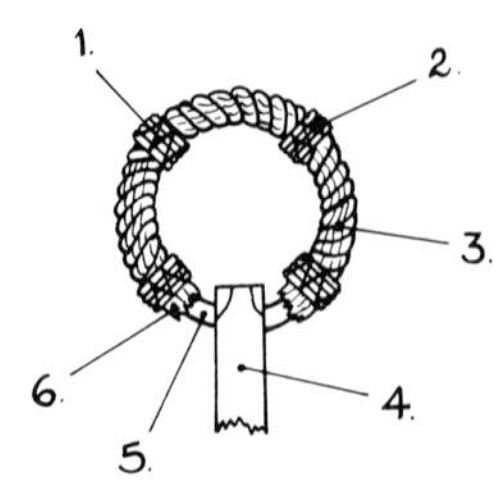

E5/15 Detail of the anchor cable at the anchor ring

1 Anchor cable
2 Seizings
3 Whipping
4 Whipped end of cable
5 Puddening of the anchor ring
6 Seizing of the puddening
7 Iron hoop
8 Anchor stock
9 Anchor ring
10 Anchor shank

E5/15

E5/16 Stowed anchor (1/64 scale)

1 Double sheaved cat block
2 Cathead
3 Additional lashing
4 Cat block tackle
5 Chain shank painter
6 Sheet anchor (bower anchors stowed in identical manner)
7 Anchor cable
8 Cat block hook
9 Anchor chock
10 Anchor stock

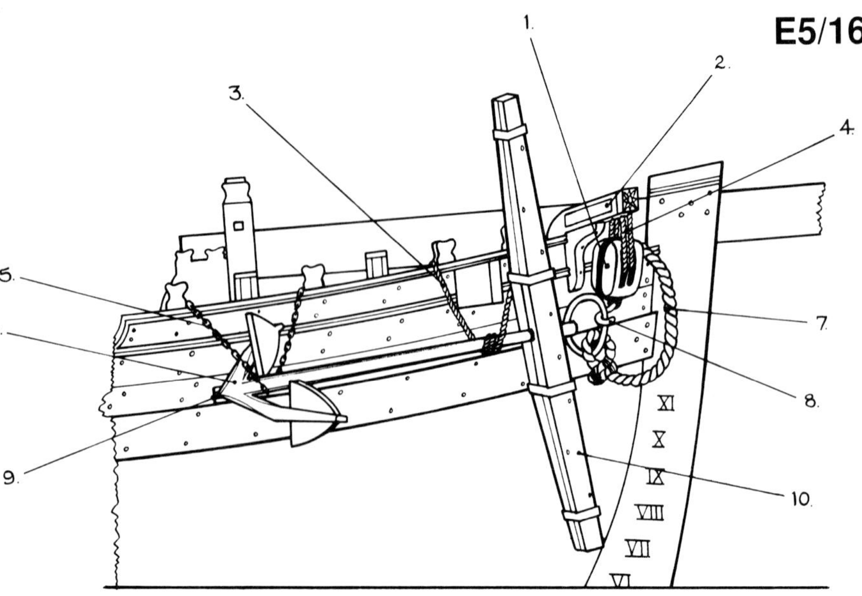

E6 IRON FIREHEARTH AND STOVE (1/48 scale)

E6/1 Cross sectional view

E6/2 Side elevation

E6/3 Front elevation

E6/4 Plan elevation – section through firehearth

E6/5 Plan elevation

1 Flue
2 Uptake canopy
3 Angle iron cross member
4 Gantry for cooking pots
5 Grate bars
6 Brick plinth
7 Grate
8 Oven door
9 Oven
10 Firehearth
11 Upper deck planking
12 Coaming
13 Support guides for spit carrier
14 Spit
15 Spit carrier
16 Catchment tray
17 Brick plinth
18 Lower deck (or fore platform) planking
19 Lower deck beam
20 Centreline stanchion
21 Centreline carling
22 Foot
23 Vertical strength members
24 Lifting eye and ring
25 Upper deck beam
26 Top surface of oven
27 Oven door in half open position

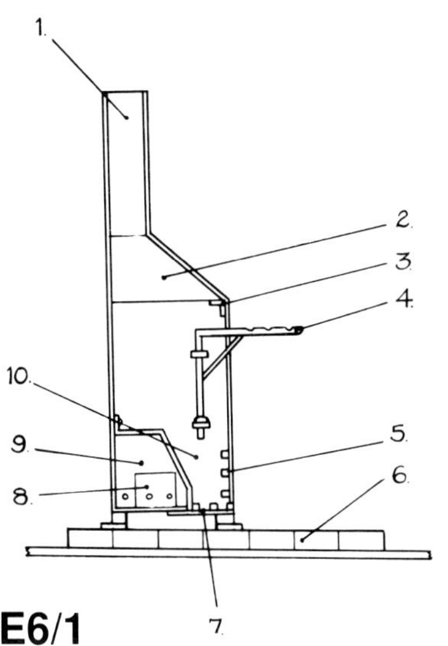

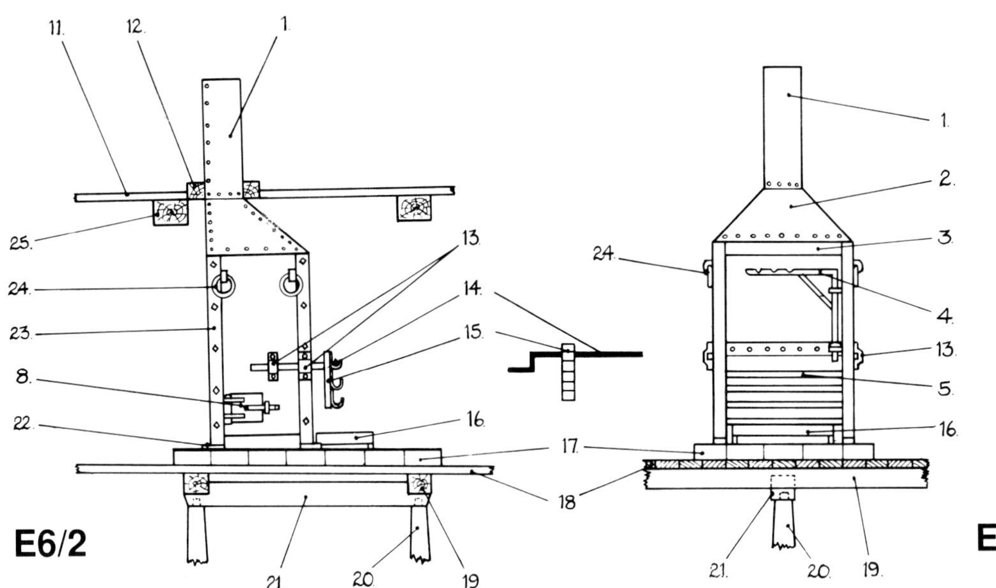

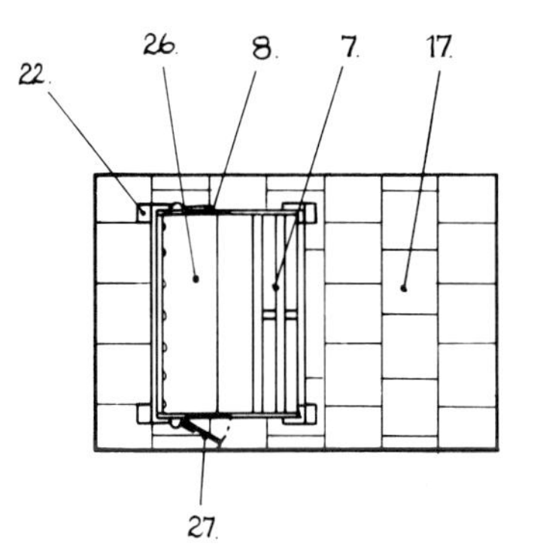

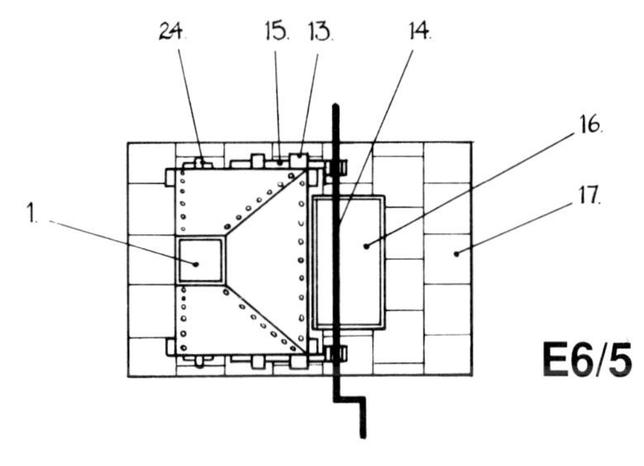

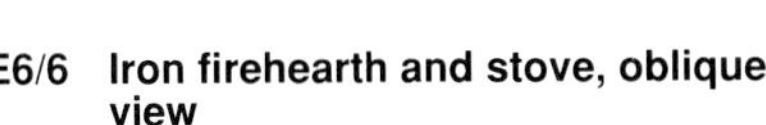

E6/6 Iron firehearth and stove, oblique view

1 Lap joint
2 Lifting eye and ring
3 Vertical strength member
4 Side face of hearth
5 Oven door (larboard side)
6 Support guide for spit carrier
7 Lower deck planking
8 Brick plinth
9 Catchment tray
10 Grate bars
11 Spit carrier
12 Spit
13 Firehearth
14 Gantry for cooking pots
15 Uptake canopy
16 Flue

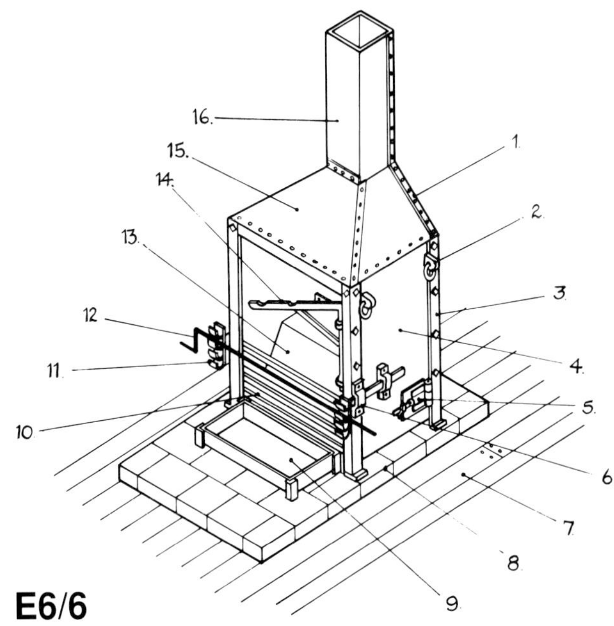

E7 HATCHES AND GRATINGS (1/48 scale)

E7/1 Fore hatchway, sectional elevation (grating omitted)

E7/2 Side elevation

E7/3 End elevation

E7/4 Plan elevation (grating omitted)

1 Head ledge
2 Coaming
3 Rabbet to support grating
4 Upper deck planking
5 Upper deck beam
6 Ledge
7 Carling
8 Grating

E7/5 Main hatchway, isometric projection (1/48 scale)

1 Grating
2 Holes for passage of anchor cable
3 Batten to support grating
4 Head ledge
5 Rabbet to support grating
6 Coaming
7 Bolts
8 Joint of head ledge and coaming
9 Carling
10 Upper deck planking
11 Upper deck beam

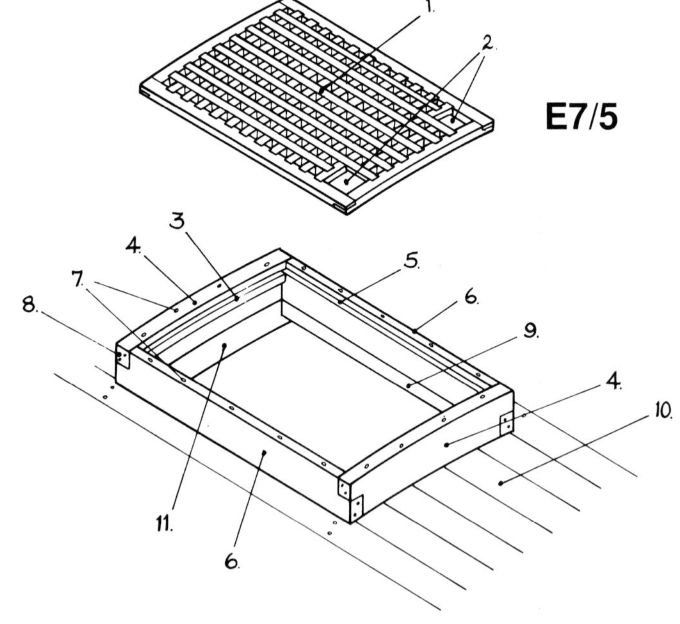

E7/6 Detail of main hatchway grating (1/48 scale)

1 Fore and aft battens (2in x 1in)
2 Athwartship edging frame (3in x 2½in)
3 Short cross batten (scored into fore and aft battens)
4 Edging frame halving joint
5 Hole for passage of anchor cable
6 Edging frames (3in x 2½in)
7 Recess in cross batten (2in x 1in)
8 Cross battens (2in x 2in)
9 Recess in edging frame (1in x 1in)

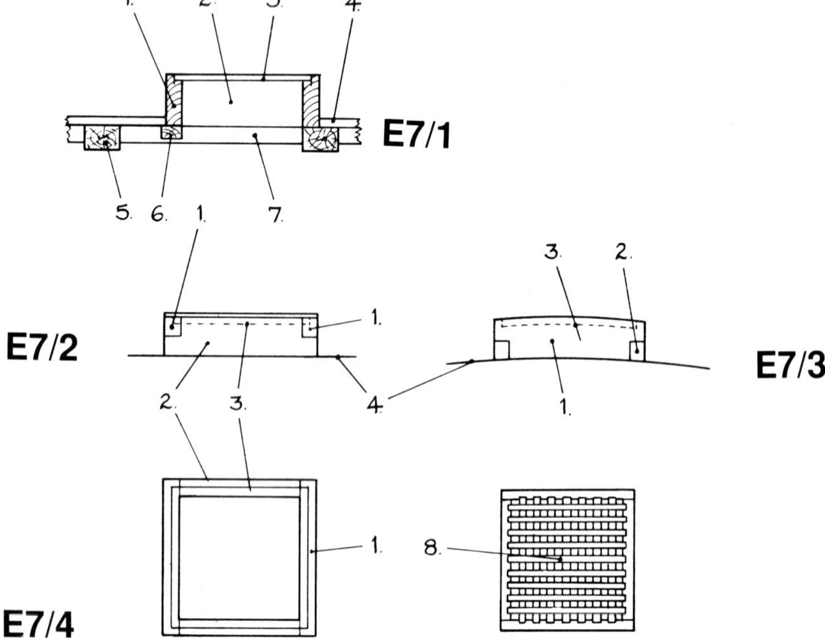

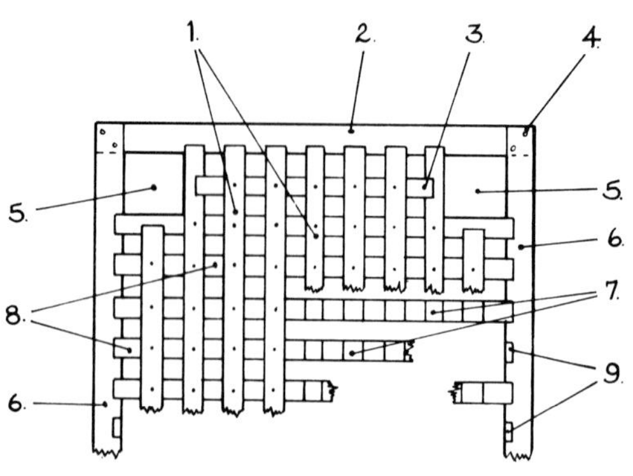

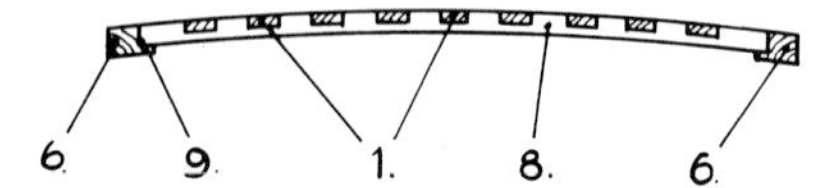

E7/6

E7/7 Companionway to after platform, sectional elevation

E7/8 Side elevation

E7/9 End elevation

E7/10 Plan elevation

1 Head ledge
2 Recess to receive fixed canopy
3 Fixed canopy
4 Strongback
5 Sliding canopy
6 Handle
7 Upper deck planking
8 Upper deck beam
9 Upper edge of coaming
10 Coaming
11 Carling
12 Lower edge of canopy recess
13 Fixed runner
14 Sliding runner

E7/11 Companionway to captain's quarters, sectional elevation

E7/12 Side elevation

E7/13 End elevation

E7/14 Plan elevation

1 Head ledge
2 Glass pane
3 Mullion
4 Recess to receive companion cover
5 Upper deck planking
6 Upper deck beam
7 Top edge of coaming
8 Carling
9 Coaming
10 Lower edge of cover recess
11 Ledge
12 Hinges
13 Cover frame

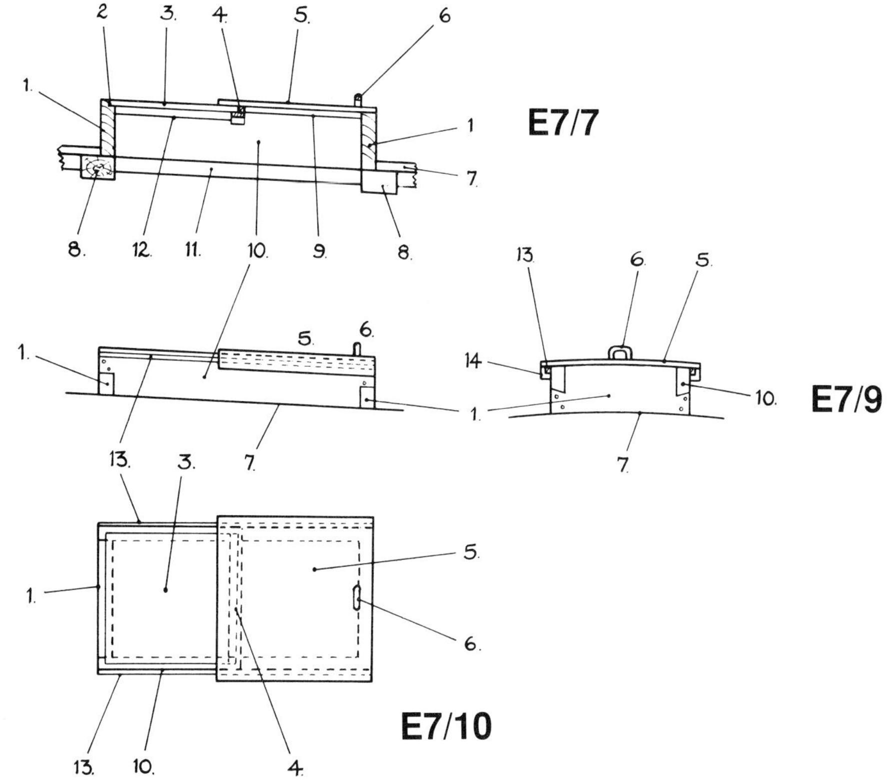

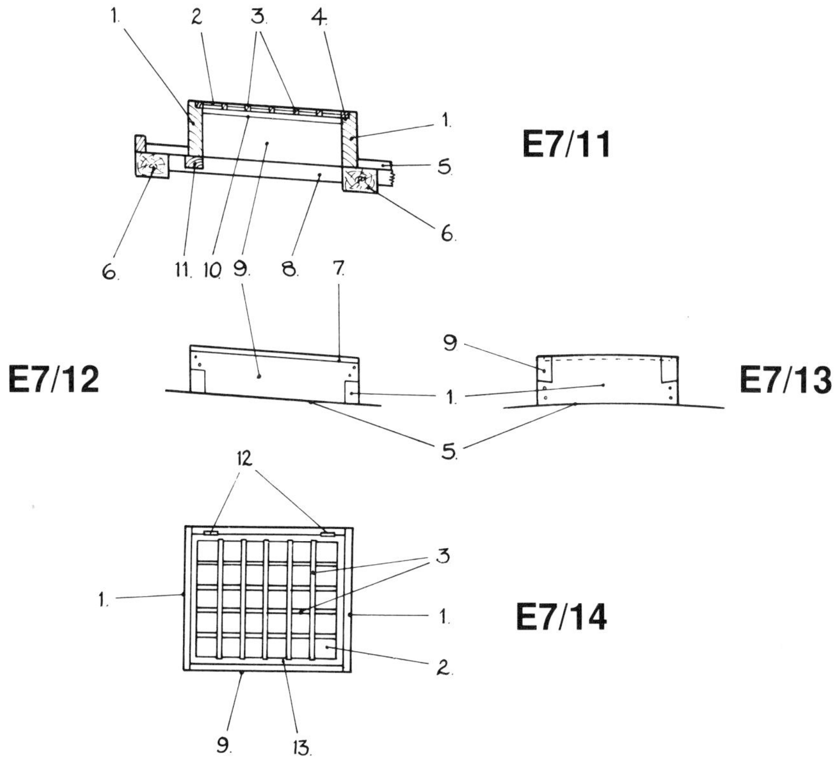

E7/15 Breadroom scuttle, sectional elevation (grating omitted)

E7/16 Plan elevation

1 Head ledge
2 Coaming
3 Batten to support grating
4 Upper deck planking
5 Carling
6 Upper deck beam
7 Grating

E8 DETAIL OF SHOT RACK (1/48 scale)

E8/1 Shot rack front elevation

E8/2 Side elevation

E8/3 Plan elevation

1 Ornate panel
2 Concave surface to contain shot
3 Shot rack
4 Bolt
5 Shot
6 Drift rail
7 Sheer rail
8 Spirketting
9 Frame
10 Ship's side planking

E7/15

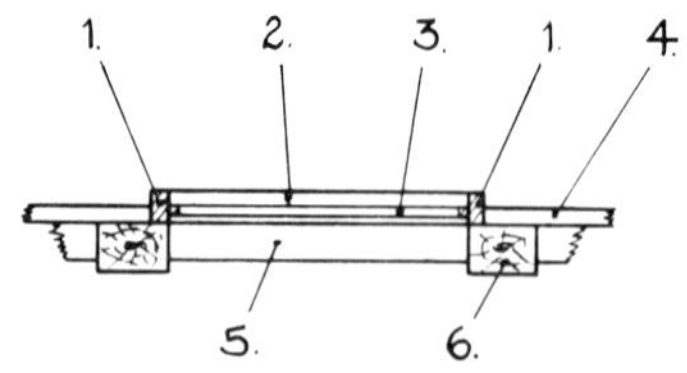

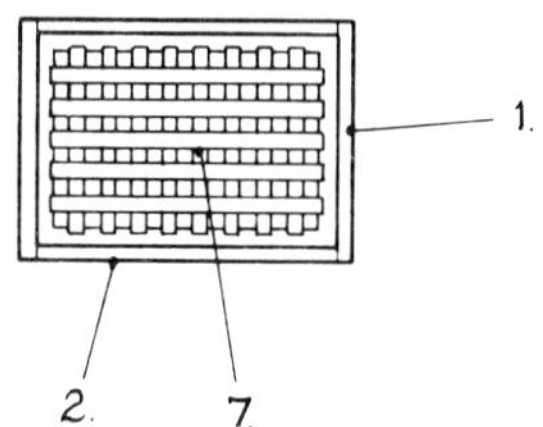

E7/16

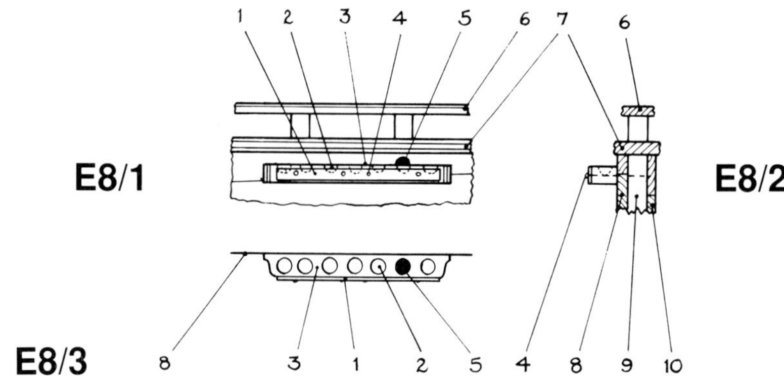

F1 4-POUNDER GUN (1/24 scale)

F1/1 4-pounder gun and carriage, side elevation

F1/2 4-pounder gun barrel, side elevation

F1/3 4-pounder gun barrel, plan elevation

1 Carriage steps, fulcrum points for handspikes when adjusting gun elevation
2 Carriage cheek
3 Cap square
4 Trunnion
5 Cap square retaining bolt
6 Cotter pin and chain for retaining cap square
7 Quoin
8 Eyebolt
9 Rear truck
10 Eyebolt for traversing tackle
11 Forelock bolt and pin
12 Axle pin
13 Front truck
14 Ogee
15 Pan
16 Vent
17 Second reinforce
18 Bore
19 Chase
20 Muzzle
21 4-pound solid shot round
22 Button
23 Vent field
24 Vent astragal
25 First reinforce ring
26 Trunnion
27 Second reinforce ring
28 Swell
29 Face
30 Muzzle ring
31 Button ring
32 Base ring
33 First reinforce
34 Royal monogram
35 Muzzle astragal
36 Muzzle moulding

F2 6-POUNDER GUN (1/24 scale)

F2/1 6-pounder gun carriage, side elevation

F2/2 6-pounder gun barrel, side elevation

F2/3 6-pounder gun barrel, plan elevation

1 Cascable
2 Breech
3 Carraige cheek
4 Trunnion
5 Cap square
6 Quoin
7 Eyebolt
8 Axle pin
9 Rear axletree
10 Rear truck
11 Eyebolt for gun tackle
12 Eyebolt and ring
13 Front axletree
14 Dowel holding truck halves together
15 Front truck
16 Cotter pin and chain to retain cap square
17 Vent hole and pan
18 Base ring
19 Vent field
20 Bore
21 Trunnion
22 Chase
23 Swell
24 6-pound solid round shot
25 First reinforce
26 Royal monogram
27 Second reinforce
28 Ogee rings
29 Muzzle
30 Face

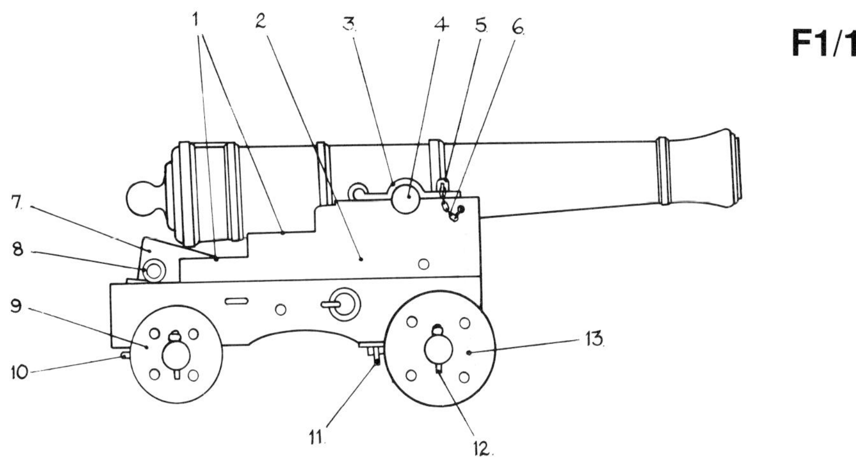

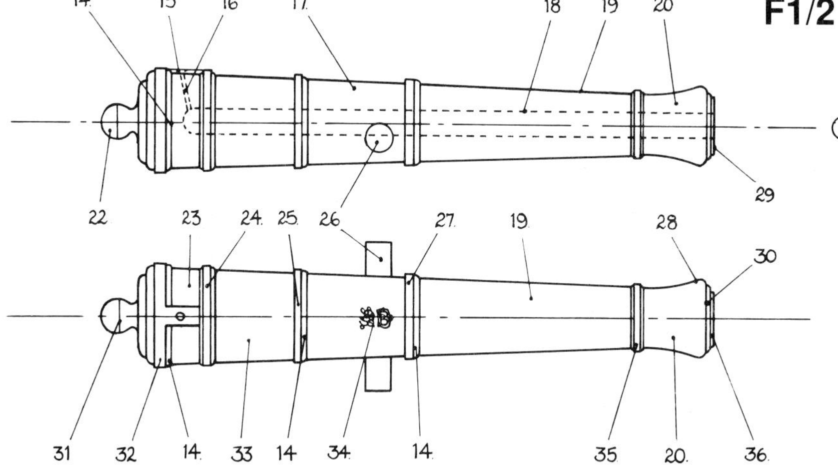

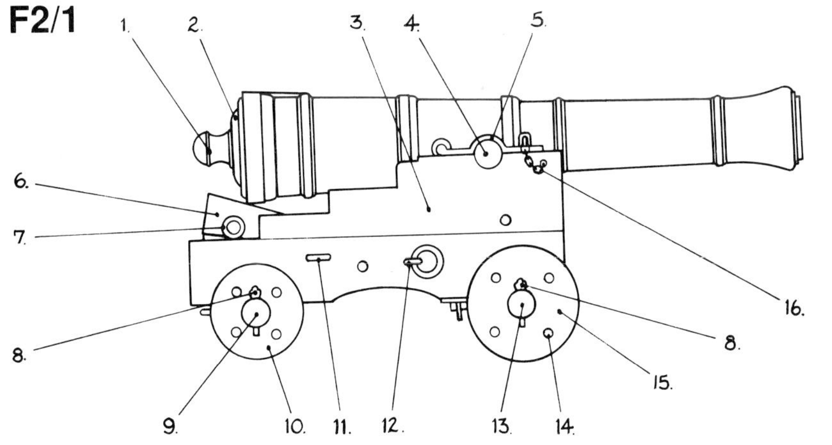

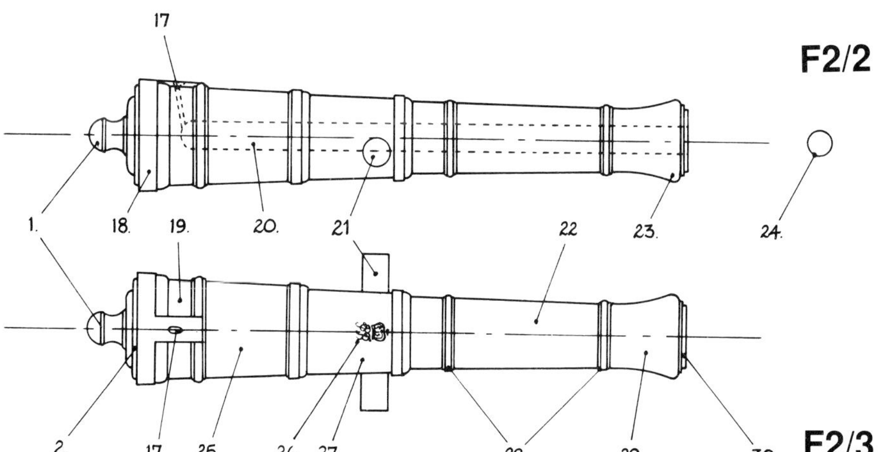

F3 GUN CARRIAGE ASSEMBLY, 4- AND 6-POUNDER GUNS (1/24 scale)

F3/1 Rear elevation of carriage

F3/2 Side elevation of carriage

F3/3 Plan elevation of carriage

1 Carriage cheek
2 Quoin
3 Transom
4 Cap square
5 Forelock bolt
6 Cap square hinge bolt
7 Cap square retaining bolt
8 Cotter pin and chain to retain cap square
9 Transverse transom bolt
10 Front eyebolt
11 Front axletree
12 Iron bracket
13 Bolt forelock pin
14 Eyebolt and ring
15 Transverse bolt
16 Eyebolt
17 Rear axletree
18 Rear eyebolt for traversing takle
19 Bed
20 Eyebolt
21 Bolster
22 Hole for axle pin
23 Rear truck
24 Front truck

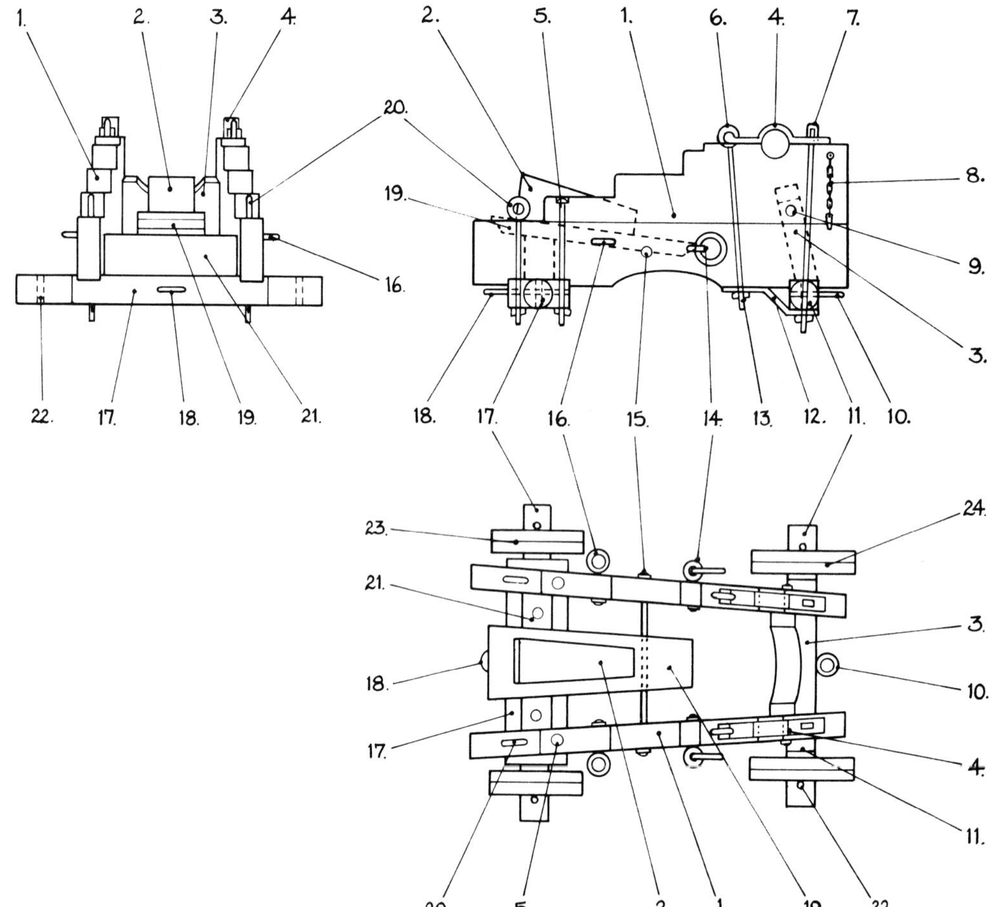

F3/4

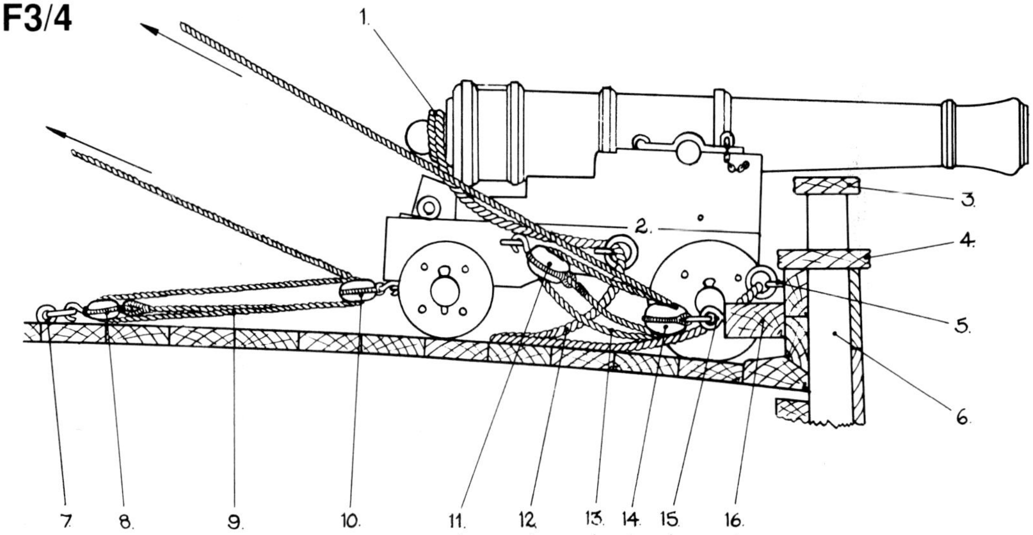

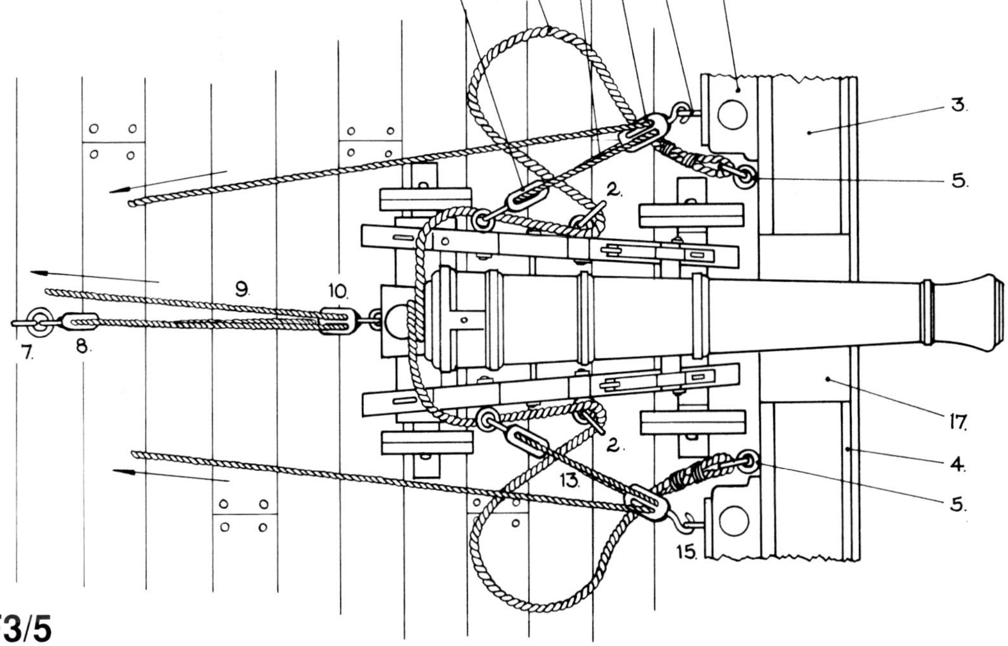

F3/5

F3/4 Gun tackle elevation

F3/5 Gun tackle plan

1 Breeching rope passed around cascable
2 Ring bolt and ring to lead breeching rope
3 Drift rail
4 Sheer rail
5 Ring bolt and ring for breeching rope
6 Ship's frame
7 Ring bolt and ring for traversing tackle
8 5in single block
9 Traversing tackle
10 5in double block
11 5in single block
12 Breeching rope
13 Gun tackle
14 6in double block
15 Eyebolt for gun tackle
16 Shot rack (or garland)
17 Gun port sill

F3/6 Detail of the royal monogram of George III (no scale)

F3/7 Cross section of 6-pounder gun (1/24 scale)

1 Breech
2 Vent
3 Bore
4 Cartridge
5 Round shot
6 Wadding (junk rope)

F3/6

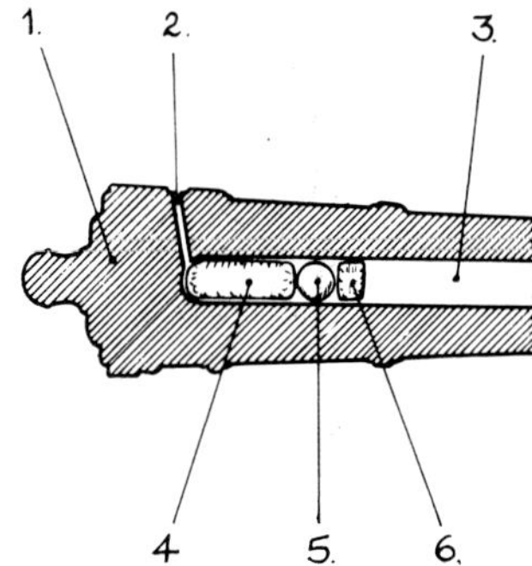

F3/7

F3/8 Shot and equipment for 4- and 6-pounder guns (1/24 scale)

1 Solid round shot
2 Chain shot
3 Bar shot
4 Expanding shot
5 Tampion and lanyard
6 Sponge
7 Ram rod
8 Worm
9 Flexible rammer and sponge

F4 HALF-POUNDER SWIVEL GUN (1/24 scale)

F4/1 Profile of gun and swivel mounting

F4/2 Swivel mounting, end elevation

F4/3 Swivel gun, plan (mounting omitted)

1 Cascable formed as a training handle
2 Flash pan and vent
3 Bore
4 Trunnion
5 End elevation of muzzle
6 Trunnion retention bushes
7 Swivel mounting pintle
8 Half pound solid shot

F4 HALF POUNDER SWIVEL GUN AND PEDESTAL (1/24 scale)

F4/4 Pedestal and railing, side elevation

F4/5 Swivel gun, pedestal and railing, end elevation

F4/6 Pedestal and rail, plan elevation

1 Socket to receive swivel pintle
2 Iron hoop
3 Cascable formed as a training handle
4 Swivel gun
5 Rough tree rail
6 Swivel mounting
7 Pedestal formed from head of toptimber
8 Drift rail
9 Drift planking
10 Lining
11 Sheer rail
12 Toptimber
13 Ship's side planking

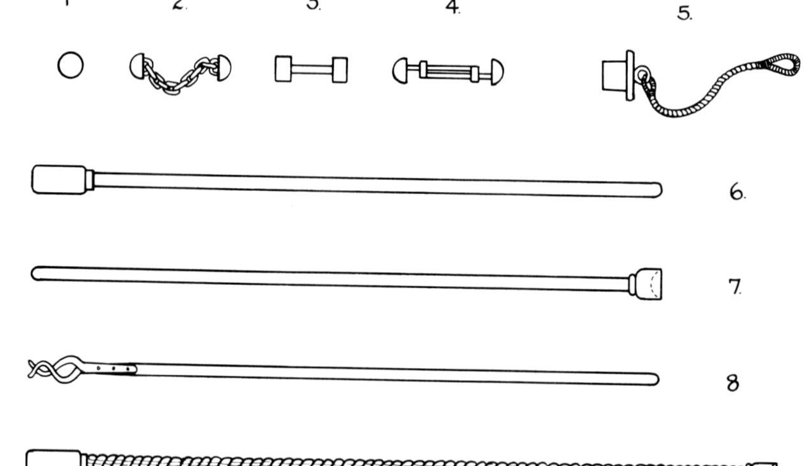

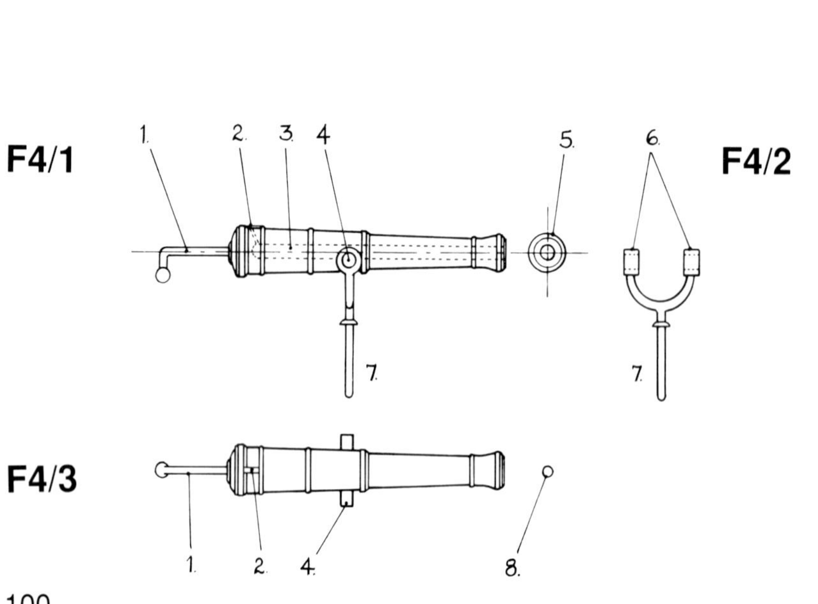

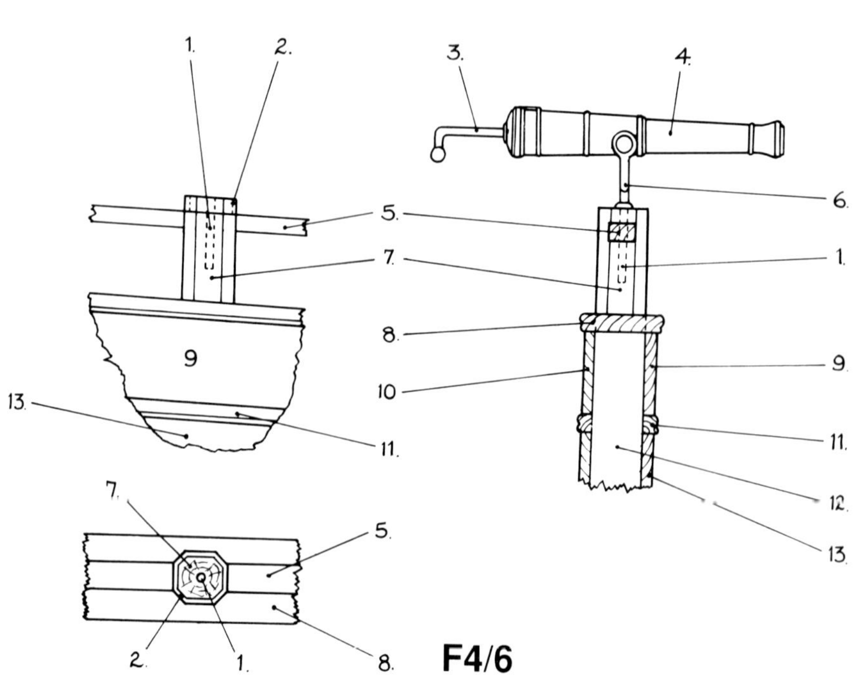

G Masts and yards

G1 MAINMAST, BOOM AND GAFFS (1/96 scale)

1 Mainmast, side elevation
2 Tenon for mast cap
3 Mast head
4 Cheek
5 Stool for boom with iron support brackets
6 Partners, denoted by 'x'
7 Heel tenon
8 Mainmast, aft elevation
9 Topgallant mast
10 Mast truck
11 Short pole head
12 Topgallant tie sheave
13 Heel
14 Top rope sheave
15 Hole to receive iron fid
16 Storm topgallant mast
17 Main boom, plan elevation
18 Main boom, inboard end, side elevation
19 Iron hoops
20 Jaws
21 Gaff
22 Eyebolt for gaff jeer tackle
23 Storm gaff
24 Driver boom
25 Storm gaff, inboard end, side elevation

G1

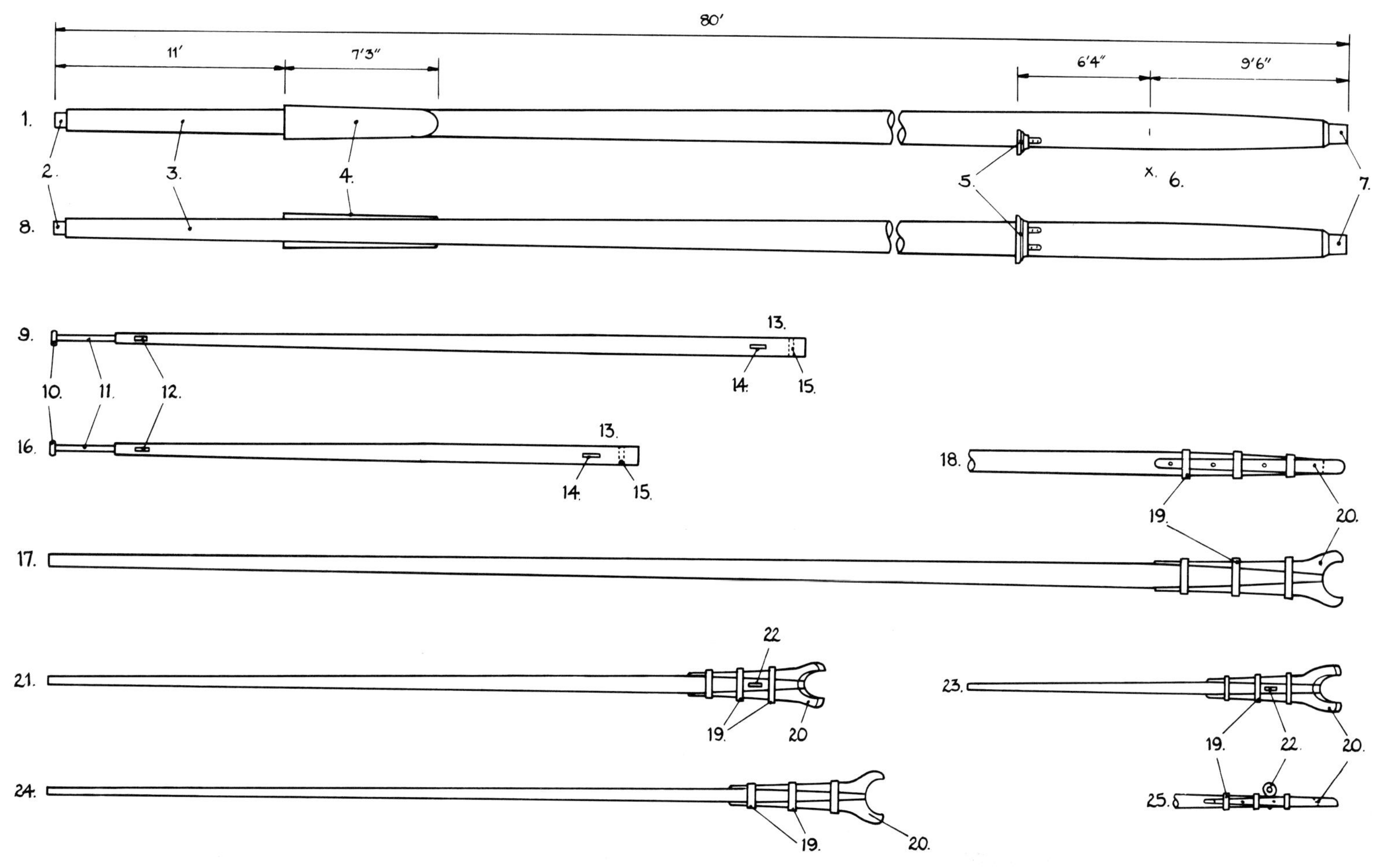

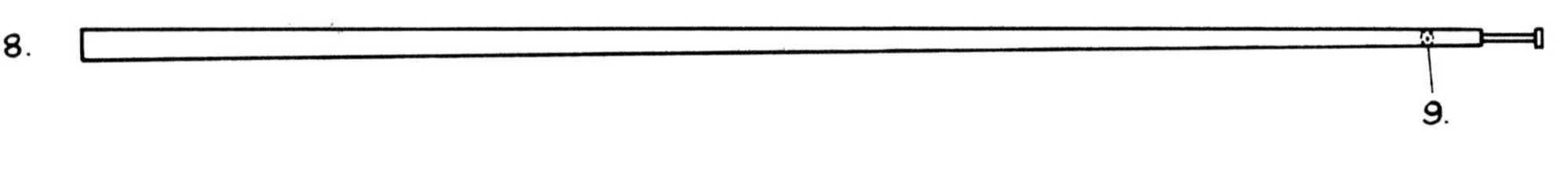

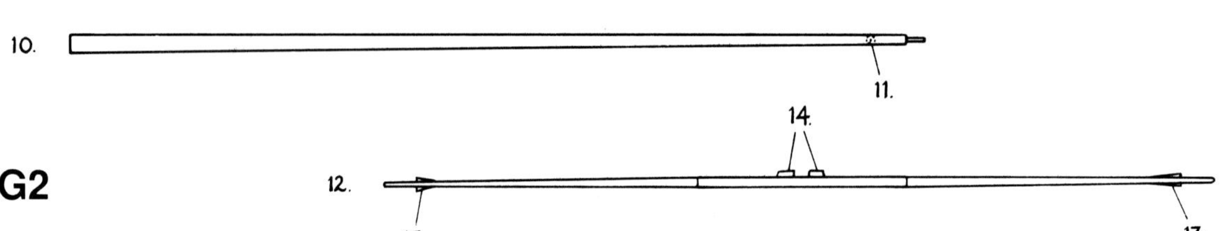

G2

G2 BOWSPRIT AND MIZZEN MAST (1/96 scale)

1 Bowsprit
2 Bowsprit heel (square in section)
3 Fid holes
4 Sheave for jib outhauler
5 Jibboom
6 Jibboom outhauler sheave
7 Sheave for flying jib outhauler
8 Mizzen mast
9 Sheave for mizzen yard halyard
10 Outrigger
11 Sheave for mizzen tug sail sheet
12 Mizzen yard
13 Yard arm cleats
14 Sling cleats

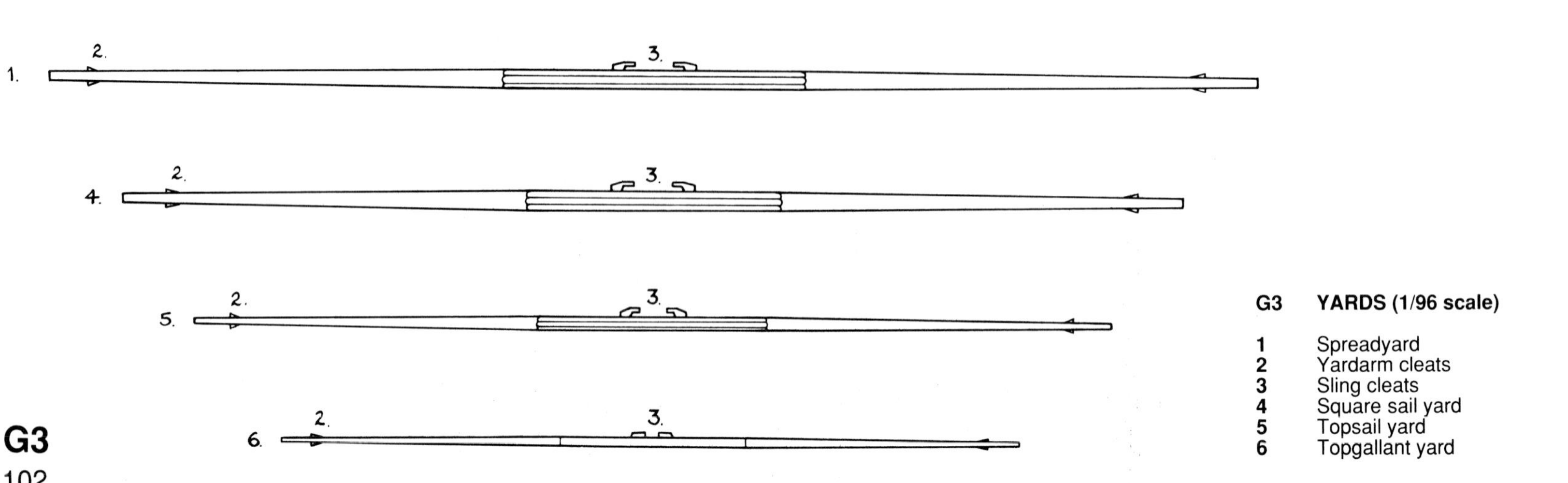

G3

G3 YARDS (1/96 scale)

1 Spreadyard
2 Yardarm cleats
3 Sling cleats
4 Square sail yard
5 Topsail yard
6 Topgallant yard

G4 MAINMAST HEAD, TRESSLETREES, CROSSTREES AND CAP (1/48 scale)

G4/1 Detail of cap, underside view

G4/2 Side elevation

G4/3 Front elevation

G4/4 Plan of tressletrees and crosstrees

1 Lower mast cap, underside view
2 Hole for topgallant mast
3 Mortice for lower mast head tenon
4 Eyebolt for topgallant mast top rope
5 Masthead tenon
6 Lower mast cap
7 Lower mast head
8 Topgallant mast
9 Sheave for top rope
10 Sheave pin
11 Topgallant mast heel
12 Fid
13 Cleat for topsail yard tie block pendant
14 Crosstrees
15 Tressletrees
16 Mast cheeks
17 Iron plate for fid

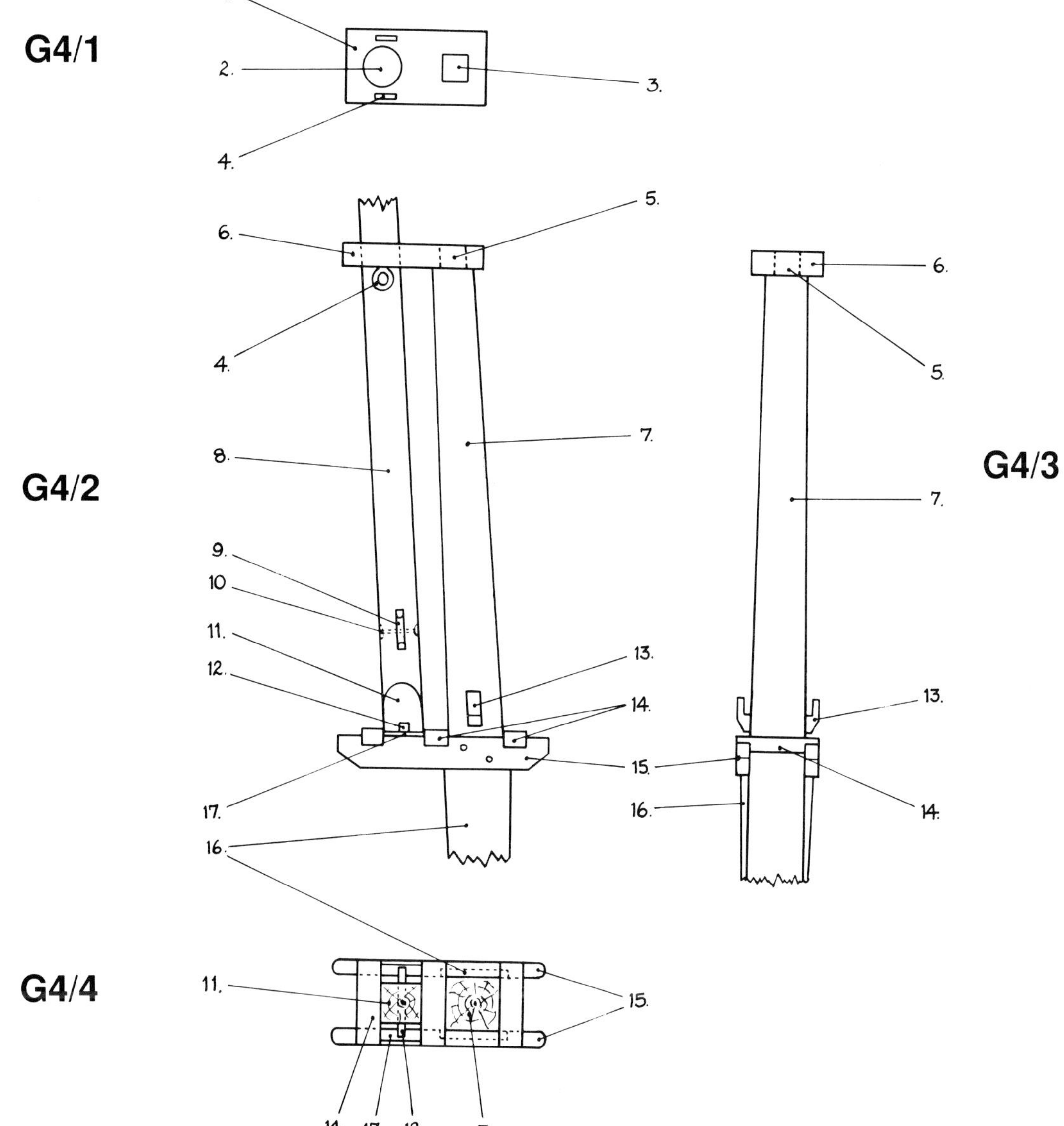

H Rigging

H1

H1/2

H1 STANDING RIGGING, MAIN LOWER MAST AND TOPGALLANT MAST (no scale)

1 Main topgallant mast
2 Main lower mast
3 Running backstay
4 Single block
5 Standing backstay
6 Standing end of running backstay
7 Fall
8 Long tackle block
9 Running backstay tackle fall
10 Running backstay tackle
11 Shroud batten
12 Deadeyes
13 Shrouds and ratlines
14 Forestay
15 Preventer stay
16 Topgallant forestay
17 Single block seized to cranse iron
18 Topgallant forestay fall
19 Bowsprit shroud
20 Forestay deadeye and lanyards
21 Shroud tackle

NB The ticked line denotes the topgallant mast breast backstay which was secured to an eyebolt fitted to the channel. This stay was not always fitted at this period.

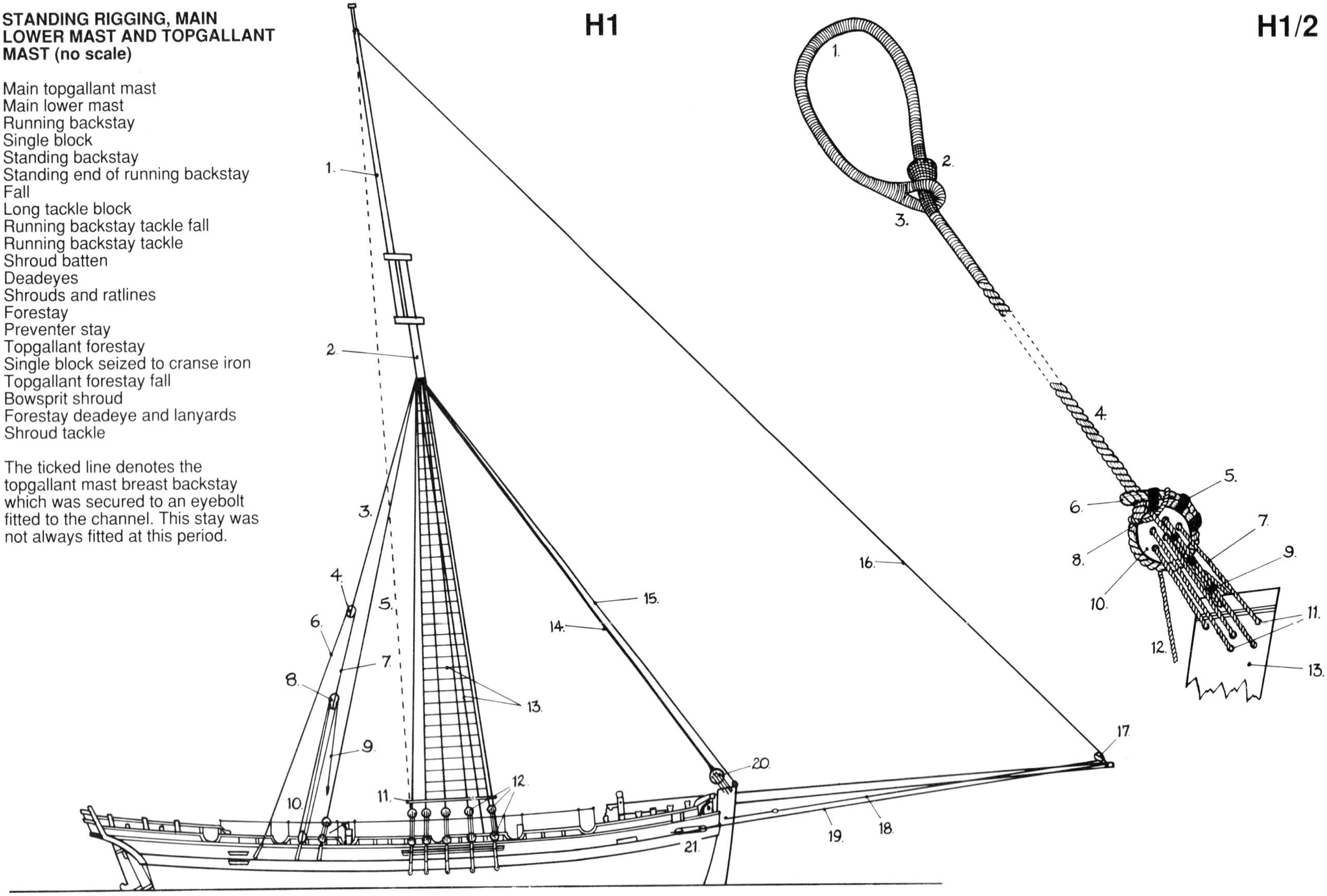

H1/2 The forestay and its associated deadeye (1/48 scale)

1 Eye, passed around mast
2 Mouse
3 Eye
4 Stay
5 Siezing
6 Stay end, passed around standing part of stay
7 Lanyard
8 Lanyard end, half hitched around stay
9 Lanyard end, siezed to standing lanyard
10 Deadeye
11 Lanyard holes
12 Standing part of lanyard, siezed to eyebolt on back of the apron
13 Stempost

H2/1

H2/2

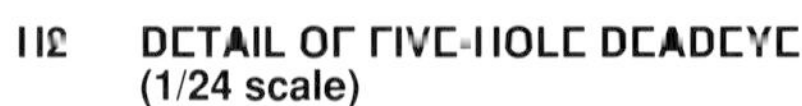
H2 DETAIL OF FIVE-HOLE DEADEYE (1/24 scale)

H2/1 Front elevation

H2/2 Side elevation

1 Lanyard hole
2 Groove for stay

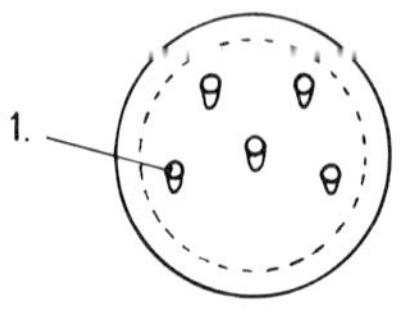

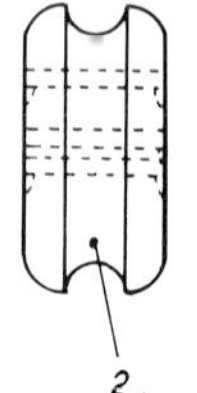

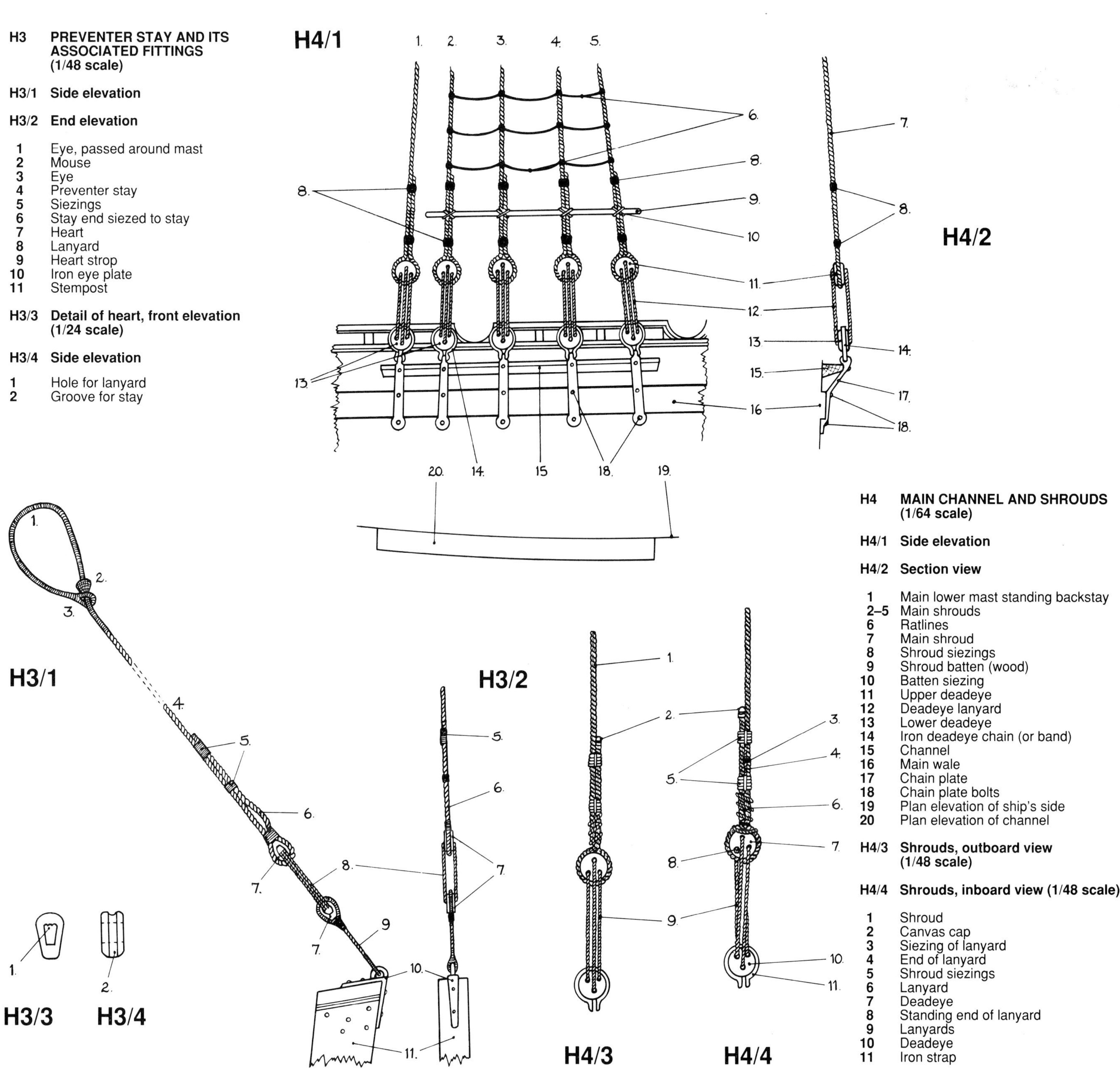

H3 PREVENTER STAY AND ITS ASSOCIATED FITTINGS (1/48 scale)

H3/1 Side elevation

H3/2 End elevation

1 Eye, passed around mast
2 Mouse
3 Eye
4 Preventer stay
5 Siezings
6 Stay end siezed to stay
7 Heart
8 Lanyard
9 Heart strop
10 Iron eye plate
11 Stempost

H3/3 Detail of heart, front elevation (1/24 scale)

H3/4 Side elevation

1 Hole for lanyard
2 Groove for stay

H4 MAIN CHANNEL AND SHROUDS (1/64 scale)

H4/1 Side elevation

H4/2 Section view

1 Main lower mast standing backstay
2–5 Main shrouds
6 Ratlines
7 Main shroud
8 Shroud siezings
9 Shroud batten (wood)
10 Batten siezing
11 Upper deadeye
12 Deadeye lanyard
13 Lower deadeye
14 Iron deadeye chain (or band)
15 Channel
16 Main wale
17 Chain plate
18 Chain plate bolts
19 Plan elevation of ship's side
20 Plan elevation of channel

H4/3 Shrouds, outboard view (1/48 scale)

H4/4 Shrouds, inboard view (1/48 scale)

1 Shroud
2 Canvas cap
3 Siezing of lanyard
4 End of lanyard
5 Shroud siezings
6 Lanyard
7 Deadeye
8 Standing end of lanyard
9 Lanyards
10 Deadeye
11 Iron strap

H4/5 Order of laying shrouds and backstays over the mast head (1/48 scale)

1 Eye over mast head
2 Larboard running backstay
3 Siezing around splice
4 Starboard running backstay
5 Serving of the eye
6 Larboard standing backstay
7 Starboard standing backstay
8 Siezing over both shrouds
9 Serving of individual shrouds
10 Larboard 5th shroud
11 Larboard 4th shroud
12 Starboard 5th shroud
13 Starboard 4th shroud
14 Larboard 3rd shroud
15 Larboard 2nd shroud
16 Starboard 3rd shroud
17 Starboard 2nd shroud
18 Larboard 1st shroud
19 Starboard 1st shroud

H4/5

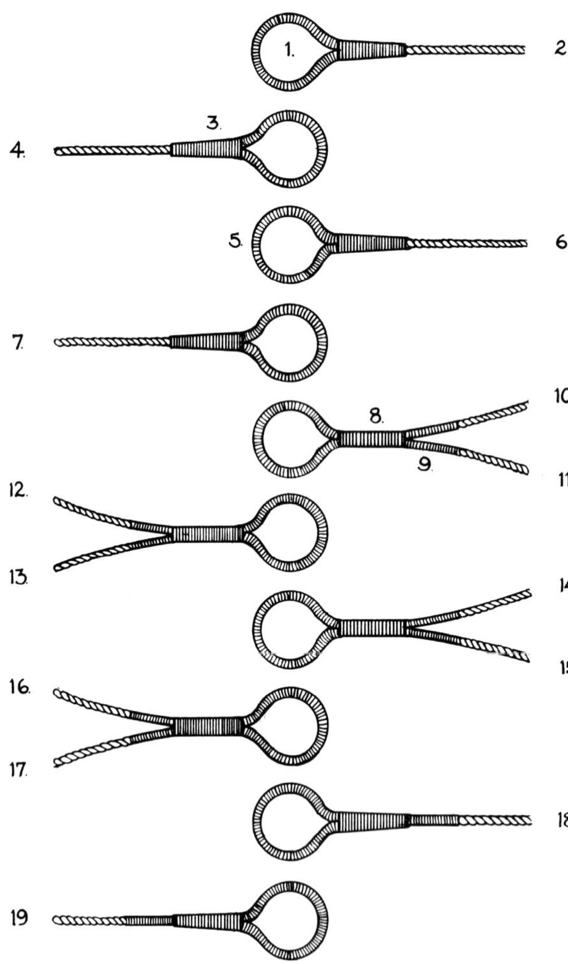

H5 MIZZEN MAST AND OUTRIGGER STANDING RIGGING (no scale)

1 Mizzen mast running backstay
2 Mizzen mast (stepped either to larboard or starboard as required)
3 Backstay tackle
4 Outrigger
5 Outrigger guy
6 Guy tackle

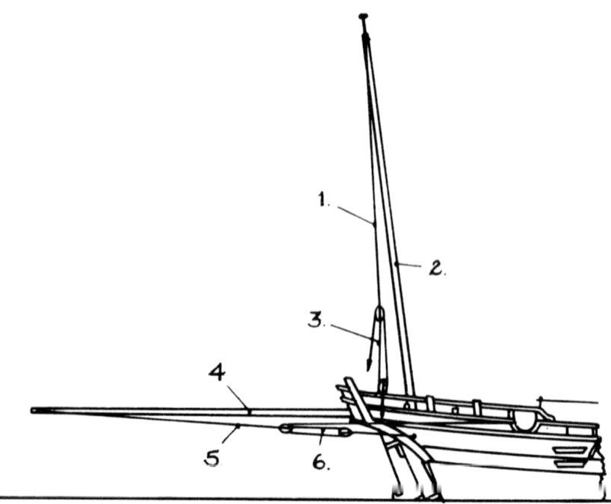

H5

H6 RUNNING RIGGING OF THE MAIN MAST (no scale)

1 Topgallant yard
2 Topgallant mast
3 Topgallant sail
4 Standing sheet block
5 Topgallant sheet
6 Topgallant sheet block
7 Topsail yard
8 Topsail
9 Standing part of topsail clewline
10 Topsail standing clew block
11 Running part of topsail clewline
12 Topsail brace pendant and block
13 Topgallant sheet fall
14 Squaresail yard
15 Topsail clewline fall
16 Topsail bridles
17 Topgallant forestay (set running)
18 Topsail sheet block
19 Spreadsail yard
20 Spreadsail yard brace pendant
21 Topsail sheet
22 Topsail standing sheet block
23 Square sail yard brace block
24 Square sail yard brace fall
25 Standing part of square sail brace
26 Topsail sheet fall
27 Square sail
28 Topsail bowline
29 Main forestay
30 Mainmast
31 Square sail bridle and bowline
32 Topsail brace inhauler
33 Topsail bowline inhauler
34 Topsail bowline standing block and pendant
35 Topsail brace standing block and pendant
36 Bowsprit
37 Square sail sheet block
38 Standing part of square sail sheet
39 Running part of square sail sheet

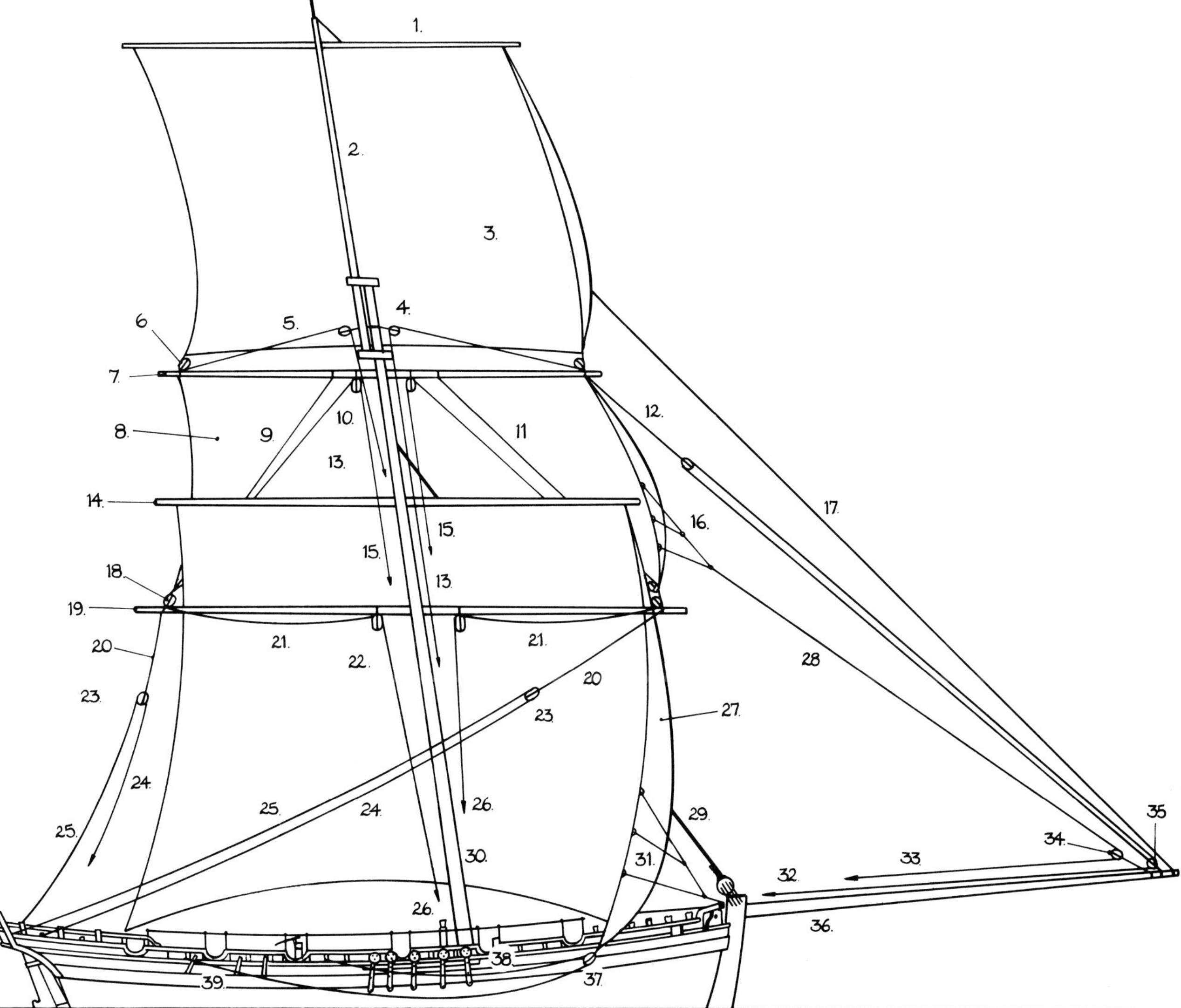

H6/1

H7 RIGGING OF SQUARE SAIL (fore side of sail to left, after side, right) (1/96 scale)

1 Square sail yard
2 Square sail yard tie block
3 Reef tackle fall block
4 Reef tackle
5 Reef tackle block
6 Reef cringle
7 Reef tackle pendant
8 Reef tackle fall
9 Bridle cringles
10 Bridles
11 Bowline
12 Running part of square sail sheet
13 Standing part of square sail sheet

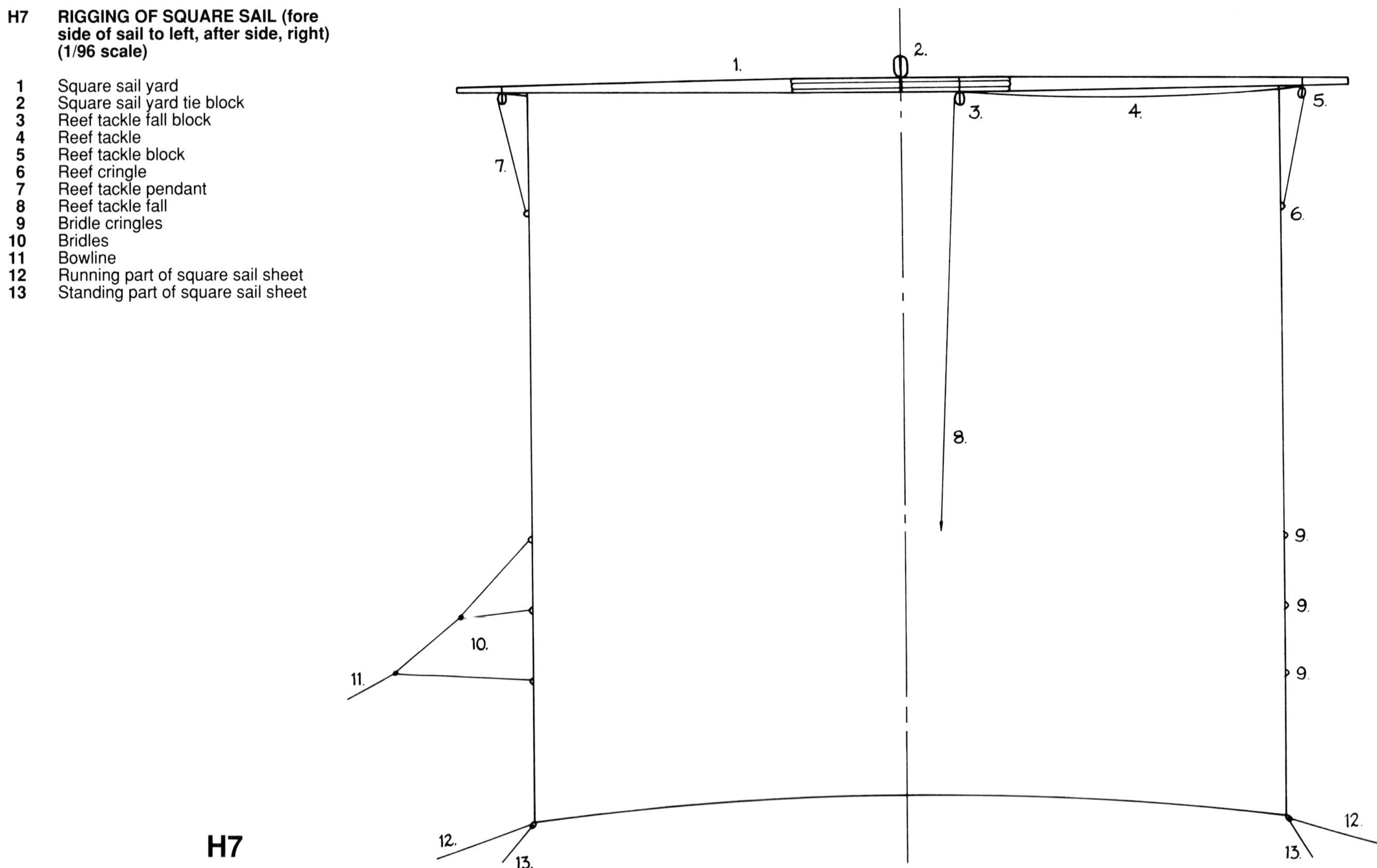

H7

H8 RIGGING OF TOPSAIL (fore side of sail on left, after side, right) (1/96 scale)

1 Topsail yard
2 Topsail yard tie block
3 Standing clewline block
4 Footrope and stirrup
5 Brace block and pendant
6 Running part of clewline
7 Standing part of clewline
8 Bridle
9 Bowline
10 Clewline fall
11 Sheet block
12 Spread yard
13 Spread yard tie block
14 Clewline block
15 Topsail sheet
16 Sheet fall block
17 Topsail sheet fall
18 Spread yard brace block and pendant

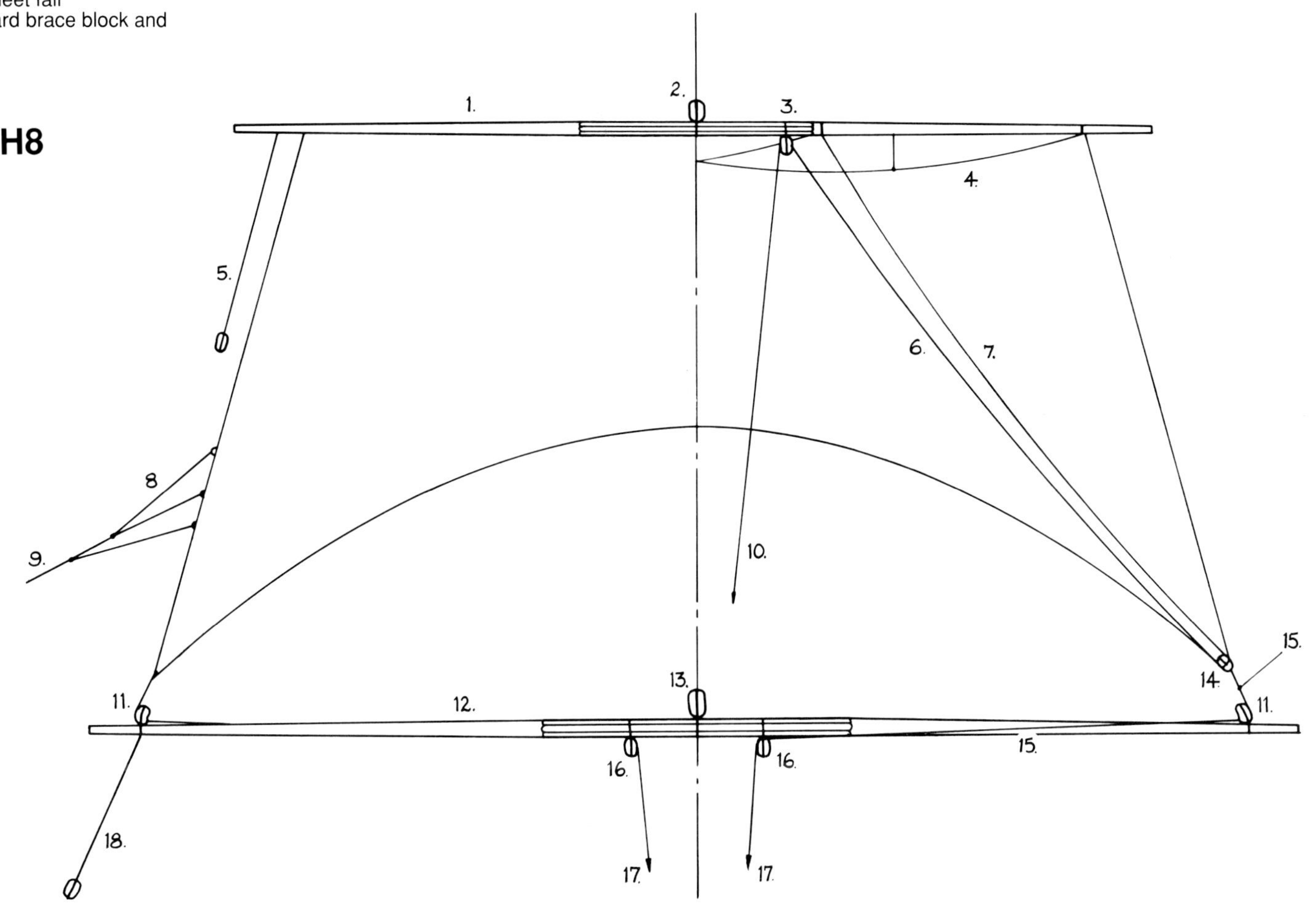

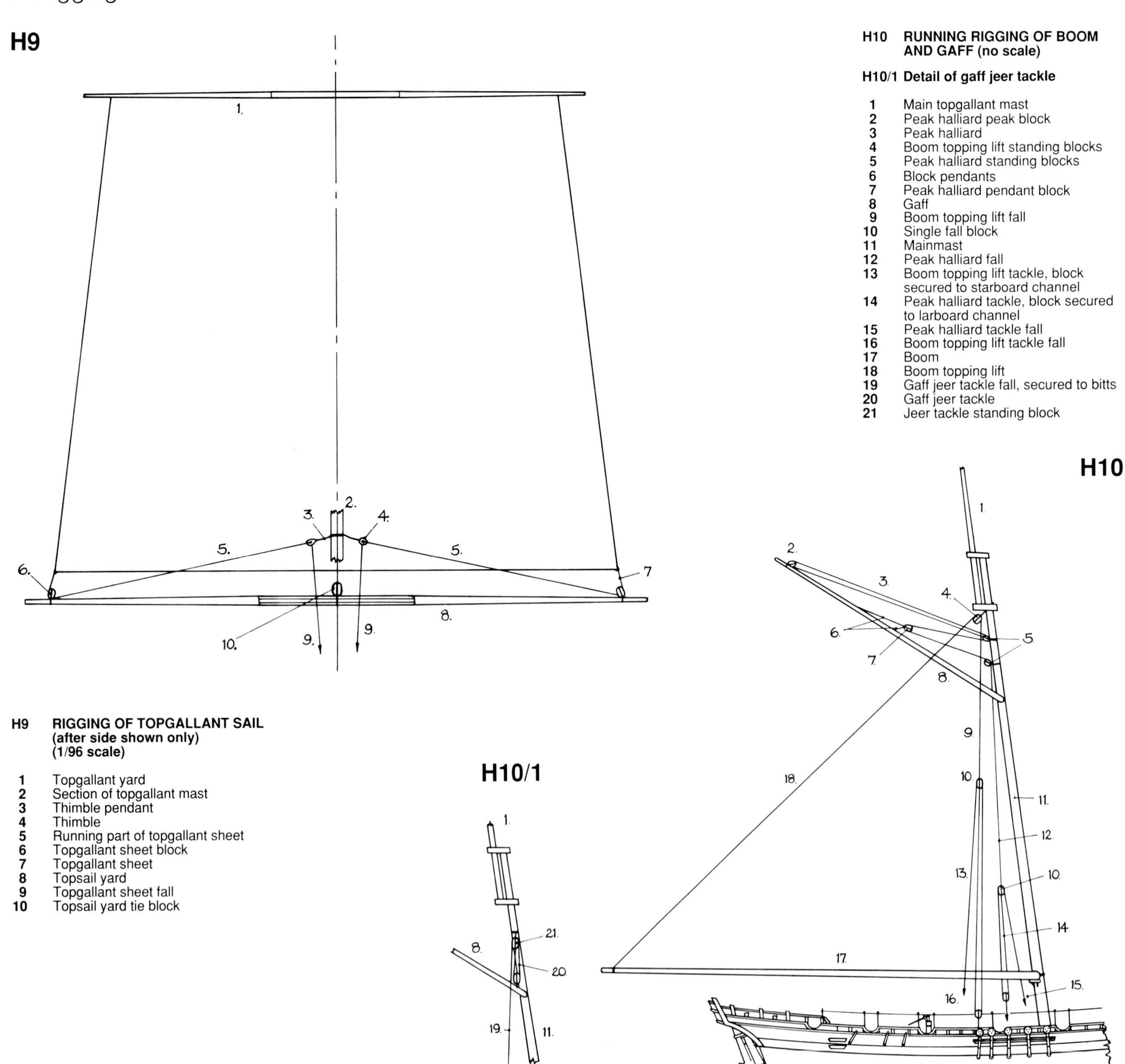

H9 RIGGING OF TOPGALLANT SAIL (after side shown only) (1/96 scale)

1 Topgallant yard
2 Section of topgallant mast
3 Thimble pendant
4 Thimble
5 Running part of topgallant sheet
6 Topgallant sheet block
7 Topgallant sheet
8 Topsail yard
9 Topgallant sheet fall
10 Topsail yard tie block

H10 RUNNING RIGGING OF BOOM AND GAFF (no scale)

H10/1 Detail of gaff jeer tackle

1 Main topgallant mast
2 Peak halliard peak block
3 Peak halliard
4 Boom topping lift standing blocks
5 Peak halliard standing blocks
6 Block pendants
7 Peak halliard pendant block
8 Gaff
9 Boom topping lift fall
10 Single fall block
11 Mainmast
12 Peak halliard fall
13 Boom topping lift tackle, block secured to starboard channel
14 Peak halliard tackle, block secured to larboard channel
15 Peak halliard tackle fall
16 Boom topping lift tackle fall
17 Boom
18 Boom topping lift
19 Gaff jeer tackle fall, secured to bitts
20 Gaff jeer tackle
21 Jeer tackle standing block

H11 RUNNING RIGGING OF STORM GAFF AND DRIVER BOOM (no scale)

1 Main topgallant mast
2 Driver boom topping lift block
3 Storm gaff peak hull and standing blocks
4 Storm gaff peak halliard
5 Storm gaff
6 Driver boom topping lift fall
7 Storm gaff peak halliard fall
8 Mainmast
9 Driver boom topping lift tackle
10 Storm gaff peak halliard tackle
11 Driver boom topping lift
12 Driver boom
13 Driver boom tackle fall (block secured to starboard channel)
14 Storm gaff tackle fall (block secured to larboard channel)

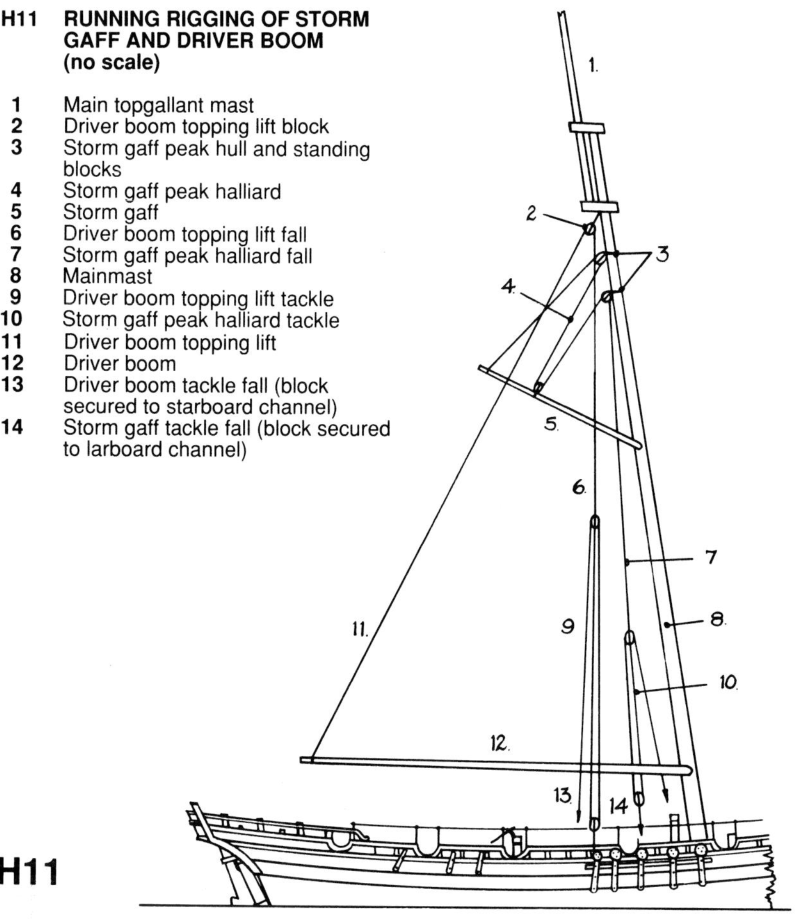

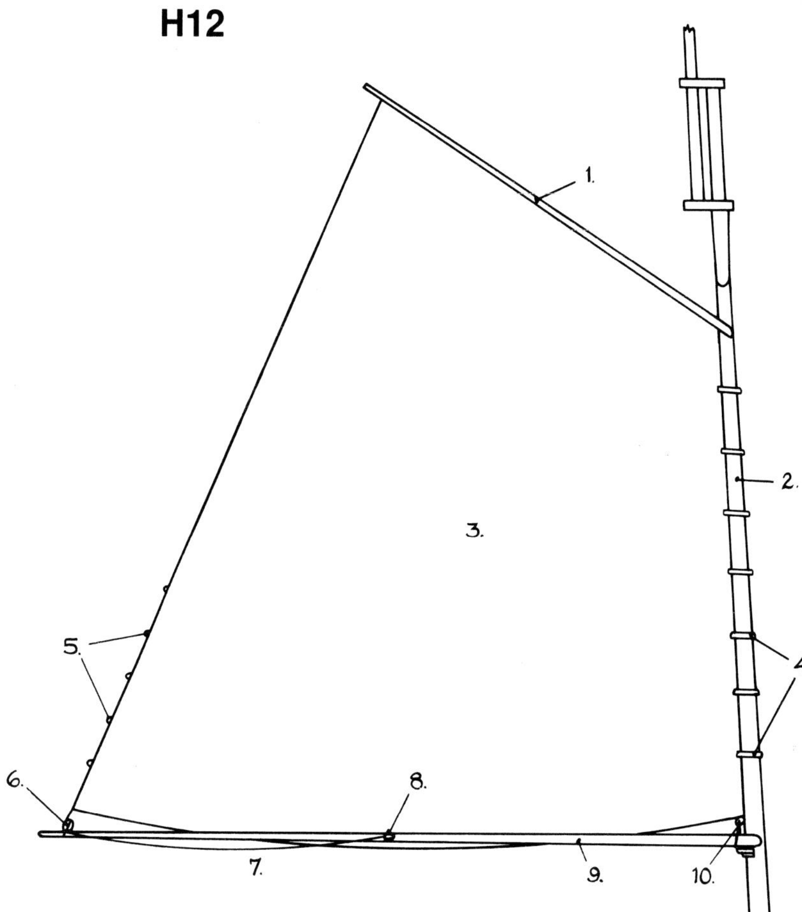

H12 RIGGING OF MAINSAIL (storm mainsail rigged in an identical manner) (no scale)

1 Gaff
2 Mainmast
3 Mainsail
4 Hoops
5 Reef cringles
6 Sheet block
7 Sheet
8 Cleat on boom for sheet
9 Boom
10 Tack

H13 BOOM SHEET TACKLE

H13/1 Boom sheet tackle – general arrangement (no scale)

1 Mainmast
2 Boom
3 Boom sheet tackle
4 Boom sheet tackle fall
NB This tackle also applies to that of the driver boom when rigged.

Continued on page 111

1.
2.
3.
4.
H13/1

H13/2 Detail of boom sheet tackle (no scale)

1 Cleat
2 Boom
3 Double block strop
4 Seizing
5 Double sheaved block
6 Standing part of sheet tackle
7 Sheet tackle fall, made fast to cleat fitted adjacent to eyebolt
8 Eye seized to strop
9 Single purchase block
10 Strop seizings
11 Block strop
12 Iron ring
13 Eyebolt, fitted onto upper surface of the rudder housing platform

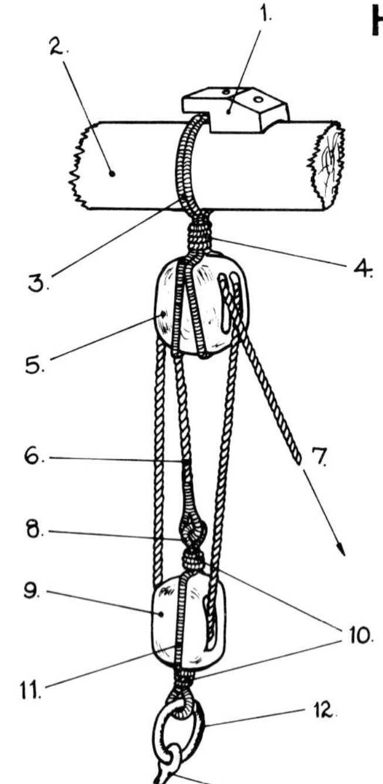

H14 RIGGING OF THE FORESAIL AND STORM FORESAIL (no scale)

1 Halliard standing block and pendant seized to forestay
2 Halliard tackle
3 Halliard block
4 Forestay
5 Downhauler
6 Foresail
7 Hanks
8 Tack secured to cleat at stem
9 Bowsprit
10 Downhauler fall
11 Sheet tackle – secured to horse
12 Mainmast
13 Halliard fall

H15 RIGGING OF THE JIB (no scale)

1 Halliard block pendant
2 Halliard block
3 Halliard
4 Peak cringle
5 Jib
6 Tack cringle
7 Tack, secured to traveller
8 Traveller
9 Outhauler, secured to traveller
10 Outhauler sheave
11 Outhauler
12 Bowsprit
13 Inhauler, secured to traveller
14 Outhauler lead block
15 Sheet blocks and pendants
16 Standing part of sheet (starboard)
17 Running part of sheet (starboard)
18 Halliard fall
19 Mainmast
20 Forestay

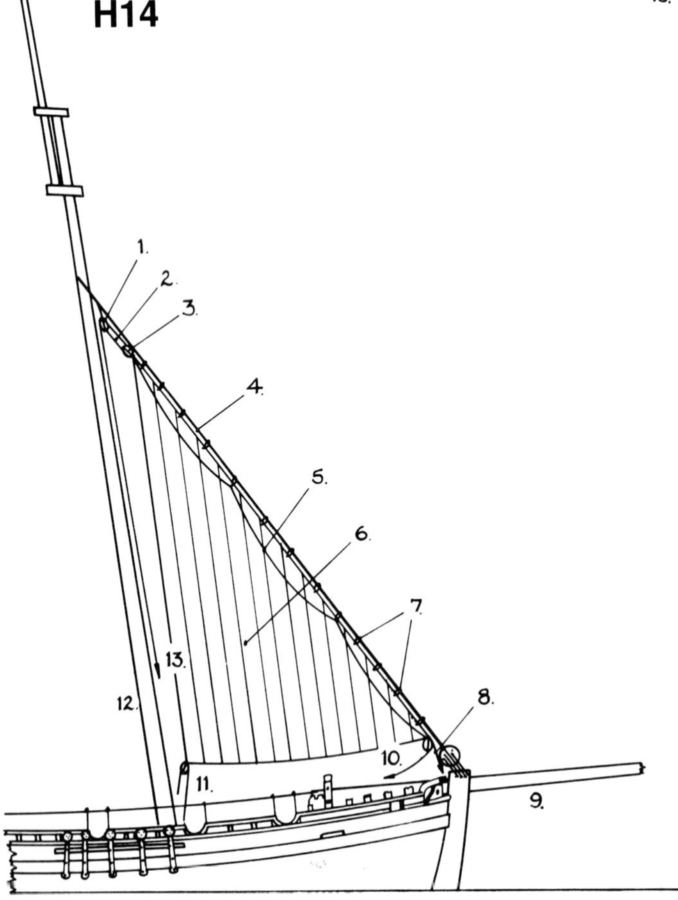

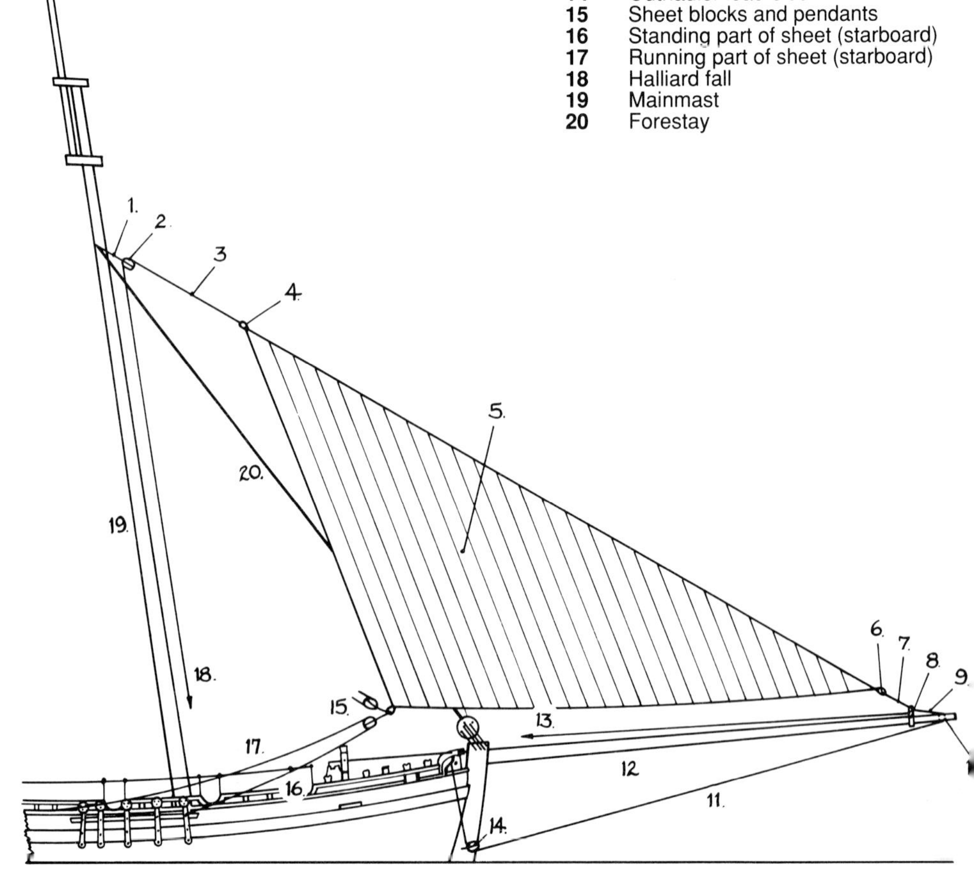

H16 RIGGING OF THE MIZZEN MAST, OUTRIGGERS AND YARD (no scale)

1 Mizzen yard
2 Halliard
3 Mizzen mast
4 Mizzen yard brace block and pendant
5 Mizzen yard brace
6 Halliard fall
7 Mizzen shroud
8 Mizzen tackle
9 Outrigger
10 Outrigger shroud
11 Shroud tackle
12 Shroud tackle block and pendant

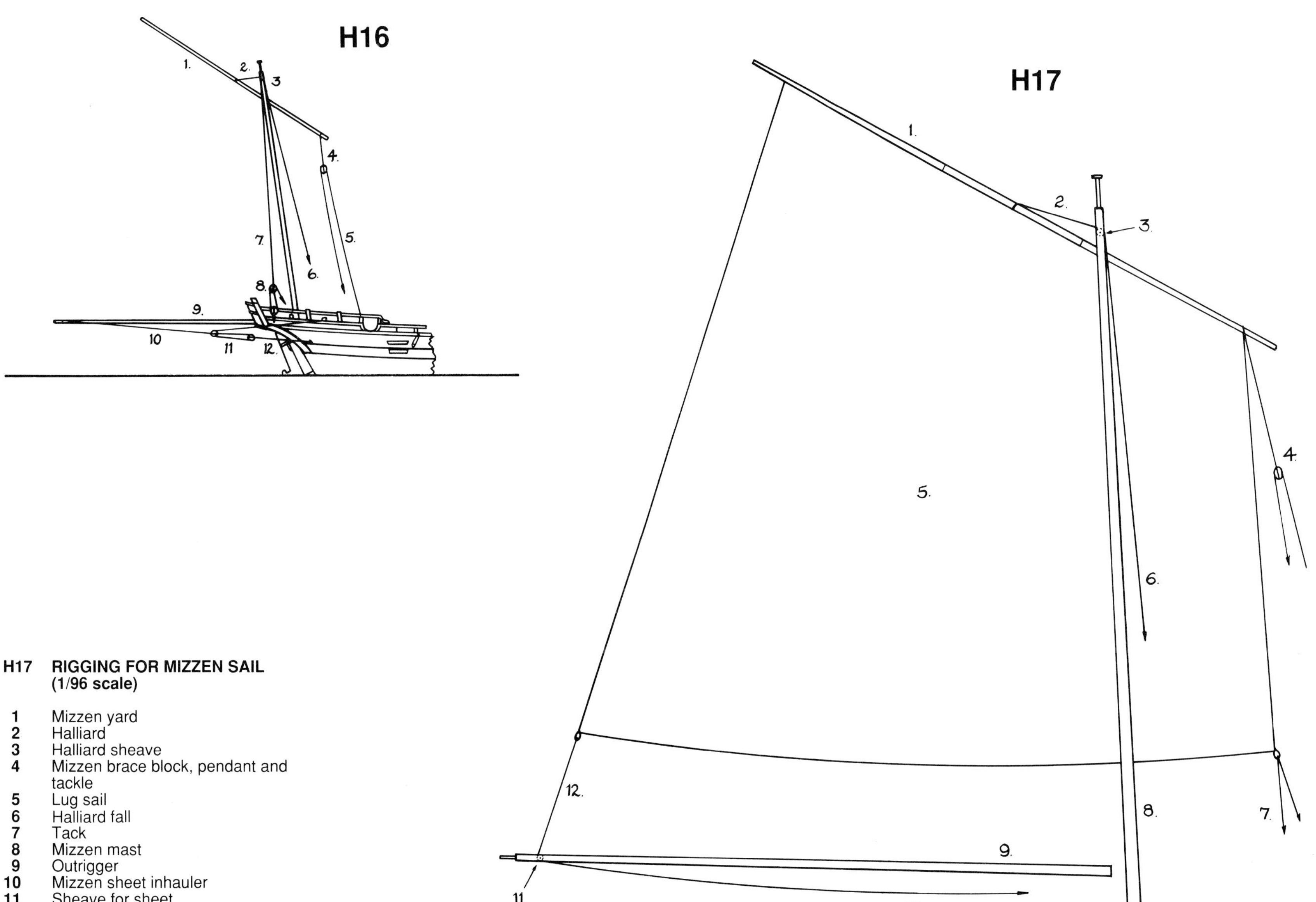

H17 RIGGING FOR MIZZEN SAIL (1/96 scale)

1 Mizzen yard
2 Halliard
3 Halliard sheave
4 Mizzen brace block, pendant and tackle
5 Lug sail
6 Halliard fall
7 Tack
8 Mizzen mast
9 Outrigger
10 Mizzen sheet inhauler
11 Sheave for sheet
12 Mizzen sheet

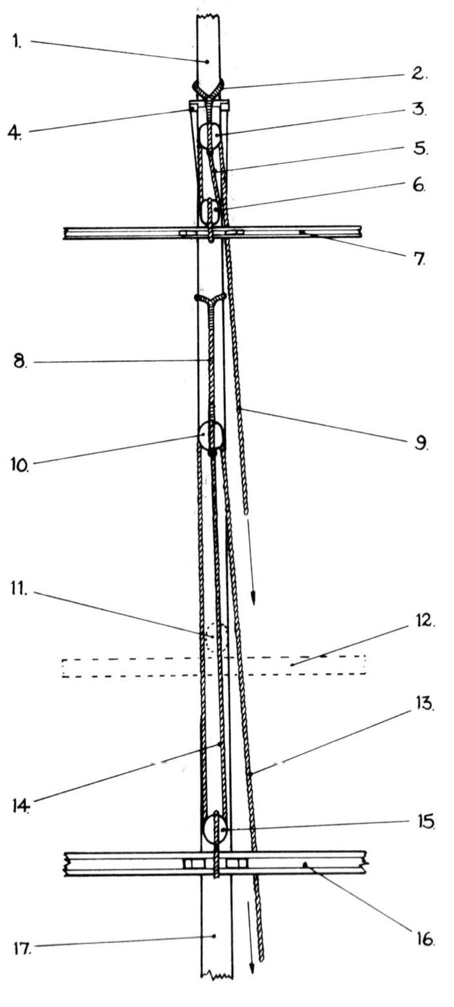

H18/1

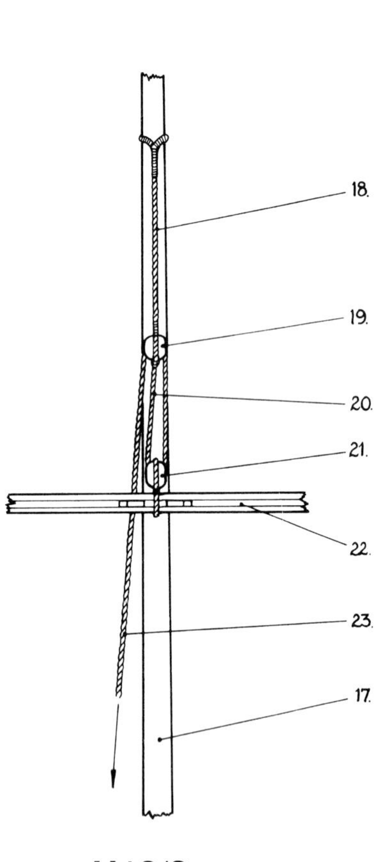

H18/2

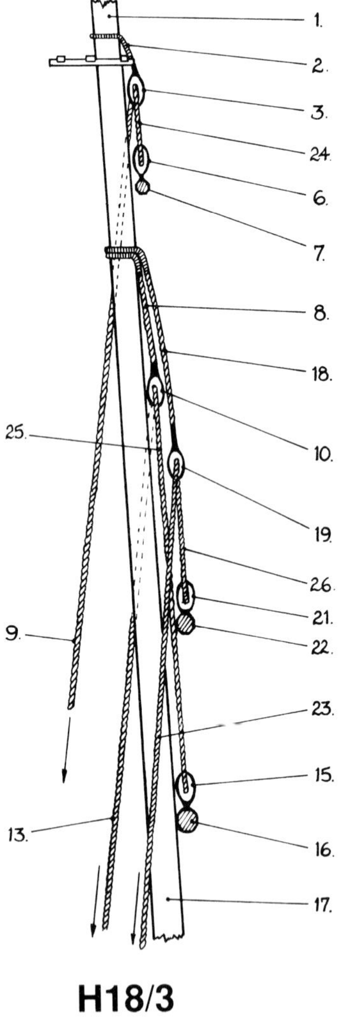

H18/3

H18 THE TIE TACKLE OF THE MAIN SPREADYARD, SQUARE SAIL YARD AND TOPSAIL YARD (1/96 scale)

H18/1 Tie tackle of topsail and main spreadyard

H18/2 Tie tackle of square sail yard

H18/3 Tie tackle of main spreadyard, square sail yard and topsail yard – side elevation

1 Main lower mast head
2 Topsail yard standing tie block, pendant and strop
3 Topsail yard standing tie block
4 Trestletrees
5 Standing part of tie tackle
6 Topsail yard tie block
7 Topsail yard
8 Spreadyard standing tie block, pendant and strop
9 Topsail yard tie tackle fall
10 Spreadyard standing tie block
11 Ticked line indicates position of square sail yard tie block
12 Ticked line indicates position of square sail yard
13 Spreadyard tie tackle fall
14 Standing part of spreadyard tie tackle
15 Spreadyard tie block
16 Spreadyard
17 Mainmast
18 Square sail yard standing tie block, pendant and strop
19 Square sail yard standing tie block
20 Standing part of squaresail yard tie tackle
21 Square sail yard tie block
22 Square sail yard
23 Square sail yard tie tackle fall
24 Running part of topsail yard tie tackle
25 Running part of spreadyard tie tackle
26 Running part of square sail yard tie tackle

H18/4 Detail of tie tackle and blocks used on the spreadyard, square sail yard and topsail yard (1/24 scale)

1 Pendant strop over mast head
2 Standing tie block pendant
3 Standing tie block
4 Eye for thimble spliced into end of block pendant
5 Thimble
6 Standing part of tie tackle
7 Running part of tie tackle
8 Running tie block
9 Strop seizing
10 Tie block strop
11 Yard, as dictated
12 Tie tackle fall
13 Ticked line denotes variation in tie tackle length as dictated by the respective yard to which it is rigged

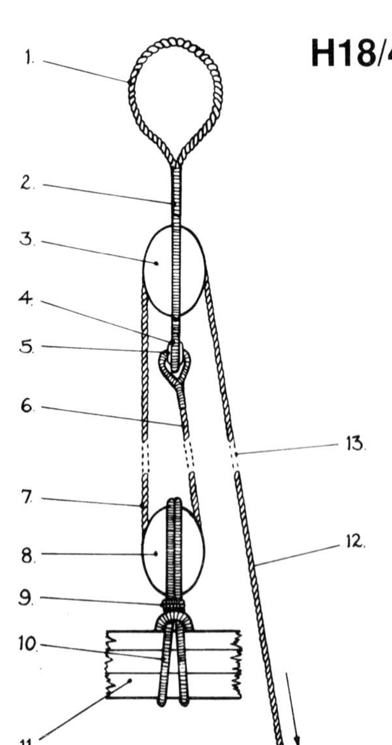

H18/4

H19 TOPGALLANT YARD TIE (1/96 scale)

H19/1 Fore elevation

H19/2 Side elevation

1 Polehead
2 Sheave pin
3 Tie
4 Topgallant yard
5 Topgallant mast
6 Rigging stop
7 Sheave
8 Strop formed at end of tie
9 Tie fall (halliard)

H19/3 Detail of strop (no scale)

1 Tie
2 Served eye
3 Seizing

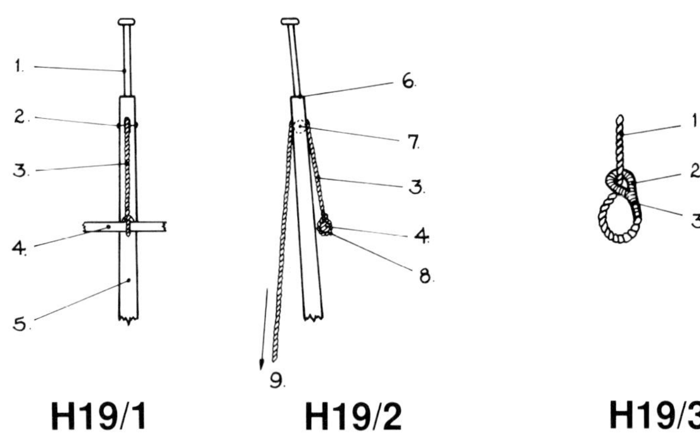

H19/1 **H19/2** **H19/3**

H20 RIGGING DETAILS OF THE BOWSPRIT, OUTBOARD END (1/24 scale)

H20/1 Side elevation of bowsprit and associated fittings

H20/2 Traveller, end elevation

H20/3 Cranse iron, end elevation

1 Topsail yard brace, starboard side shown only
2 Topgallant forestay
3 Jib
4 Bolt rope of jib
5 Tack clew
6 Topsail bowline, starboard side shown only
7 Jib tackle
8 Seizings
9 Tack hook
10 Topsail bowline inhauler (starboard)
11 Single sheaved topsail bowline block (starboard block shown only)
12 Treble sheaved block for topgallant forestay and topsail yard braces
13 Block strop
14 Topsail yard brace inhauler, starboard
15 Traveller eye
16 Traveller inhauler
17 Topgallant forestay inhauler
18 Eye for treble block strop
19 Strop and pendant for larboard topsail bowline block
20 Cranse iron
21 Eyes for bowsprit shrouds
22 Strop and pendant for starboard topsail bowline block
23 Sheave slot in bowsprit
24 Sheave for traveller outhauler
25 Starboard bowsprit shroud
26 Traveller inhauler running forward to sheave
27 Iron traveller
28 Traveller inhauler, running aft
29 Bowsprit

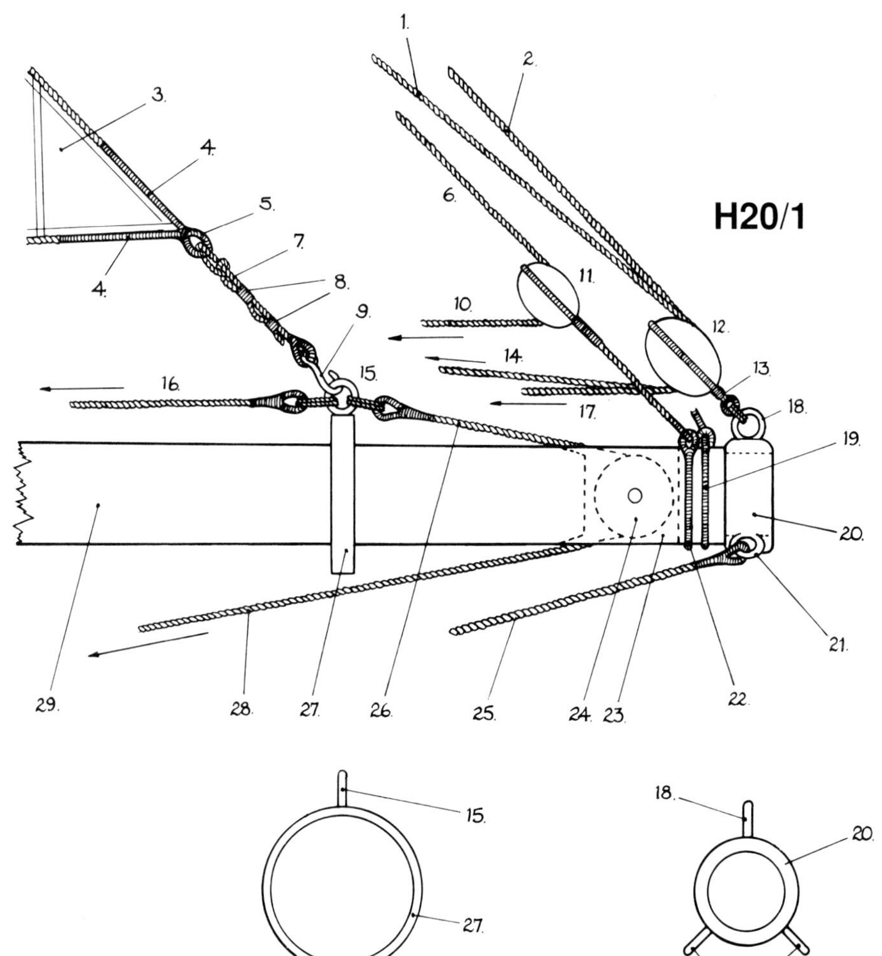

H20/1 **H20/2** **H20/3**

H20/4 Cranse iron and treble sheaved block, end elevation (1/24 scale)

1 Starboard topsail yard brace
2 Topgallant forestay
3 Larboard topsail yard brace
4 Block strop
5 Trebled sheaved block
6 Eye
7 Cranse iron
8 Bowsprit

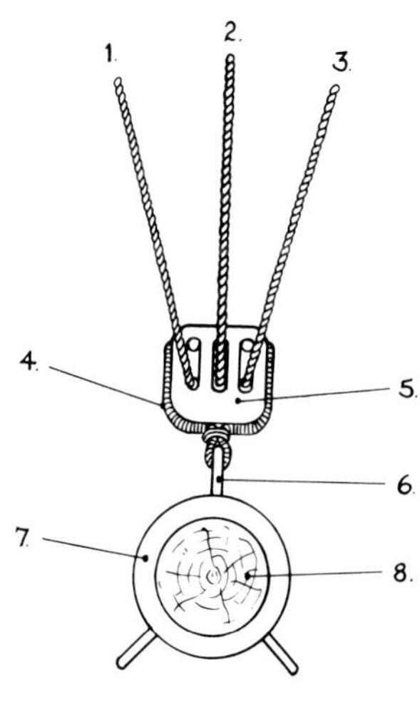

H20/4

H21 BOOM AND GAFF JAWS (no scale)

H21/1 Gaff jaws

1 Gaff
2 Gaff jeer tackle
3 Mainmast
4 Iron hoop
5 Jeer tackle block and hook
6 Eyebolt (for above)
7 Jaws
8 Monkey fist end of parrel rope passing through jaws
9 Parrel truck
10 Parrel rope

H21/2 Boom jaws

1 Boom
2 Iron hoops
3 Mainmast
4 Parrel truck
5 Parrel rope
6 Jaws
7 Mast saddle
8 Monkey fist end of parrel rope passing through jaws
9 Mast saddle support brackets

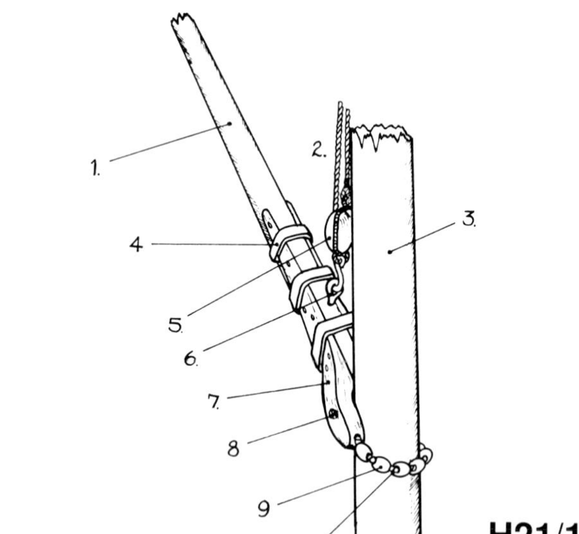

H21/1

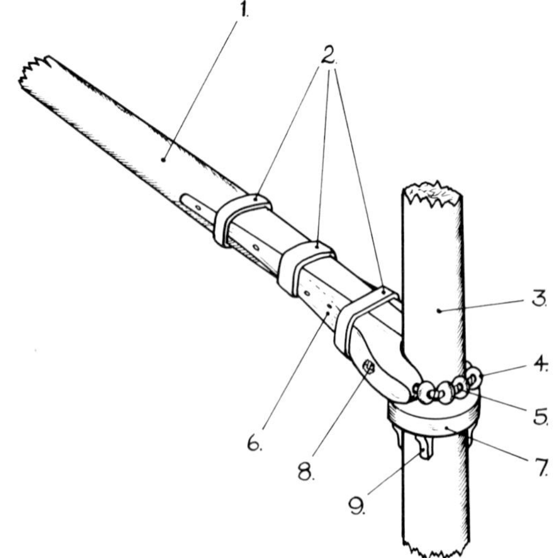

H21/2

H22 MAST HEAD DETAILS

H22/1 Details of the main lower mast head (no scale)

Note: shrouds, stays and other standing rigging, topping lift and gaff halliard rigging omitted for clarity.

1 Topgallant mast
2 Main lower mast head tenon
3 Main lower mast cap
4 Eyebolt for top rope block strop
5 Top rope block strop
6 Top rope block
7 Main lower mast head
8 Top rope
9 Strop for topgallant sheet thimble pendant
10 Cleat
11 Running part of top rope, passed through sheave and secured to eyebolt on mast cap opposite side
12 Topgallant sheet thimble pendant
13 Crosstree
14 Top rope sheave
15 Topsail yard standing tie block strop
16 Tressletree
17 Topgallant mast heel
18 Thimble
19 Topgallant sheet
20 Iron fid
21 Topsail yard standing tie block
22 Standing part of topsail yard tie tackle
23 Running part of topsail yard tie tackle
24 Topsail yard tie block
25 Topsail clew block strop
26 Strop of standing part of topsail clewline
27 Topsail yard
28 Sling cleats
29 Topsail yard tie block strop
30 Clewline block
31 Standing part of clewline
32 Running part of clewline
33 Main lower mast
34 Clewline fall
35 Topgallant sheet fall
36 Top rope fall
37 Topsail yard tie tackle fall

H22/2 Details of the mainmast head (1/48 scale)

1 Topgallant mast
2 Mainmast head
3 Cleat
4 Topgallant mast fid
5 Crosstree
6 Tressletree
7 Topsail yard tie block pendant
8 Gaff halliard
9 Boom topping lift standing block
10 Topsail yard standing tie block
11 Gaff halliard standing block (upper)
12 Boom topping lift
13 Boom topping lift fall
14 Strops for gaff halliard blocks
15 Gaff halliard standing block (lower)
16 Gaff halliard fall
17 Strop and pendant for jib halliard block
18 Jib halliard block
19 Strop and pendant for standing gaff jeer tackle block
20 Rigging stop (iron hoop)
21 Jib halliard
22 Standing gaff jeer tackle block
23 Ratlines
24 Square sail yard standing tie block, pendant and strop
25 Spreadyard standing tie block, pendant and strop
26 Foresail halliard block, pendant and strop
27 Preventer stay
28 Forestay
29 Foresail halliard
30 Foresail halliard fall
31 Spread-yard standing tie block
32 Running backstay
33 Standing backstay
34 Shrouds
35 Mainmast

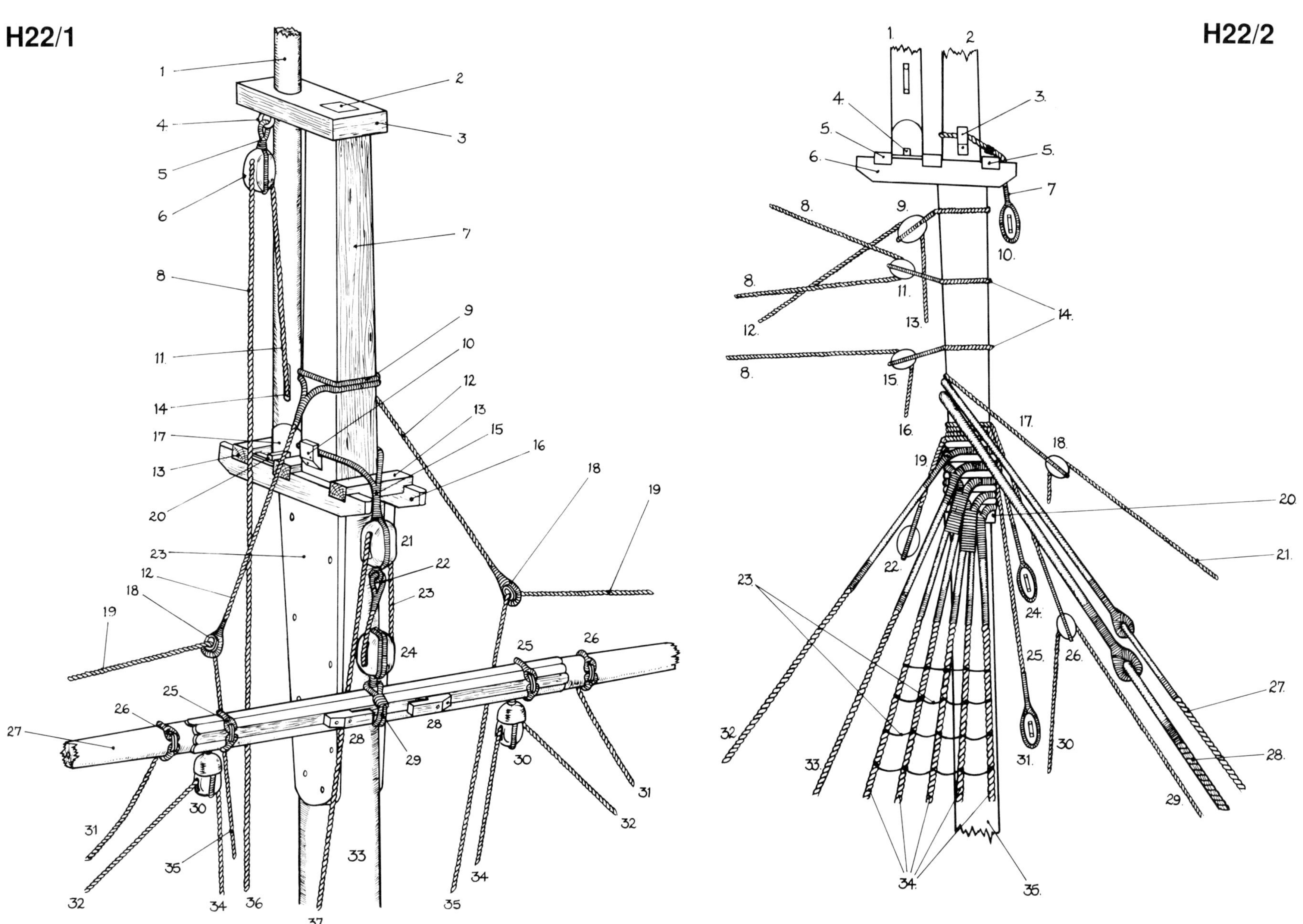
H22/1
H22/2

H23 DETAIL OF TOPGALLANT MAST HEAD (1/48 scale)

Note: drawing includes details of both breast backstays and flying jib halliard which were not always rigged

1 Small sheave for pendant halliard
2 Truck
3 Polehead
4 Strop for topgallant forestay
5 Seizing for flying jib halliard block pendant (if rigged)
6 Eye for larboard breast backstay (if rigged)
7 Rigging stop
8 Starboard breast backstay (if rigged)
9 Flying jib halliard block pendant
10 Topgallant forestay
11 Flying jib halliard block (if rigged)
12 Flying jib halliard (if rigged)
13 Flying jib halliard fall (if rigged)
14 Sheave for topgallant yard tie
15 Topgallant yard tie
16 Topgallant yard tie fall
17 Topgallant mast

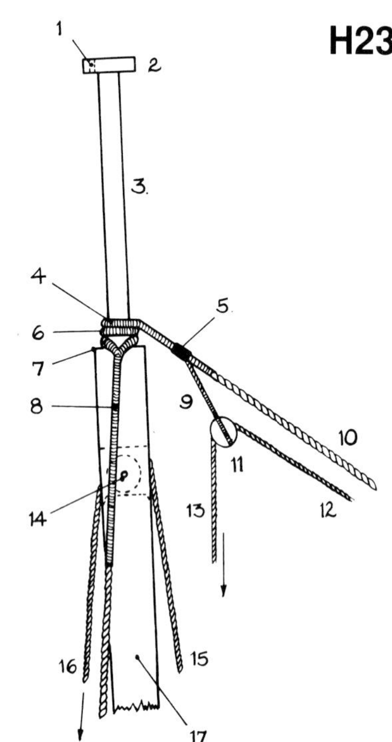

H24

H24 VARIETIES OF BLOCK (1/16 scale)

1 Common single-sheaved block, side elevation
2 Common single-sheaved block, end elevation
3 Double-sheaved block (type used for jeers)
4 Treble-sheaved block (type used for catblock)
5 Sister block
6 Long tackle block
7 Sheet block
8 Shoulder block (not commonly used on cutters)
9 Shoulder block (type used for clewlines)
10 Deadeye with concave groove for shrouds
11 Deadeye with flat groove for chain plates
12 Shoe block
13 Lignum vitae sheave
14 Sheave pin
15 Score for pendant rope

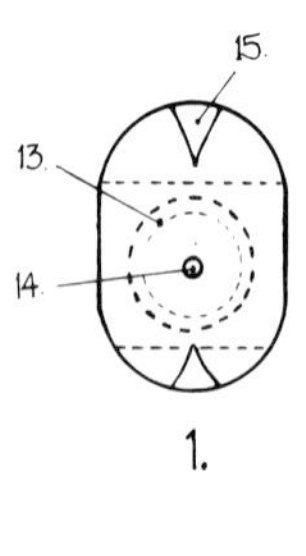

1.

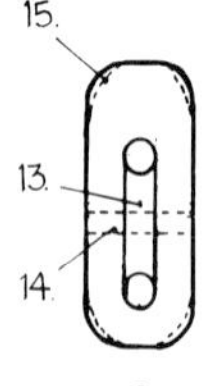

2.

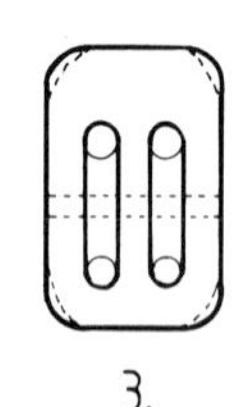

3.

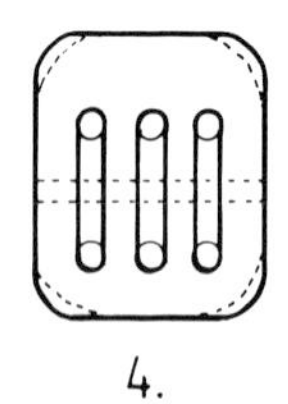

4.

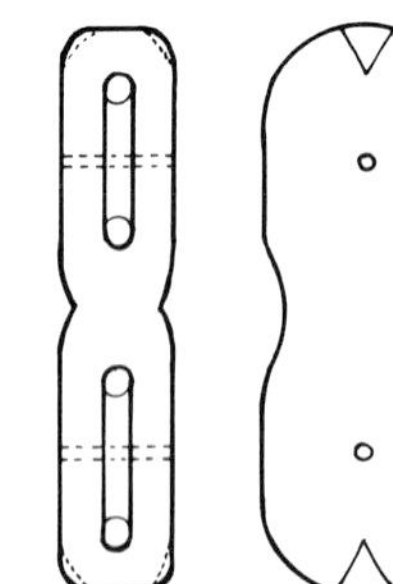

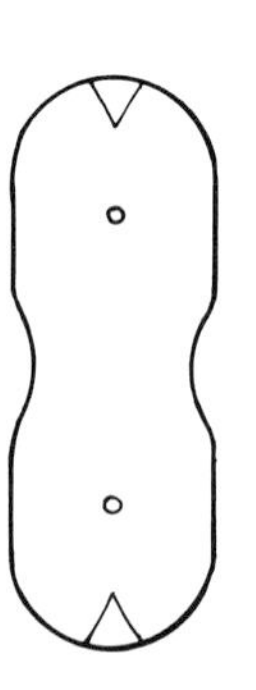

5.

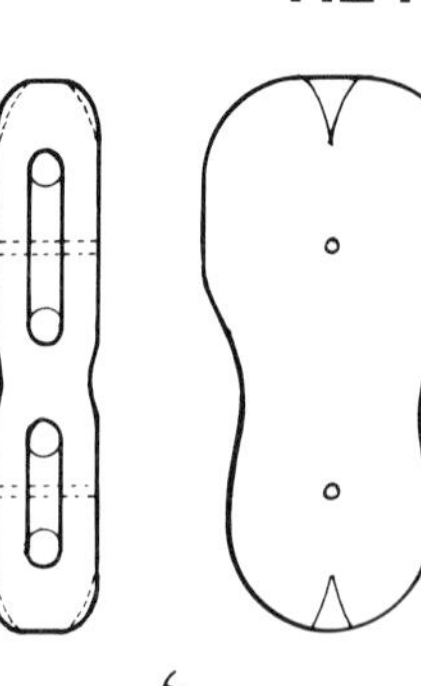

6.

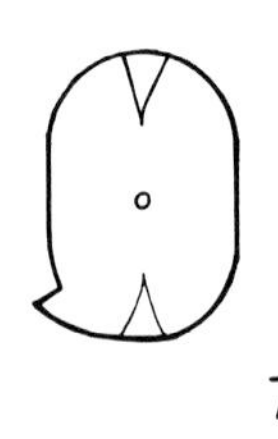

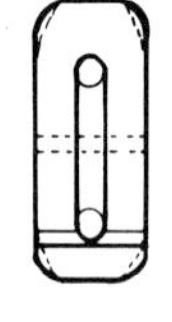

7.

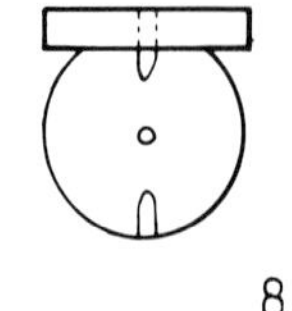

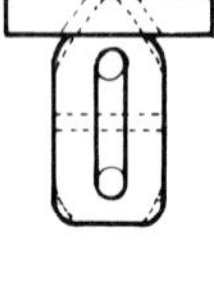

8.

9.

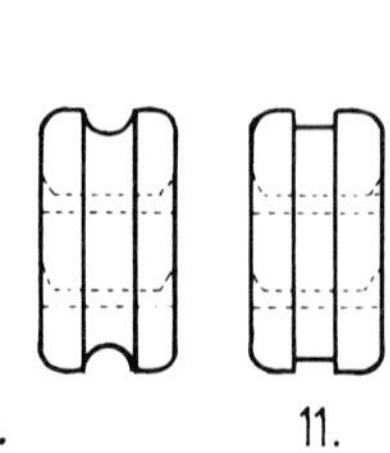

10.

11.

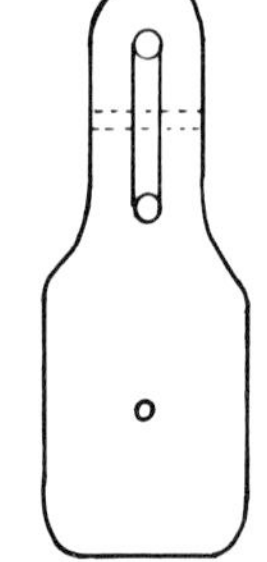

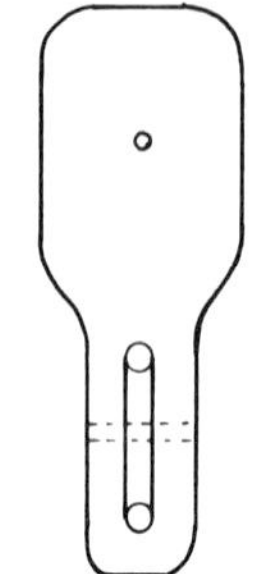

12.

I1 SQUARE SAILS OF THE MAINMAST (1/128 scale)

I1/1 Main topgallant sail

I1/2 Topsail

I1/3 Squaresail

1 Earing
2 Head seam
3 Head bolt rope
4 Roband eyes
5 Earing lining
6 Leech seam
7 Leech bolt rope
8 Clew lining
9 Clew
10 Foot seam
11 Foot bolt rope
12 Reef lining
13 Reef cringle
14 Reef points
15 Bowline and bridle cringles

I1/1

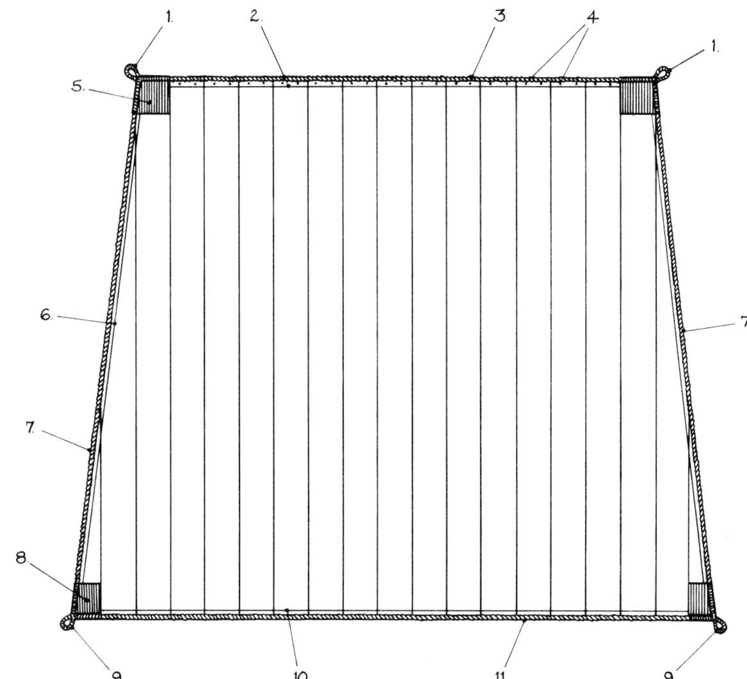

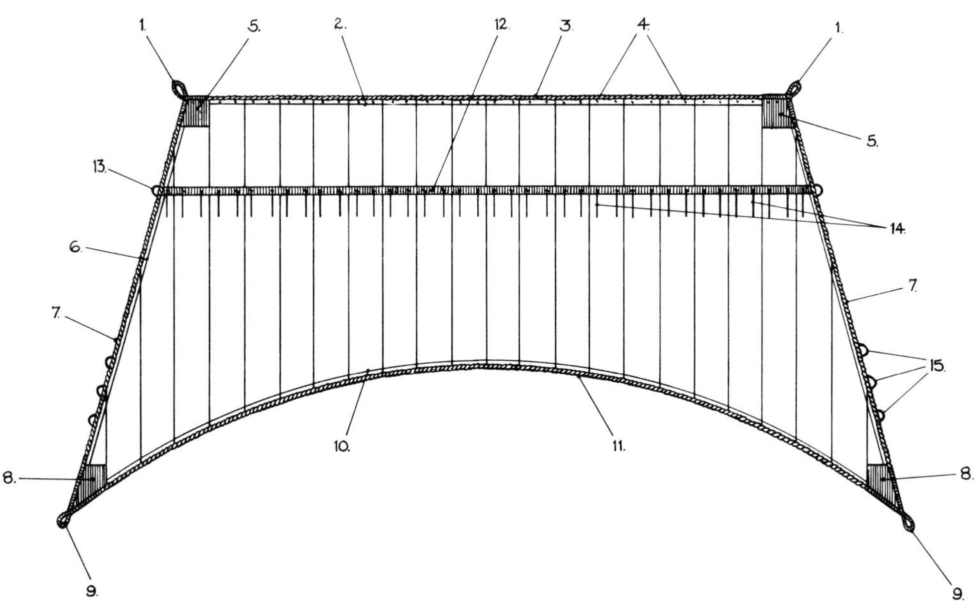

I1/2

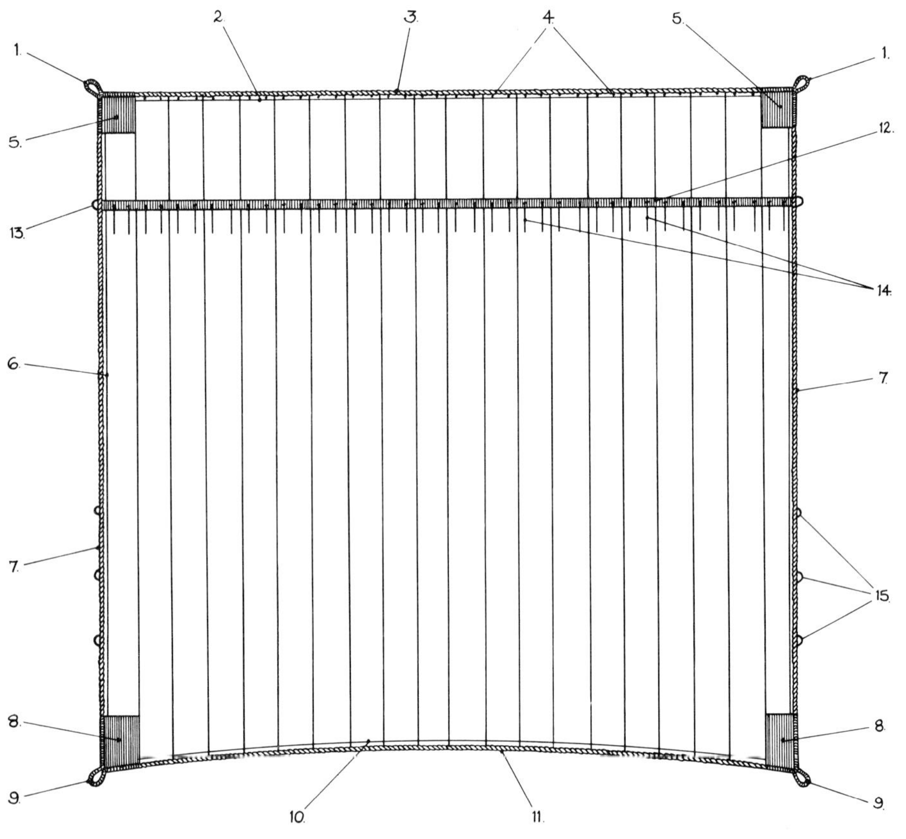

I1/3

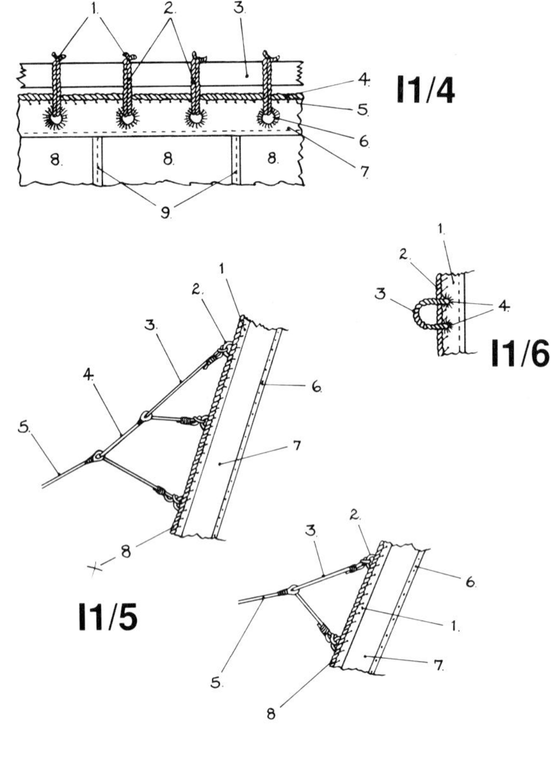

I1/4

I1/5

I1/6

I1/4 Details of robands and gaskets (no scale)

1 Reef knots
2 Robands
3 Yard
4 Head bolt rope
5 Stitch of sail to bolt rope
6 Roband gasket
7 Head seam
8 Sail cloths
9 Cloth tabling

I1/5 Detail of bridles (no scale)

1 Leech seam
2 Bridle cringle
3 Bridle
4 Second bridle
5 Bowline
6 Cloth tabling
7 Sail cloth
8 Bolt rope

I1/6 Details of cringle (no scale)

1 Leech seam
2 Bolt rope
3 Cringle
4 Cringle gaskets

I1/7 Main squaresail clew details (no scale)

1 Leech bolt rope
2 Tabling of the cloth
3 Leech seam
4 Foot seam
5 Monkey fist end of tackle
6 Foot bolt rope
7 Clew
8 Running part of the sheet
9 Tack
10 Sheet block pendant
11 Sheet block
12 Standing part of the sheet

I1/8 Topsail clew details (no scale)

1 Running part of clewline
2 Standing part of clewline
3 Leech bolt rope
4 Leech seam
5 Clew block
6 Tabling of the cloth
7 Clew block strop
8 Seizing
9 Foot bolt rope
10 Foot seam
11 Monkey fist end of sheet
12 Clew
13 Sheet

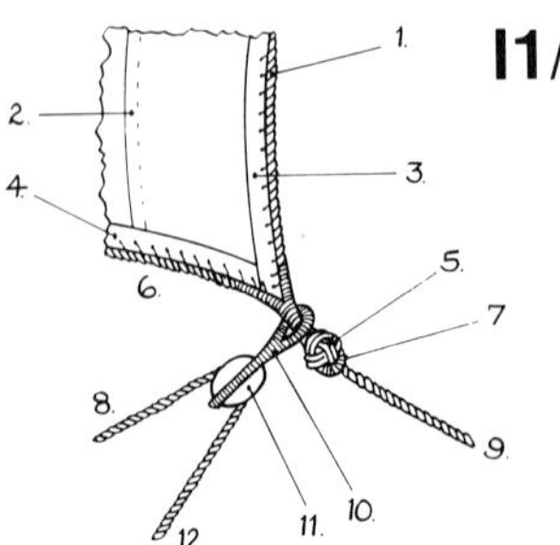

I1/7

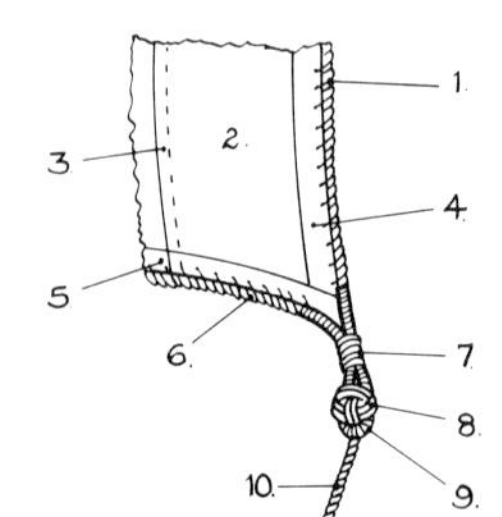

I1/9

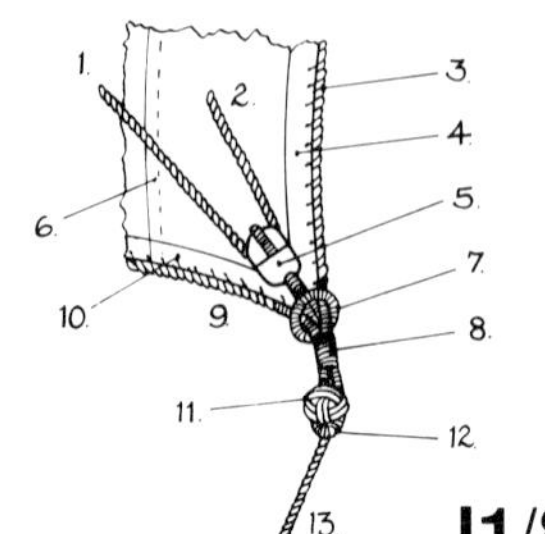

I1/8

I1/9 Topgallant sail clew details (no scale)

1 Leech bolt rope
2 Sail cloth
3 Tabling of the cloth
4 Leech seam
5 Foot seam
6 Foot bolt rope
7 Seizing of the clew
8 Monkey fist end of the sheet
9 Clew
10 Sheet

I2/1

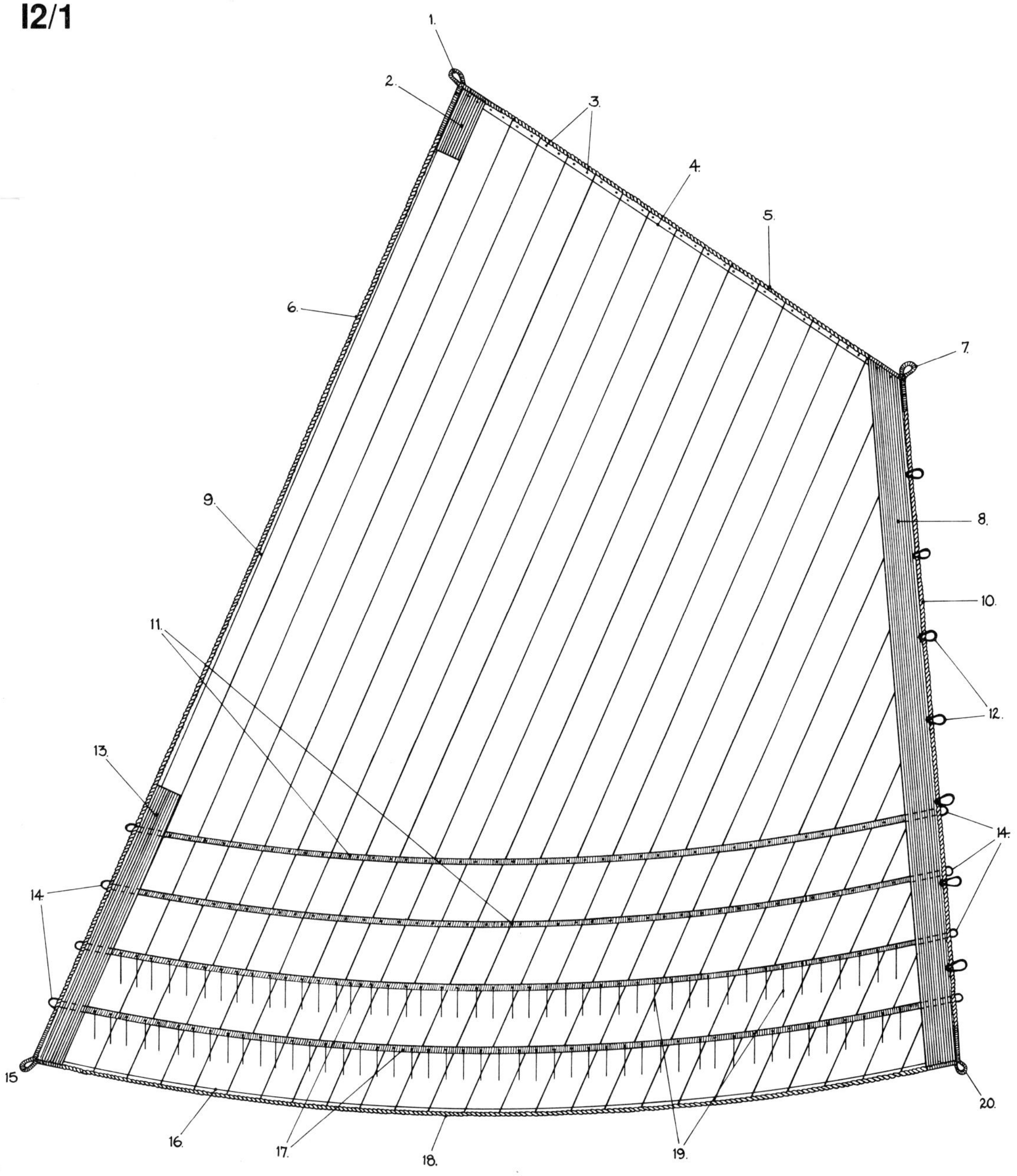

I2/2

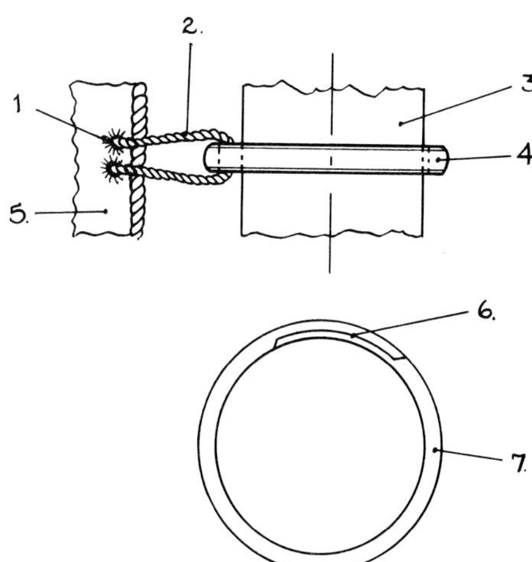

I2/2 Mainsail mast hoop and cringle, side and plan elevation (1/24 scale)

1 Cringle gasket
2 Hoop cringle
3 Mainmast
4 Wooden mast hoop
5 Luff seam of mainsail
6 Hoop joint, upper
7 Mast hoop, plan view

I2 MAINSAIL (1/128 scale)

1 Peak cringle
2 Peak lining
3 Roband eyes
4 Head seam
5 Head bolt rope
6 Leech bolt rope
7 Throat cringle
8 Luff lining
9 Leech seam
10 Luff bolt rope
11 Upper reef band with reefing eyelets
12 Mast hoop cringles
13 Leech lining
14 Reef cringles
15 Sheet clew
16 Foot seam
17 Lower reef bands
18 Foot bolt rope
19 Reef points
20 Tack clew

I3 STORM MAINSAIL (1/128 scale)

1. Peak earing
2. Head bolt rope
3. Head seam
4. Roband eyes
5. Throat earing
6. Luff lining
7. Luff
8. Luff bolt rope
9. Tack clew
10. Reef linings
11. Foot seam
12. Foot
13. reef points
14. Foot bolt rope
15. Sheet clew
16. Reef cringles
17. Leech lining
18. Lining (or strengthening band)
19. Leech seam
20. Leech
21. Peak lining

I4 FORESAILS (1/128 scale)

I4/1 Main foresail

I4/2 Storm foresail

1. Peak cringle (for halliard)
2. Peak lining
3. Luff bolt rope
4. Leech bolt rope
5. Hanks
6. Luff seam
7. Leech seam
8. Tack lining
9. Clew lining
10. Clew cringle (for sheets)
11. Foot bolt rope
12. Foot seam
13. Tack cringle

I4/1

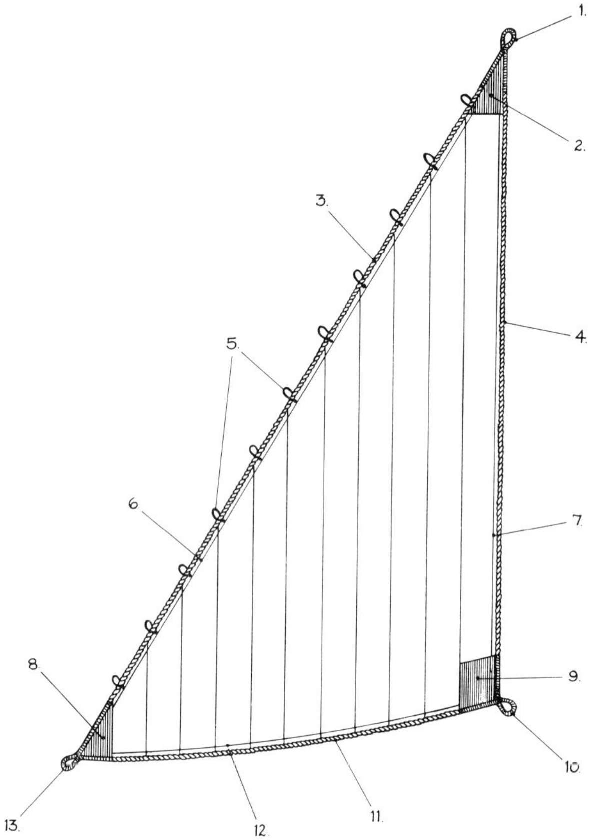

I4/2

I3/1

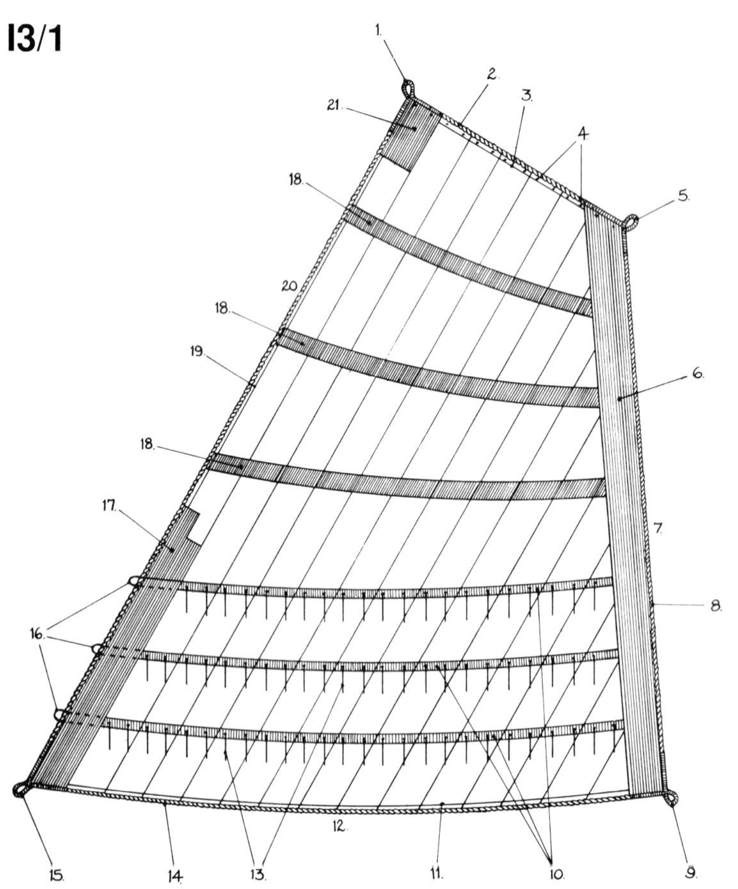

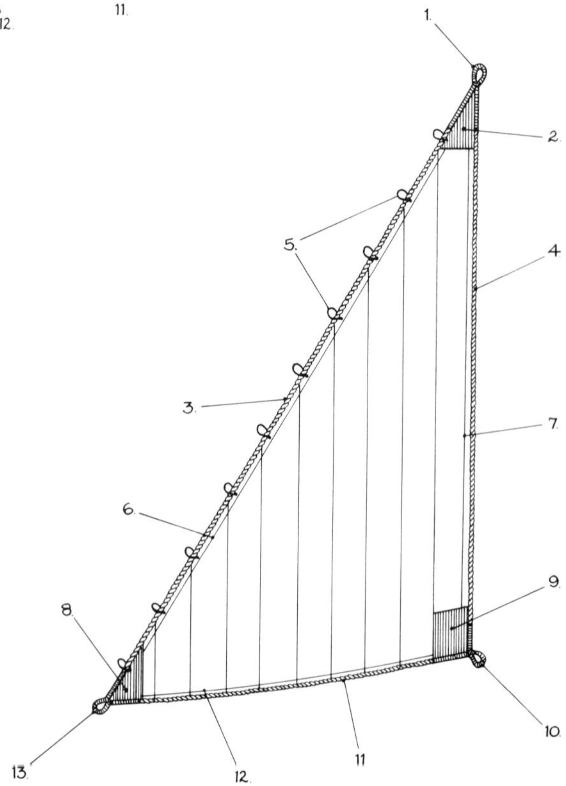

I5 JIBS (1/128 scale)

I5/1 Jib

I5/2 Flying jib

1 Peak cringle
2 Peak lining
3 Luff bolt rope
4 Leech seam
5 Luff seam
6 Leech bolt rope
7 Clew lining
8 Clew cringle for sheets
9 Foot bolt rope
10 Foot seam
11 Tack cringle
12 Tack lining

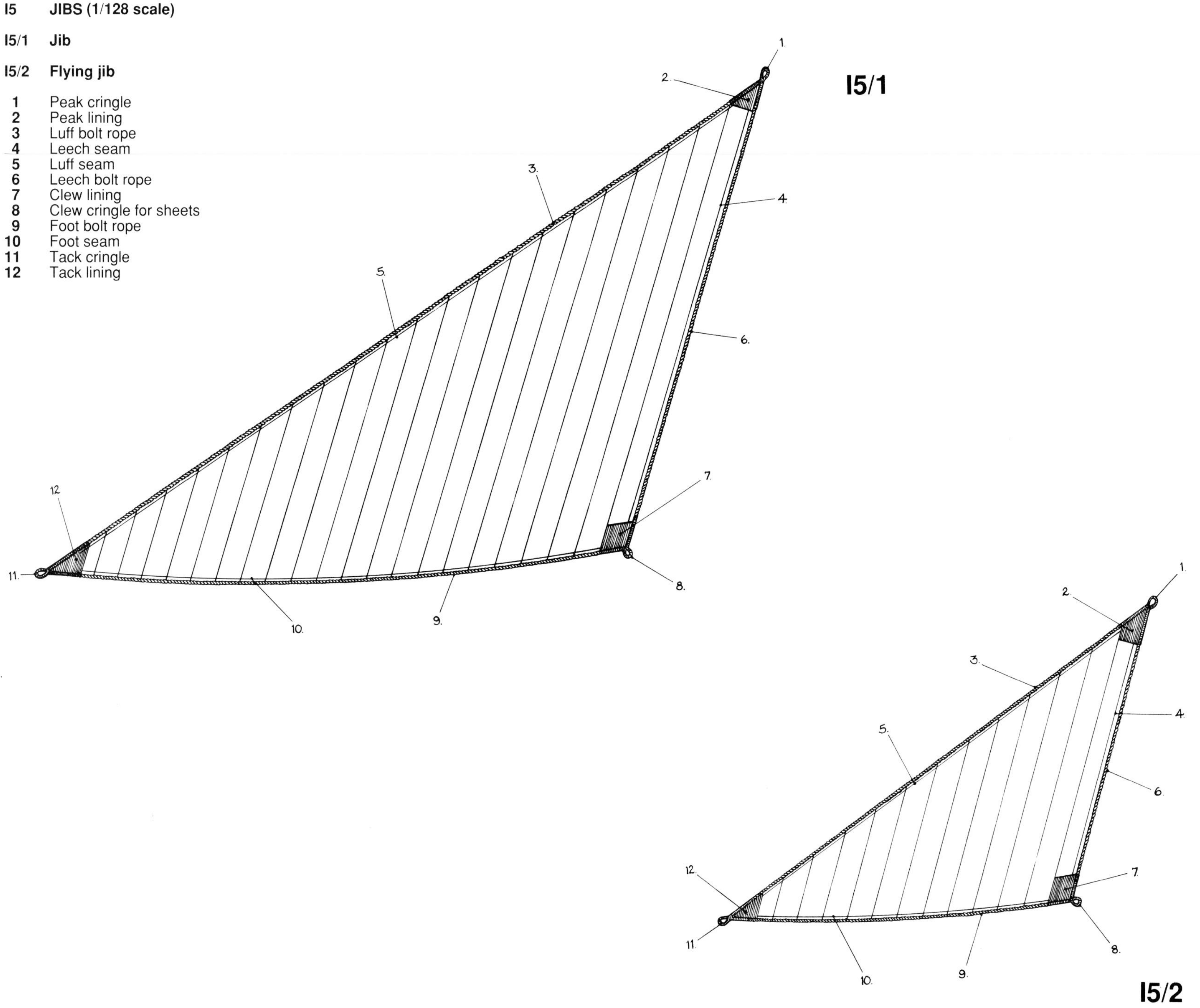

I6 MIZZEN SAIL (LUGSAIL) (1/128 scale)

1 Peak earing
2 Roband eyes
3 Head seam
4 Head bolt rope
5 Throat lining
6 Throat earing
7 Luff bolt rope
8 Luff seam
9 Tack lining
10 Tack clew
11 Foot bolt rope
12 Foot seam
13 Clew cringle for sheet
14 Sheet lining
15 Leech seam
16 Leech bolt rope

I6/1

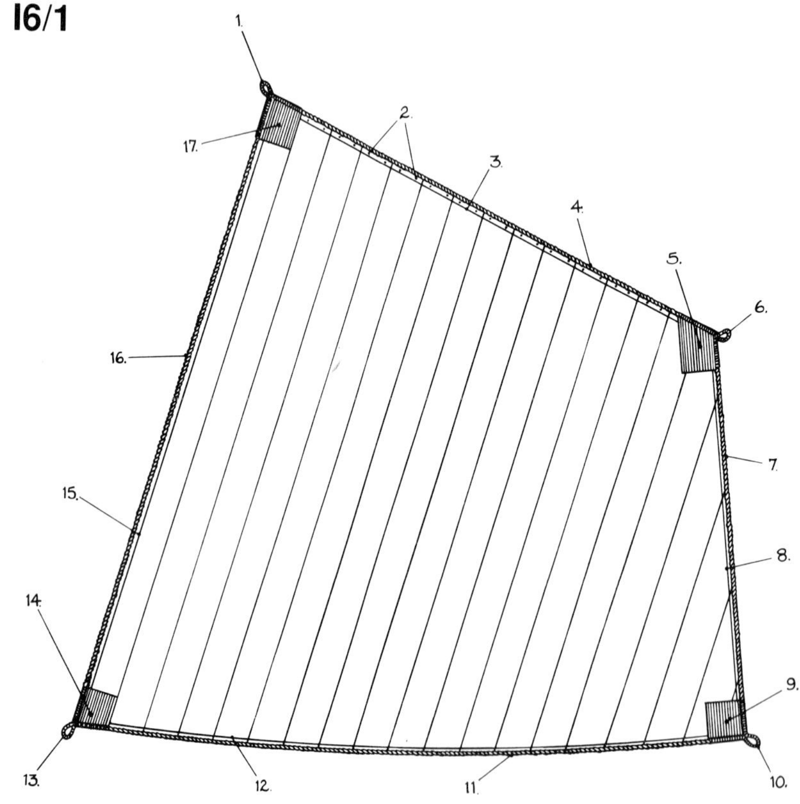

J The ship's boats

J1 18FT CUTTER (1/48 scale)

J1/1 Body plan

J1/2 Sheer and profile

J1/3 Half breadth plan

J1/4 Detailed plan

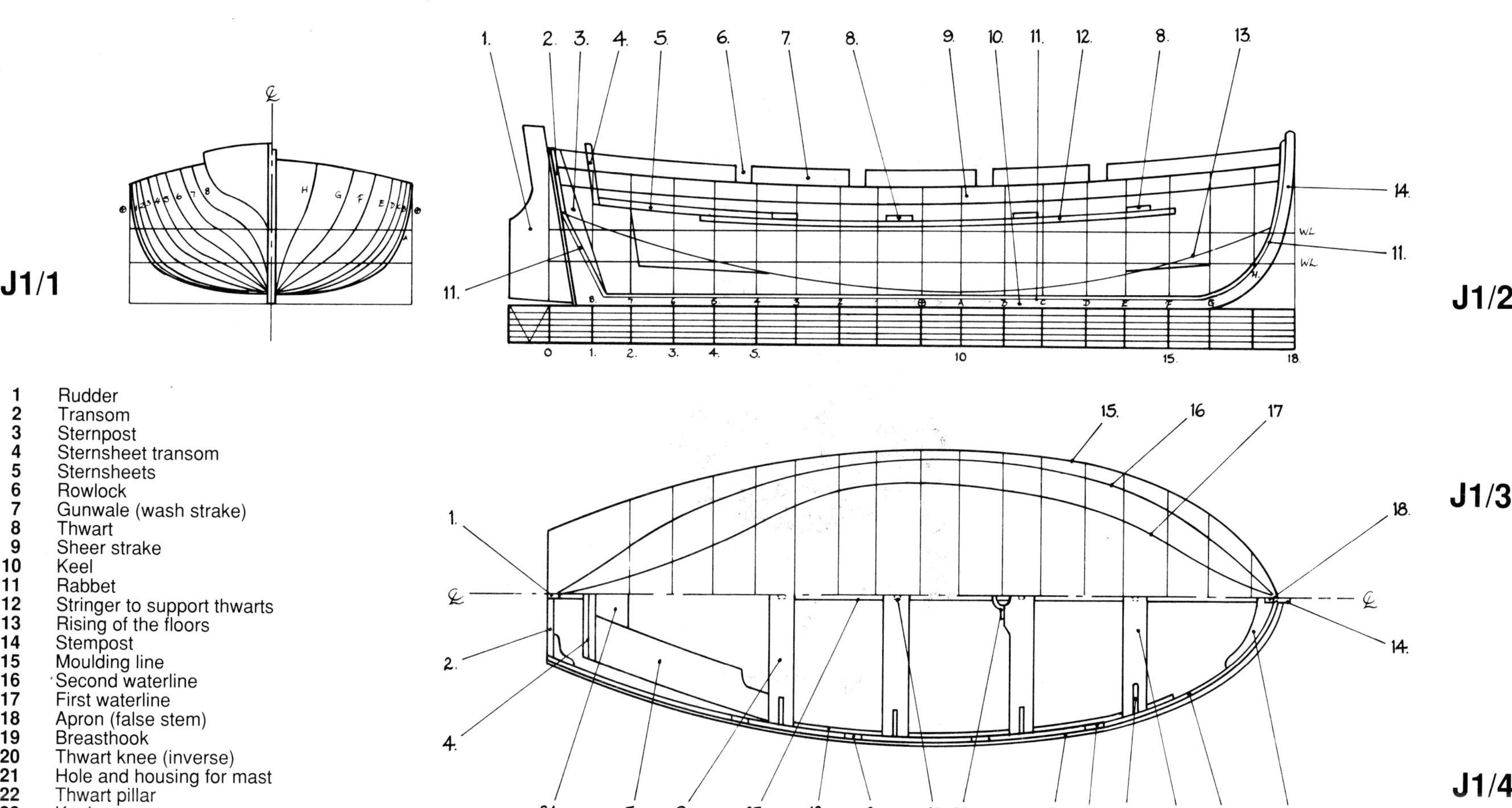

1 Rudder
2 Transom
3 Sternpost
4 Sternsheet transom
5 Sternsheets
6 Rowlock
7 Gunwale (wash strake)
8 Thwart
9 Sheer strake
10 Keel
11 Rabbet
12 Stringer to support thwarts
13 Rising of the floors
14 Stempost
15 Moulding line
16 Second waterline
17 First waterline
18 Apron (false stem)
19 Breasthook
20 Thwart knee (inverse)
21 Hole and housing for mast
22 Thwart pillar
23 Keelson
24 Transverse sternsheet thwart

J The ship's boats

J2 RECONSTRUCTION OF A 16FT LONG BOAT (1/48 scale)

J2/1 Body plan

J2/2 Sheer and profile

J2/3 Half breadth plan

J2/4 Detailed plan

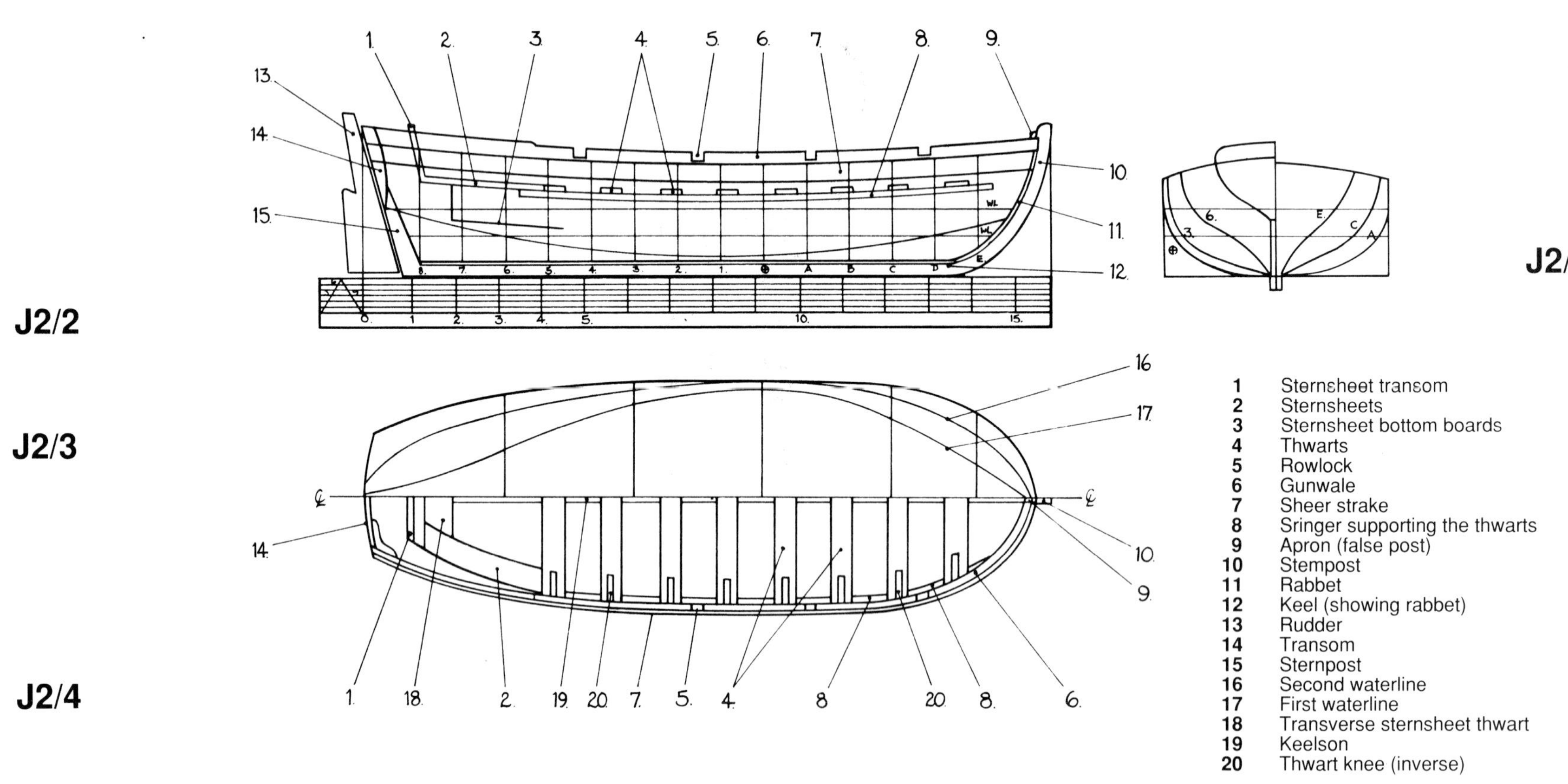